W9-ADL-970

SUNDAY HOMILIES

BOOKS BY HERBERT F. SMITH, S.J.

Living for Resurrection
God Day by Day
The Lord Experience
The Pilgrim Contemplative
How to Get What You Want from God
Hidden Victory (A Historical Novel of Jesus)
Prayer and Personality Development
Homosexuality (co-authored)
Sunday Homilies, Cycle A
Sunday Homilies, Cycle B

SUNDAY HOMILIES

CYCLE C

Herbert F. Smith, SJ

ALBA · HOUSE   NEW · YORK

SOCIETY OF ST. PAUL, 2187 VICTORY BLVD., STATEN ISLAND, NEW YORK 10314

Library of Congress Cataloging-in-Publication Data

Smith, Herbert F.
   Sunday homilies. Cycle C / Herbert F. Smith.
      p.   cm.
   ISBN 0-8189-0582-4
   1. Church year sermons.   2. Catholic Church — Sermons.
 3. Sermons, American. I. Title.
   BX1756.S595S863   1991
   252'.6 — dc20   91-17927
                                      CIP

Designed, printed and bound in the United States of
America by the Fathers and Brothers of the
Society of St. Paul, 2187 Victory Boulevard,
Staten Island, New York 10314, as part of their
communications apostolate.

© *Copyright 1991 by the Society of St. Paul*

Printing Information:

Current Printing - first digit 1 2 3 4 5 6 7 8 9 10 11 12

Year of Current Printing - first year shown
1991   1992   1993   1994   1995   1996   1997   1998

CONTENTS
Cycle C

Preface xiii
1st Sunday of Advent
Our Unique Christian Waiting 3
ABC — Immaculate Conception
Mary's Uniqueness in all History 6
2nd Sunday of Advent
Are there Substitutes for Catholicism? 9
3rd Sunday of Advent
Invitation to Joy 13
4th Sunday of Advent
What Can I Expect of Christmas? 16
ABC — Christmas
Vigil Mass *(See Cycle A)*
Midnight Mass *(See Cycle B)*
Mass at Dawn
A Christmas of Love 19
Mass during the Day
Ascending to Him Who Descended to Us 22
The Holy Family
Secrets of the Happy Family 25
ABC — Solemnity of Mary
Knowing Him and Us through Her 29
ABC — Epiphany
Doing the Epiphany 32
Baptism of the Lord
Jesus Revealed 35

2nd Sunday of the Year
  Surprises at Cana of Galilee 38
3rd Sunday of the Year
  Winning to Sunday Joy 41
The Presentation
  The God-Hero is Recognized 44
4th Sunday of the Year
  Angry with God 47
5th Sunday of the Year
  Discovering I'm Called 51
6th Sunday of the Year
  The Wealth of the Poor and Poverty of the Rich 54
7th Sunday of the Year
  Hearts that Know only Peace 57
8th Sunday of the Year
  The Power and Glory of the Tongue 61
1st Sunday of Lent
  Who Wins the Victory? 64
2nd Sunday of Lent
  No Cross, No Crown 67
3rd Sunday of Lent
  History in God's Hands — and Ours 70
4th Sunday of Lent
  Coming Home 74
5th Sunday of Lent
  The Prodigal Daughter 77
Passion (Palm) Sunday
  Recovering the Purpose of Suffering 80
ABC — Easter Vigil
  Passing Over with the Lord 83
ABC — Easter Sunday
Morning Mass
  The Necessary Resurrection 86

2nd Sunday of Easter
  Propagating the Resurrection 89
3rd Sunday of Easter
  Our Mysterious Relationship to Jesus 92
4th Sunday of Easter
  Vocation — Hearing the Good Shepherd's Call 95
5th Sunday of Easter
  Love's Way of Life 99
6th Sunday of Easter
  Walking with God 102
The Ascension
  What Jesus and We are Doing 105
7th Sunday of Easter
  Our Family in Heaven and on Earth 109
ABC — Vigil of Pentecost
  The Necessary Holy Spirit 112
ABC — Pentecost Sunday
  Life in the Spirit 115
Trinity Sunday
  The Trinity: Faith's Family Model 119
C — Corpus Christi
  Sacrament of the Heart of Jesus 122
Solemnity, Sacred Heart
  Through His Heart to the Trinity 125
10th Sunday of the Year
  God: For or Against Our Suffering? 129
11th Sunday of the Year
  Forgivers and Repenters 132
ABC — John the Baptist *(See Cycle A)*
ABC — Sts. Peter and Paul *(See Cycle A)*
12th Sunday of the Year
  Discovering Discipleship 135
13th Sunday of the Year
  The Way of Discipleship 139

14th Sunday of the Year
Attainable Happiness 142
15th Sunday of the Year
Unrecognized Calls to our Calling 145
16th Sunday of the Year
The Heart of Jesus and the Apostleship of Prayer 149
17th Sunday of the Year
Friends in High Places 152
The Transfiguration
The Mystery of the God-Man 155
18th Sunday of the Year
Prayer: The Road out of Materialism 159
19th Sunday of the Year
Fixed and Fleeting Prayer 162
ABC — The Assumption
Woman Victorious 165
20th Sunday of the Year
Overcoming Alcoholism 169
21st Sunday of the Year
Conscience and Authority 172
22nd Sunday of the Year
Elevating Humility 175
23rd Sunday of the Year
The Cost of Discipleship 179
ABC — Triumph of the Cross
The Healing Cross 182
24th Sunday of the Year
Forgiveness in the Family 185
25th Sunday of the Year
RCIA — The Business of All Catholics 189
26th Sunday of the Year
The Non-negotiable Mandate to Share 192
27th Sunday of the Year
The Christian Response to Abortion 195

28th Sunday of the Year
The Prayer of Glorious Thanksgiving 199
29th Sunday of the Year
Prayer, the Road to Fool-proof Joy 202
30th Sunday of the Year
How to Pray and not to Pray 205
ABC — All Saints
The Day to Look Homeward 209
ABC — All Souls: Mass One
The Almighty to the Rescue 212
ABC — All Souls: Mass Two
A Soul's Journey: Purgatory to Paradise 215
31st Sunday of the Year
The Faith that Underlies Conversion 219
ABC — St. John Lateran
God's Home and Ours 222
32nd Sunday of the Year
Removing Roadblocks to Resurrection Faith 225
33rd Sunday of the Year
Stock Taking for the Final Report 229
Christ the King
Knowing the Heart of our King 232

TABLE OF ABC HOMILIES

(Since each ABC homily can be used for the given Feast in any year, only one homily is available for some ABC Feasts; but for more celebrated feasts, two or even three homilies are provided for variety. The table below lists the homilies available for each ABC Feast, and the Book(s) in which they appear).

Immaculate Conception — A, B, C
Christmas:
   Vigil Mass — A
   Midnight Mass — B
   Dawn Mass — C
   Mass During the Day — A, B, C
Solemnity of Mary, Mother of God — A, C
Epiphany — A, B, C
Presentation — C
Easter Vigil Mass — C
Easter Sunday Mass — A, B, C
Pentecost Vigil Mass — C
Pentecost Sunday — A, B, C
Solemnity, Sacred Heart (has distinct A, B, and C readings but this
   homily is generic enough for use with any of the three) — C
Birth of St. John the Baptist — A
Solemnity of SS Peter and Paul, Apostles — A
Transfiguration (has distinct A, B and C Gospels, but this
   homily is generic enough for all) — C

Assumption — A, B, C
Triumph of the Cross — C
Feast of All Saints — A, C
All Souls:
    First Mass — C
    Second Mass — C
St. John Lateran — C

PREFACE

How better highlight the homily's privileged nature than to see it as the servant of the Word of God? It serves up the Word in ways that apply it practically to our lives. It illumines the contemporary path to God. It becomes most powerful when it serves the Word most faithfully.

No wonder, then, that Saints as diverse as the Curé of Ars and St. Francis Xavier the missionary could not say enough of the power of preaching. No wonder St. Teresa of Avila wrote that she listened with pleasure to even the poorest sermons, and always felt affection for a preacher who preached well and with feeling.

And, in view of the homilist's wide-ranging tasks, no wonder the Lord himself called stewards of the Gospel to bring forth new things and old from their storerooms. We need wide nets to gather material for our homilies.

How tell a good homily from a poor one? Here's one valid norm: A poor homily conveys only information and theory; a good homily gives faithful instruction in the practical Christian life. I have tried to follow that norm.

Many of these homilies are substantially the same as I preached them, but better. Why? Because, hoping they would be widely used, I took the time to strip them to leanness, and search out illustrative stories that would pulse with their essence.

Still, the best of homilies is lacking if the preacher himself does not pulse with the message it contains. Before he delivers it he must make it his own by prayer. Preaching should be the fruit of the preacher's own prayed experience, to convey that feeling which St. Teresa so appreciated. Once made one's own by prayer, a borrowed sermon is less borrowed. An hour of prayer over it will make the difference between serving up store-bought bread and a fresh loaf from the oven, hot and aromatic, with crusty fresh texture. Recently, after making a retreat, I found my preaching so much more fervent and effective that only then did I realize how it had declined before the retreat. Prayer and good preaching are inseparable.

A good homily serves up something to think about, something to emote over, something to aspire to, something to smile at, and something to believe: We present a problem to solve, a value to cling to, a goal to reach, a touch of humor to relax over, and a truth of faith to live by.

Recently I met a popular young pastor who seemed an admirable priest. Then I was told by one of his thoughtful parishioners that his pastor was so upbeat in his preaching that he didn't deal with the issues. No doubt he was pleasing to hear, but on reflection one realized that while the glad hand was extended, the issues had not been joined, and the needed help not given. Who wants a commander who sends his troops onto the battlefield with a light heart but no mention that a war is going on, and neither the training nor the armaments of survival, much less of victory?

Doubtless, some, or even many, will be pleased because they have heard no reminder that Christian life is a warfare, have no intention of going into battle, and feel confirmed in their drifting. After all, when did they last hear the warning, "If your hand leads you into sin, cut it off"? When did they last hear the prominent sins of the day denounced? Perhaps the Pastor has come to agree with the culture that such ways of proceeding are not sins but necessities? No need to inquire further, since the Pastor has exonerated them from the task, at least by his silence.

Of course, there is a problem of confronting issues that the layman mentioned had not considered, but every preacher has faced: the need to deal with such a range of topics that if he had the theological knowledge of St. Thomas Aquinas and the wisdom of Solomon he'd still find homilies a problem without a good grasp of current affairs.

How do we solve the problem? Often, by default, like a priest friend I heard denouncing contraception without mentioning Natural Family Planning. I asked him why, since there is truth in the contention of John Kippley, co-founder of the Couple to Couple League, that to mention the condemned practice without informing people of the God-given way out is immoral. The priest friend said simply, "I know nothing about it."

Though the knowledge of Natural Family Planning is so critical I have studied it thoroughly and written and spoken on the topic (See the Thirty-second Sunday for a homily that brings up the subject), I have at times avoided other ideal topics for given Sundays because I didn't have time to do the research and preparation to treat them creditably.

In keeping with my commitment to write these three volumes of homilies, I have taken that time where necessary, time which the busy parish priest often cannot find to do the same. So these homilies cover a great range of important doctrinal, moral, spiritual, social, and family topics and issues of the day. May they assist many a priest to preach on the "ideal topic" when he might otherwise circumvent it.

While dealing in these homilies with issues that must be faced, I avoid derailment. Religion is about God and life. God is love. Life is a mystery of love. Our faith finds that love centered in the Heart of our Redeemer, and so it is Christ we preach in season and out of season. We are devoted to his love only when we are devoted to his truth. His truth comes through revelation. Faith, hope and love, then, keep us on course in our journey home to the Father, and they should be the refrain of all our homilies.

In the Preface of Cycle A, I presented a brief treatise on homilies; in the Foreword of Cycle B, Fr. George A. Maloney,

S.J., generously provided his thoughts on preaching and his assess-ment of the book. I refer the reader to those more adequate treatments. Here I have singled out only those central guiding truths and convictions that help me keep my own preaching on course. Homilists who agree with them should find valuable help between these covers.

CYCLE C

OUR UNIQUE CHRISTIAN WAITING

What is Advent all about? It is a time of Christian waiting. This waiting has a uniqueness about it, but it does bear some resemblance to other types of waiting. If you dine out you're only too familiar with the type captured in an epitaph of one waitress. On her tombstone is the inscription, "God finally caught her eye."

Waiting involves expectation, and there's something "unreal" about an expectation. To wait is to long, expect, believe and hope for something, but it remains unreal in the sense of being as yet *unrealized*. If we had it we wouldn't have to wait for it. When we finally do have some great thing we've waited for, it still seems unreal. You know the saying, "Pinch me. I can't believe it's true!" One pilgrim who finally made it to Jerusalem felt that way. When he saw the banner in the chapel that read, "And now my feet are standing within your walls, O Jerusalem," he had a sense of unreality. Could he really be there? That, he thought, must be the way we will feel when we finally get to heaven!

We've waited for waitresses, buses, planes and guests. We've waited for graduations, diplomas and paychecks. From these experiences we can learn something about Advent waiting.

There are two types of waiting, passive and active. In passive waiting, we can do nothing but stand watch, as when we gaze anxiously from the curb stone to see if the bus is coming. In active waiting, such as that for overdue friends, we keep busy about the home, making doubly sure all is disposed for a royal welcome.

That second type of waiting applies to Advent season. Before we consider it, I have a question to ask and answer: Besides waiting, what is Advent all about? It is about the investment of our lives in the three comings of Christ. He came the first time by his birth on the first Christmas. In extension of that First Coming, he continues to enter our lives daily, as he will this coming Christmas. Then there is his awaited Second Coming, when he will wrap up the affairs of time and escort us into eternity. And, for those of us who do not survive until then, there is the coming that consists in his meeting each of us individually at our death. These are the comings of Jesus for which we long and prepare and wait.

Advent is a time of waiting for our most loved of friends. It is a time to grow and prepare him the most fitting of welcomes. St. Andrew, whose feast we celebrate in this season, is a model for us. When Jesus ascended to heaven, he didn't passively await his return. He went out and labored the rest of his life to bring the kingdom of the Father to the earth and its people. He worked to speed the return of the Savior, and the day when all will be taken up to the Father. Andrew and all the Saints teach us that Advent is far from passive waiting. It is a time to serve Jesus, and to grow closer to him.

The waiting Christian is much like a young man or woman who enters college. Students wait for graduation, but if they do nothing but wait there will be no graduation. They must study and learn and earn their diploma. We bring Christ to us on Christmas by removing the obstacles, loving and serving and praying our prayers of longing.

But Advent waiting is also unique. Unlike our waiting for other friends, we're not without Jesus as we await him. He promised to live with us as we await his full coming. He said, "Whoever loves me will keep my word, and my Father will love him, and we will come to him and make our home with him." We find this mystical presence of his through prayer; and we find his still more wonderful presence in the Mass and the Eucharist.

Let us look more closely now at Christ's different comings. God promised for ages, through prophet after prophet, that he would send a Savior. As the days, the years and the centuries dragged on, he seemed to the people to fail his promise. Then God sent his prophet Jeremiah to insist the day was coming, as we heard in the first reading. And the months and the years and the centuries dragged on again — then suddenly the angel was in Mary's home! The time had come. She conceived the Infant Savior by the power of God, and gave birth to him in Bethlehem.

What looks like delay, as the first letter of Peter explains, is in reality a grace-time given us to repent and prepare. What God promises, he always does.

Christ's daily comings into our lives are the focus of our Advent preparations. If we open ourselves to him daily, we'll be full of holiness and readiness to greet him with joy on Christmas day, and on the coming of the eternal day.

In its deepest meaning, Advent is both a longing to have Christ with us here on earth, and a yearning to return with him to heaven. When we're away from home, no matter how much we enjoy it, there's a tension, a looking forward to our return home. Heaven is our home. Advent stirs our love and longing for God and for home. That's why, in the Postcommunion Prayer, we'll beg our Father to make Communion guide our way on earth, and teach us love of heaven.

You probably know that the Bible ends with the Book of Revelation. The second-last verse is the plea, "Come, Lord Jesus." That's the prayer of Advent. "Come, Lord Jesus! I'll pray and work and renounce my sins to prepare your way." That is Advent, with its active and passive waiting. We go more frequently to Mass and Holy Communion; we draw closer to our Blessed Mother. We recognize in her Immaculate Conception the final preparation for the Son of God's Incarnation.

The very sun and the season help us. Twilight falls early. Quiet descends on human affairs. We remember Jesus' call to guard against drunkenness and worldly cares. We feel the call to Bible reading, reflection and prayer.

All of this prepares us for Jesus' daily coming, his Christmas coming, and his final coming. Of that final coming, Jesus speaks in today's Gospel, and he gives its signs. Many Christians in the past thought those signs were fulfilled. We don't know when they will be fulfilled, but this we know: Jesus will come to each of us in our lifetime, whether in his triumphant Second Coming, or in his coming to each individually, at the time of our death.

Preparation, then, is a firm necessity, because his coming to each of us is an absolute certainty. Advent is a lesson for life. If we live in preparation for the coming of Christ daily, we will certainly have a merry Christmas, and a merry eternity.

"ABC" — Immaculate Conception   Gn 3:9-15, 20
                                                            Ep 1:3-6, 11-12
                                                                Lk 1:26-38

MARY'S UNIQUENESS IN ALL HISTORY

What is the Immaculate Conception? That was the "double jeopardy" question once asked on the TV program of that name. A group watching the program threw money into a pot, winner take all. No one won. No one could give the right answer. Can you? If any here cannot, how can they have the joy of intelligently honoring Mary and celebrating with her today?

A Catholic girl who was part of the group that couldn't give the correct answer said that she thought it was the Virgin Birth. The Virgin Birth is in fact the mystery the angel is explaining to Mary in today's Gospel. She will conceive Jesus in her womb by the power of God, without a human father. And that is the faith of the Church, that Mary conceived and gave birth to Jesus while remaining a Virgin. So the Virgin Birth involves both Jesus and Mary. He was conceived without a human father; she remained a Virgin in conceiving and giving birth to him.

What then is the Immaculate Conception? The first thing to say is that it has to do with Mary herself. It has to do with her at the moment *she* was conceived by *her* parents. It is the dogma of faith recalled in today's Opening Prayer. God prepared Mary to be the worthy Mother of his Son by making her share beforehand in the salvation Christ would bring. Christ came to take away our sins, but for Mary he did even more. From the very moment Mary was conceived, God preserved her from original sin. But the mystery can be put in the more personal, beautiful way Mary herself once phrased it. When she appeared to Bernadette at Lourdes, she declared, "I *am* the Immaculate Conception."

The Virgin Birth of Jesus is a manifest miracle of nature, but the Immaculate Conception is a hidden miracle of grace. Jesus had no human father, and that is certainly a miracle of nature. Mary had a human father and mother in the ordinary way; but at the very moment she was conceived in her mother's womb, God sanctified her. He never allowed Adam's sin to stain her. Sometimes when a bride comes up the isle dressed all in the purest white, she looks immaculate. Think, then, of Mary's soul coming forth from the hand of God pure and immaculate at the moment she was conceived in Ann's womb. That is the Immaculate Conception.

To this day, if you walk the streets of old Jerusalem, you can come upon a placard which reads, "The Virgin Mary was born here." In the courtyard beyond is the noble Church of St. Ann, the mother of Mary. St. Ann and St. Joachim are the parents of Mary. Perhaps in that very place, they gave her being and life in that embrace of married love by which all devout parents give life to their children. But at the very moment they became parents, God blocked out the influx of original sin from Mary, and filled her soul with the grace that made her the Immaculate Conception.

Today let us honor Mary by recalling her unique role in all of salvation history. For Mary is model for the whole Church and for each of its members. From the moment she was conceived, she possessed the sinlessness we're all destined to arrive at one day if we keep the faith. In that second reading, St. Paul tells us that before God created the world he chose us in Christ to be holy and blameless and full of love. At our baptism, we were cleansed of original sin, and made adopted children of God. To share at last in Mary's sinlessness, we must struggle against all sin until sinfulness itself is behind us, and we have been purified of any last stains in Purgatory.

Let us compare Mary to Eve, the first woman. Eve is the mother of all the living. But when she passed life on to us, she passed on death as well. Mary became the new Eve, the true Mother of all the living. She is the Morning Star who gave birth to the "Sun of Justice" from whom we all receive the life that overcomes death.

Now, compare Mary to the Church. Mary is both a member of the Church and the Mother of the Church. She gave birth to the divine Bridegroom from whose pierced side the Church was born.

Mary is the loved and admired model for the Church. She is God's gift and sign to the Church of everything God intends for the Church. Mary was sinless, and that the Church struggles to become. Mary was most pleasing to the Father, and the Church is trying to please him. Mary gave Christ to the world, and the Church is doing the same through all ages. Mary said *yes* to all God asked; so the Church longs to do; Mary served her Son and suffered with him in the work of redemption. The Church finds its very identity in trying to do the same. Mary was taken body and soul to her divine Lord, where she is enjoying the eternal Sabbath. The Church, too, longs for the everlasting day when, cleansed of every stain and wrinkle and glorified in the risen bodies of all her members, she will be taken up to her place in the home of her divine Bridegroom forever.

Praise of Mary is right and good. The danger is that we will give empty praise. The danger is that we will gaze at her from afar as though she is beyond imitation. The Church knows how wrong that is. There is only one Mary, and there will never be another.

The Church knows that, but she knows too that we are all Mary's children, all called to grow into her likeness as children do.

There was once a young man who used to kneel at a distance from a lovely statue of Mary and observe her with her bowed head, seemingly taken up in her unique relationship with God. But one day need and love forced him to go and kneel at her feet. Looking up, he saw her gazing into his eyes with tender love. How beautifully the sculptor of that statue taught that young man that you can't know our Lady from a distance. Like the Child Jesus, we have to be close and familiar with our sweet Mother. Like Joseph, we have to care for her needs and the needs of her Son whom she shares with us.

Mary is unique in the history of salvation. She is unique also in this, that there is no creature more humble, more approachable, more loving and more concerned for each of us. If we want to praise her, we certainly have to know that and tell her that. Otherwise, she will say, "He means well, but he doesn't know me." By our love, our imitation, our rosaries, our giving, our serving, let us prove that we do.

"C" — Second Sunday of Advent

Ba 5:1-9
Ph 1:4-6, 8-11
Lk 3:1-6

ARE THERE SUBSTITUTES FOR CATHOLICISM?

Are Catholics aware and concerned that thousands of idealistic young members abandon the Church and join fundamentalist Christian or non-Christian sects? If these wayward members challenged the average Catholic to tell them why they should remain, how many could give a compelling answer?

Advent is a time of joy, a time for homecoming, a time for the return of prodigals and lost sheep, a time to look to Christ and prepare his way, and a time to look homeward to our eternal Father. It is a time to reflect on whether we who are not lost are giving the wayward and the lost convincing witness to our faith in Christ.

John the Baptist was the witness for many. He believed with passion and preached with power that the time had come when "all mankind shall see the salvation of God." The first Christians, brought to Christ with John's help, took up John's task. In the second reading, St. Paul rejoices that the believers he addressed "have all continually helped promote the Gospel from the very first day." When will today's Catholics see they are held by Christ to do the same, promoting the self-same Gospel?

The light of the Church has shone in the past. Many stories tell of the rugged "Road to Rome" taken over the ages by men and women who by heroic effort and flashing lights of grace discovered the Church most of us inherited at birth. Now the "Road *from* Rome" is heavily trafficked. Can anyone guarantee he or his children will not join that traffic if he does not know and appreciate and communicate the faith he has received?

We can forward our Advent preparation by reflecting on the fact that there is only one true Church, that we are its witnesses, and that Advent calls us to become worthy witnesses.

First, there is only one true Church. Catholics who consider themselves broadminded have been known to tell those on the Road from Rome to do what they think best, instead of helping them to think right. "Broadminded" indifference to the truth about Christ and his Church is faithlessness.

St. Peter says of Jesus, "There is no salvation in anyone else." Jesus said to Peter, "You are Rock (Peter in Greek), and on *this* rock I will build my Church." And at the Last Supper Jesus prayed that there would be only one flock, as he is the one Shepherd. St. Paul taught that there is "one Lord, one faith, one baptism, one God and Father of all." Pope Innocent III defined as dogma that "There is but one universal Church of the faithful, outside of which no one at all can be saved."

How can these truths be reconciled with the ecumenical movement? This way: We honor all who believe in God, and are happy for all who believe in Christ. We respect their consciences, but also our own. Our respect does not prevent them from giving witness, and must not prevent us, since it is commanded by Christ.

St. Paul taught that all who believe in God as just Judge, and live by their lights, can be saved; but he worked like a Hercules to make them know Christ. Vatican II taught that baptized and believing Christians are part of the Catholic Church, even though they don't know or admit it. They should be treated as brothers. But it adds what we should never forget, that "It is through Christ's Catholic Church alone, which is the all-embracing means of salvation, that the fullness of the means of salvation can be obtained." Only the Catholic Church is one, holy, Catholic, and founded by Christ on the Apostles.

John Henry Newman, who was declared Venerable by the Church on January 22, 1991, is a light to the religiously indifferent. He sought religious truth passionately. He began as an Anglican, defending his belief against Catholicism. Then doubts arose. He made an arduous search of the whole Christian development through the centuries, which he recorded in his *An Essay on the Development of Doctrine*. He sent the book to press, but before it came off, he was so influenced by the religious truths he had investigated and thought and written about that he had to add a postscript: "Since the above was written, the author has joined the Catholic Church."

If indifference to the scientific quest, which adds so much to our knowledge and culture, would be folly, how much greater is the folly of indifference to religious truth? It is our faith that Christ is the world's Redeemer, and the Catholic Church is his creation, and eternal life hinges on those facts.

Secondly, we are the Church's witnesses. By our lives the

Church is judged. By our lives Christ is judged. If our light hides under a bushel basket for lack of courage, or grows dim because the oil of faith has run low, Advent is the time to pluck up our courage and lay in a supply of faith.

Meditation on Jesus and his Church can revitalize us. The beautiful hymn of the Divine Office composed by Cardinal Newman provides the sentiments to be sought: "And I love supremely, solely / Christ who for my sins has died. / And I hold in veneration / For the love of him alone / Holy Church as his creation, / And her teachings as his own."

Finally, Advent calls us to be worthy witnesses. We prepare the way of the Lord by preparing ourselves for the Lord. If we deny our sins, we deny Christ; if we admit them, renounce them and confess them, we give witness to our Savior who removes them. The Christian who ponders the faith and looks with eager anticipation to Christmas will, even unawares, radiate a joy that witnesses to Christ. One priest likes to tell of a busy businessman who edified him when he was a boy by trudging through the winter snows to Mass on First Fridays. Attendance at even occasional Advent daily Mass not only expresses one's longing to Christ; it gives the kind of witness others will long remember to their profit.

The Catholic who purifies and renews himself becomes a window of the holiness of the Church of Christ and the Apostles. He is practicing the first principle of ecumenism and performing the most basic work of the missionary. As our Psalm today says, may his life be "filled with laughter" and his "tongue with rejoicing."

"C" — Third Sunday of Advent

Zp 3:14-18
Ph 4:4-7
Lk 3:1-18

INVITATION TO JOY

A Catholic psychiatrist asked a colleague what he did to promote joy in his patients. "Joy?" the man repeated. "I know nothing about joy."

May God save us from such an attitude. Everyone desires joy, every Christian is called to joy, and today we are given God's own invitation to rejoice. "But," someone might challenge me, "who has ever captured joy, and made it do his bidding, so he can have it whenever he wants it?" Let us ponder that challenge. Has God given us the answer?

We've all known many joys, but they slip away. Yet surely we have learned something about joy that will help us have and hold it. With the help of today's scriptural call to joy, I will ask and try to answer three questions: What is joy, so that we can cultivate it as the Lord exhorts us? What are the causes of Christian joy? What is the deepest joy we can hope for?

First, then, what is joy and how can we cultivate it? Did you ever make the determined resolution, "Today I'm going to be joyous"? And find that it doesn't work? In contrast, we *can* resolve to be more patient or more kind and, in a few weeks, if we persist, we will succeed. Patience and kindness are virtues, and virtues are good habits, and we *can* cultivate habits by repeating them over and over. Why can't we cultivate joy head-on in the same way? The reason is that joy is not a virtue.

If joy is not a virtue, what is it, and how do you get it? To search out the answer, think of the most joyous people you have known. What is their secret? Don't you always find joy at the wedding of lovers, the birth of a little child, the ordination of a devout priest, the vows of a loving Sister? The fountain of joy is pure love. If you find joy without love, a bird can fly without wings. Joy and happiness are found when we love and are loved. We find the greatest joy when we give ourselves to the greatest lover, God himself.

Here then is a deep secret of joy. Just as we cannot grow oranges but only orange trees, we cannot grow joy, but only love, the tree on which joy grows. Joy is the delightful emanation of pure and true love.

Pope Paul VI sang the praise of the joy of St. Francis of Assisi. For love of God, St. Francis left everything. In his poverty he tasted the joy of Adam and Eve on the day of creation. When poor and half blind, he chanted his unforgettable *Canticle of Creatures*. For when he no longer clung to creatures he could see through them to the glory of the Creator he loved so well.

Second, what are the sources and causes of Christian joy? The main cause is that God loves us. In that first reading, the prophet Zephaniah pictures God like a joyous young lover singing with all his might in the presence of his beloved, his people.

In the Gospel, God expresses the greatness of his love for us by telling everybody to treat us right: If we are poor, share with us; if under obedience, don't cheat or bully us.

In the psalm, God tells us that we "will draw water at the fountain of salvation." To us Christians, that is the fountain of the open heart of Christ, pouring out his love.

If that doesn't bring you joy, think of this: What if God had said, "I'm not going to become man. I'll appoint the Baptist their Savior, and what little he can do I'll accept as payment for all their sins." Doesn't it give you a sinking feeling just to think of it? But thank God, he gave us his Son. That is our joy. We are *loved.* Our religion is not some*thing* but Some*one*. Our salvation comes not merely by holding to the law, but only by holding to Christ.

Finally, what is the deepest joy we can hope for? Our deepest joy is expressed in our Advent longing for the Incarnate God. Today,

Gaudete Sunday, we rejoice because Christmas is near. Christmas is the joy of God coming to us as one of us, and the promise of one day going to him. Then our joy will be greater than our wildest dreams.

We must prepare for that day by struggling to increase and purify our love. In writing on joy, Pope Paul VI said that "the combat for the kingdom necessarily includes passing through a passion of love." Jesus and all his Saints make that truth evident.

Sunday is a day given us to think of these things, and grow closer to God. Sunday helps us to prepare for the eternal Sabbath. And if we love God, we long for the eternal Sabbath, and find joy in the remembrance of things to come. When St. Francis lay dying he was singing with such exultant joy that one of his silly followers cautioned him he might scandalize people.

Finally, consider two obstacles to joy. The first is knowingly refusing God what he wants of us. Love is union of wills. How can we be one with God and divided in wills? The second obstacle to joy is failure to believe how much God loves us. We are like ugly little caterpillars incapable of believing that the beautiful butterfly soaring above can find anything in us to love. But like the caterpillar, we too will sleep in the cocoon of death, and then awaken to find that we have taken on the glory of a new life like to our divine Lover's.

God made the caterpillar that becomes a butterfly to help us believe in the resurrection and the life. He even made a comparison himself. Through Isaiah he says, "Fear not, O worm, Jacob, O maggot Israel; I will help you." If we think God can't do for us what he does for the caterpillar and more, remember the word of the angel at the Incarnation, the beginning of it all. "All things," he said to Mary, "are possible with God."

One final thought. In his *Exhortation on Joy,* Pope Paul said that our Christian joy can't be dissociated from the Mass and Eucharist. In them, he says, we have the first taste of the joy we will have in eternity. May that joy be ours today and prepare us for Christmas.

"C" — Fourth Sunday of Advent   Mi 5:1-4
                                                 Heb 10:5-10
                                                 Lk 1:39-45

WHAT CAN I EXPECT OF CHRISTMAS?

We're all preparing for Christmas, and many are out buying Christmas presents. Perhaps you heard of the father who returned from Christmas shopping, drew his last five dollars from his pocket, and said, "I'm going to give this present to the man who needs it most." Then he put it back in his own pocket.

Today's readings are all about our final preparation for Christmas. Like all sound preparation, it involves giving. Christmas is the feast on which God gave everything. He gave himself. Instinctively, his people imitated him by originating the admirable practice of giving Christmas presents.

Let us see from the readings how Mary is preparing for Christmas, how Jesus is preparing, and how we should prepare.

First, we look at how Mary prepared for Christmas. As soon as the angel was gone, she hurried away to visit her cousin, Elizabeth, who was sixth months pregnant.

Let's reflect on that. Here is Mary, a young woman, just experiencing the most profound event in all religious history. If ever a woman had cause to stay secluded and ponder and pray and guard from a dangerous journey the Child conceived within her, that woman was Mary. And yet, she sped off to serve.

Mary teaches us by being what she is — selfless in her loving service of others. And so she set out on a three-day journey to a town near Jerusalem which tradition identifies as Ein Karim. Israel is in many regions a desert country, but Ein Karim, which means "Fountain Spring," is in a lovely, verdant little valley in the hill country of Judea.

Note the miraculous thing that happened at the meeting. At this early stage, Mary showed no external signs of her pregnancy.

Yet the child in Elizabeth's womb leaped for joy, and Elizabeth was inspired by the Holy Spirit to realize what had happened. As the paten bears the consecrated host, Mary bore within her the long-awaited Messiah. And so, inspired by the Holy Spirit, Elizabeth spoke the words that have become part of the *Hail Mary*: Blessed is the fruit of your womb.

Do you realize what this meant to Mary? Her faith that she was carrying a child was now being confirmed by a woman to whom she had said nothing but a word of greeting.

Let us reflect on the other infant, John, who stirred in his mother's womb. A gynecologist reported the case of a pregnant woman who used to listen to a certain soap opera. Shortly after her child was born, it would turn with intense interest to the TV set whenever the theme song of that soap opera came on. The conclusion was that the baby remembered the song from its days in the womb. So it seems likely that John heard the gladness of the redemption in Mary's greeting, and jumped for joy. The Holy Spirit used the very sound of Mary's voice as a sacrament.

Observe how central mothers and families are to God's plan to redeem us all. Mary sings of that in her Canticle of Praise: God lifts up the lowly. These housewives, not considered much by the world, are God's close helpmates in his saving action.

Notice, too, Elizabeth praising Mary because she believed and trusted God. Are we not inspired to do the same?

Second, let us look at how Jesus is preparing for Christmas. In the first reading we hear from Micah, a prophet who lived six hundred years before Christ. He tells us that a Ruler will be born in David's town. That Ruler, though new-born, will be of ancient origin. What can this mean? In the light of the Gospel we see here a prophecy that this new-born Ruler will be the eternal Son of God. And yet Jesus' preparation for his Christmas birth is the same preparation every unborn baby makes for birth. Nourished and warmed and sheltered by his mother, he continues to grow until he has the strength to enter this world.

When he enters it, Paul tells us, in our second reading, he will offer God his will in a new covenant. But so eager is Jesus to begin his work that he inspires his mother to carry him to be revealed to John and Elizabeth.

Finally, we think about our own preparation for Christmas. We are helped by the realism of the readings. Did you note the Bethlehem-Calvary connection in the second reading? We are told why Jesus came into the world. It was to do the will of the Father who loves us, and wants our salvation. So Jesus gives the Father his will, and surrenders his body to God for the work of our redemption. He was born in Bethlehem to pour out his blood on Calvary, and to be our offering in an unbloody manner in the Mass through the ages. Already the cross is appearing on the horizon. It is always present. We cannot so much as buy a Christmas present without making a sacrifice. How blessed are those who do it willingly and lovingly as Jesus did.

To prepare for Christmas, we need to be realistic about its meaning. In the Opening Prayer we begged the Father to fill our hearts with love to follow Jesus through suffering and death to resurrection and glory. Jesus became human, and we follow him as humans through sorrows and sacrifices as well as joys.

My brothers and sister, let us keep Christmas and resurrection connected. If we divorce the two, we will expect from Christmas things it is not meant to give us. Like Jesus born in a cold stable, our lives on Christmas are often mixed with sufferings and sorrows. There may be people here today who are afflicted by cancer or some other tragedy. That need not take away the fundamental joy of Christmas.

The joy of Christmas is Christ, given us by the Father, given as our way. If we accept that with deep faith and a most heartfelt love of Jesus Christ, Christmas can't disappoint us. We will be like Jesus, who found joy even in his sufferings. He rejoiced that through his life he could bring us redemption. And we, through our lives, can give joy to the Father by our irrepressible love of his Son.

And we can give joy to Christ by helping him bring joy to the world.

Let us keep Christmas what it is. It isn't the fulfillment of all our desires, but only a beginning and promise. In Christ and his cross we have to work out our salvation until we reach eternal joy with him. In the meantime, we have in the Eucharist a taste of the joy of Mary. We have Emmanuel, God with us.

"ABC" — Christmas Dawn Mass

Is 62:11-12
Tt 3:4-7
Lk 2:15-20

A CHRISTMAS OF LOVE

While the eternal Father in heaven gazes on his divine Son with him forever, Joseph bends over the Son newborn, lying in his mother's arms in the quiet of Bethlehem. Love is poured out in heaven, and love is poured out on earth, for God has become one of us, a member of our human race.

Religion is always about love, even when we fail to mention it. God is love, God created out of love, God calls us home to eternal love. In love God gave us his only Son.

Poets and lovers sing of the marvels of love. Here, in the baby of Bethlehem, is love that is, in truth, out of this world. Love stories tell of the prodigious feats of love, of its epic journeys to unite lover and beloved, of its banning of the word "impossible" as it undertakes its Herculean tasks. The Christ Child has indeed completed an immense journey, of Creator into his creation, of Eternity into time. Such wonders has he wrought that only people who know both God and love are able to believe.

If I said this babe was made of stardust, would I be talking in fables? Science tells us that we are all made of stardust, that the elements of our bodies were forged in the early stars. Whatever the source of the elements, this baby is our flesh and blood born of Mary, passed on through the line of David, received from Adam and Eve, formed of the earth by the hand of God. He is one of us. ''A Child is born to us, a Son is given to us.''

Let us join the shepherds as the angels depart, and hasten with them the two miles up the slope of the hill of Bethlehem to the cave where Jesus was born. ''Once they saw, they understood what was told them concerning this child.'' By prayer and thought we can understand the more, for have not we his life and teaching? What did they see? What did they hear? And what does it mean for us?

What did they see? They saw a strong husband with his lovely wife and her tender Child. God has now spoken in the language of family, a language in which we are all fluent, a language which makes us feel at home with the mystery of Christmas. They saw that the baby was newborn, wrapped in swaddling clothes and lying in a manger. But they saw far more. They saw God's love and kindness visible in the flesh. They saw their long-awaited Christ the Savior and Lord.

What did they hear? They heard his name pronounced. *Jesus!* They heard that they, poor, unwashed shepherds, were welcome. They realized that they, common folk and common sinners, had been called to him and given him as their own.

Is it any wonder that St. Paul tells us that God our Savior saved us not because of any righteous deeds we had done, but because of his mercy? In the presence of this Child all distinctions between saint and sinner, rich and poor, cultured and uncultured, jar like impertinent strangers, and fade away like mist in the morning sun. He is the holiness, the riches, the wisdom of us all. The poor, sinful, unlettered person who receives him possesses infinitely more than all the wealthy and wise men and self-proclaimed ''saints'' who reject him. All who receive him are brothers and sisters. In him, the unity which the human family has always sought in vain is now within our reach.

What does it all mean for us? The day anyone understands that is the day his life changes. That day came for the shepherds on Christmas morning. It came for the disciples when they followed him. It has come to millions through the ages. It is the day that they were freed from slavery to the earth and became its masters. It is the day they discovered they are not so much citizens of the earth as pilgrims on the way to their homeland in heaven.

Mary is the model of those who possess this knowledge. She held Jesus in her arms, and the flames and thunder of Sinai faded into the past. God was as gentle and approachable as her little Son, for her little Son was God.

The ten commandments had taken on a new form, and were living and breathing in her arms. All of God's law and all the prophets were wrapped in those swaddling clothes. He was her way, and he is ours.

In her family, she found a likeness of the Holy Trinity, and love taught her to make that likeness grow. Those who wish to plunge more deeply into the Trinitarian hints in this mystery may wish to ponder how the virgin motherhood of Mary and the solely spiritual fatherhood of Joseph reflect the divine Father's fatherhood; and how the Holy Family's poverty, which could not dim their joy, reflects the Holy Trinity, where there is full joy in the possession of nothing but one another.

If we see the meaning of Christmas for us, we see that we can claim the Savior for our own as Mary did. He who was born in Bethlehem, which means "house of bread," and laid in a manger, a place of feeding, gives himself to each of us under the form of bread. Holy Communion is the Christ Child's Christmas gift to us. How could Christmas be complete without it? But Holy Communion itself is not complete unless, receiving him, we give him our hearts.

One day while St. Thomas More was at Mass, King Henry imperiously summoned him, not once but three times. More's response was, "Tell the king I am with the King." We too are with the King who was born this day.

The day would not be complete unless we share his love with others. One Christmas card suggest ways of doing it: Mend a quarrel, seek out a forgotten friend, write a love letter, encourage youth, keep a promise, find the time, be kind and gentle, laugh a little, laugh a little more, go to Church, welcome a stranger, gladden the heart of a child, and take pleasure in the beauty and wonder of the earth.

Christ is born. Earth is so mingled with heaven that joy is the watchword. Today and forever, let there be rampant joy.

"ABC" — Christmas Mass During the Day   Is 52:7-10
                                                              Heb 1:1-6
                                                              Jn 1:1-18

ASCENDING TO HIM WHO DESCENDED TO US

One priest tells of the time he was taken to church as a child and seated at the end of the pew. It had a beautifully curved arm-rest, and he considered what a great race-track it would make for one of his toy cars to speed down and fly off into thin air. But, though he was such a tiny little boy that no adult would suspect he could have a worth-while thought in his head, he also felt how wonderful it was to be in God's house, so close to God. That's the way we should feel today — how wonderful it is to be in God's house, at Mass, with the very Lord Jesus who was born on Christmas day.

Another little child was so happy on Christmas night he said, "I wish every day was Christmas!" The marvel is that every day can be a kind of Christmas. Now that God has become one of us, he never leaves us. He's always present in the Eucharist.

Today we celebrate a mystery so wonderful that even the angels can't praise it enough. For all eternity we'll rejoice more and more in what God did for us on the first Christmas.

The three Christmas Masses of midnight, daybreak and this daytime Mass are a kind of serial repetition of what happened on the first Christmas, and are made for us to attend them all if we can. Let's review them. At Midnight Mass, the Gospel tells how Jesus the Savior, Messiah and Lord was born in a stable and laid in a manger. The angels rushed to the shepherds, gave them the good news, and sang their hearts out about what the Lord had done. But even they must have felt tongue-tied. How praise so great a wonder as God becoming less than they, God for love of us becoming one of us of the human race. So the angels "sing a new song," the Song of the Incarnation.

At the dawn Mass the Gospel describes the shepherds rushing up to the hill-town of Bethlehem to find the Child, and worship him, their Messiah and Lord, who had been promised for so long.

The readings and prayers of this third Mass review the whole mystery of Christmas and what it means. In this Gospel we get the tough job. It's so profound it makes our heads spin. It calls us up to visit the God who came down to us. But I'll return to that.

Christmas means that the prophecies and promises have been fulfilled. Let us not miss the wonder. Only God knows the future, and in that first reading Isaiah foretold what would happen: The Lord himself would come to redeem us. And so in the psalm we're invited to "sing the new song," the song the angels sang on the first Christmas night, the song of God becoming a little baby in Bethlehem. The second reading tells us that the Son of God and of Mary came to save every one of us, to bring his salvation to the ends of the earth. He became man for each of us as though there were no one else. He was born to give us rebirth as children of God. He suffered our troubles to give us peace. He shared our weakness to give us a share in his glory and kingdom.

And now the hard part: In the Gospel of this Mass we're

invited to go up in our minds and hearts to him who came down to us by becoming man. It wouldn't be so hard for us if John had said, "In the beginning was the Son of God and he was God too." But John didn't say that. He said, "In the beginning was the Word, and the Word was God — and the Word became flesh." Why did the Holy Spirit make him say that? Because he wants us to go up into the mystery. Every lover wants to be known. We want to be known by our Savior, and he assures us he knows us by becoming one of us. Now he wants us to know and love him for what he is as God and not just for what he became by being born of Mary. He wants us to know him and even become like him. That's what our sacraments are, mysteries to make us become like the Word.

It's not easy for us to wrestle with what John is saying, but we at this Mass are stuck with it; let's not be lazy; let's do it for love. It wasn't easy for the Son of God to become one of us strugglers either. An early Father of the Church, a genius named Origen, encourages us. He said that when we struggle to understand one of our religious mysteries, and suddenly succeed, it is the Word kissing our souls. Because we can't really understand by ourselves, but when we try the Word rewards us by suddenly manifesting himself to our minds or hearts.

We begin by trying to grasp why John called him The Word. Let's go to our use of words. What is a word? It's something we sound with our lips or write with a set of letters. We use words to communicate to others. A word is a communicator.

But did you ever think of this: Sometimes we have a thought or feeling we want to express, and *we just can't put it into words.* That tells us that a word is spiritual before it's embodied in sounds or letters. Do you see what this helps us discover? A word is really a spiritual reality that contains an understanding, a nature, an experience. We even speak of "conceiving" a thought, or "generating" ideas, as though we were talking about having spiritual children.

Doesn't that give us some inkling of what the Holy Spirit is teaching us in St. John's Gospel? He is telling us that God conceived or generated an image of himself. Since God is a pure Spirit that likeness of himself is just like him, pure Spirit, and it's everything he is except to be Father. It is his Son. But to distinguish him from a human child, he is called The Word. He is ''true God of true God, fathered, not made.'' This Child of God is neither man nor woman, but a Divine Being.

And the final step is this: When we have a spiritual word to communicate, we give it a ''body.'' That is, we flesh it out in sounds or letters. So, too, God gave his Divine Word a body of flesh in the womb of the Virgin Mary. Of course, ''flesh'' here means human nature, as when we say, ''It's good to see you in the flesh!'' Jesus, who is everything God is, became everything we are in the womb of his Mother. And he calls us by the mysteries of our faith to share what he is as God. We can never be God, but we can participate in his divinity.

After I'm all finished someone might feel, ''Yes, but I'd still like to take the Child in my arms as the shepherds must have done.'' So would I. But we have something better. In Holy Communion we have the very Child of God and Mary, grown, risen from the dead, giving himself to us to be our Life, the Father's best Christmas present to us all. Merry Christmas!

''C'' — Holy Family

Si 3:2-6, 12-14
Col 3:12-21
Lk 2:41-52

SECRETS OF THE HAPPY FAMILY

Years ago when the Duke of York visited the U.S. he said with tongue in cheek, ''I notice something very unusual about American parents — how well they obey their children.'' Another

Englishman, Charles Dickens, described his age with the words, "It was the best of times, it was the worst of times." That is a kind of summary of family life. It brings us our happiest experiences and our most sorrowful. Today, we see a painful experience even in the best of families, the Holy Family.

The readings invite us to make a serious reflection on family life. I propose it under three headings: Family life and children; Family life and God; Family life and lifestyle.

First, then, family life and children. We adults know that we are called to live in an ordered society that requires obedience to God and human authority. Surely, we also know that a rebel against authority is like a square wheel crashing through life, unhappy and causing unhappiness. One psychiatrist touched on a common psychiatric theme when he said, "I never had a patient who knew how to handle authority."

Many parents dislike disciplining their children, and fail to train them in obedience. The failure can end in battered children. The years of neglect go on, and the breaking point comes when the children become so unmanageable the parents fly into a rage and lose their own self-control. With gentle and firm persistence, parents must require obedience from the first. It's necessary to their own happiness, and to the responsibility they owe to God, to their children, and to society.

One young husband found his little girls were leaving toys strewn on the floor. He feared his pregnant wife would trip over them, and told the little ones they must pick up after themselves. He warned them they would lose their toys if they didn't. Finally, he put the toys in a barrel, and nailed it shut until his wife delivered. Wasn't that a needed and never to be forgotten lesson in obedience, done with kind firmness?

Our Lord Jesus obeyed his parents and God. Though Son of God, he learned obedience to those who stood in the place of his heavenly Father. Does that not teach us that to obey is at least as honorable as to command?

But never abuse parental authority. Don't nag with constant orders. They are your children, not your servants. Praise them often. Show you love them and do everything for their good. What more disheartens children than to hear only blame? One psychiatrist said, "I never had a patient who did not have a bad self-image." Constant criticism can turn children into psychos.

Secondly, we consider the family and God. One sometimes gets the picture that families see God as the great servant created for the sake of family life, instead of seeing families as created for the honor and glory of God. God must be first in our families in everything. The family that thinks worldly happiness more important than eternal life with God is headed for tragedy and disaster. Do you want happy family life? Then see family life as part of your pilgrimage to God.

In today's readings, God's wisdom gives us norms for family life. Each family makes its choice of following his wisdom or the world's. Families broken by following the wrong choice are legion. Families should sit and read today's scriptural passages, and pray and discuss and come to a mutual understanding of their views of family life in Christ. Do it, and be surprized at how God will bring you unity and peace.

Once, a certain doctor was the "bible" on raising children for millions of parents. He virtually absolved them from teaching obedience. Years later he changed his mind — too late for those formed in the way he now renounces. The real Bible's teaching does not change. It is right to begin with.

Families should learn to respect one another's consciences and calls from God. To our surprize, even Mary and Joseph had to learn this, as we see in today's Gospel. We all have to learn it, particularly in families where God calls a son or daughter to religious vocation. Some parents stand against God. A young boy began to write letters to a priest-author about his desire to be a priest. Later, he wrote and said, "I told my father, and you'd think I had committed murder." Soon, he wrote no more.

Consider what young John the Apostle would have been cheated of if his parents had forbidden him to follow Jesus. Wasn't that boy letter-writer deprived of essentially the same?

God claims first place in every family, and family happiness consists in respecting that claim. The widely-loved Saint Thomas More knew that and always put God first. He considered religious vocation, but felt no call, so he married. He became a loving husband and father, and Chancellor of England and martyr for the faith. A biographer wrote, "The strange fascination exerted by More, which has made even the foes of his religion speak of him both reverently and affectionately, is probably due to the details of his domestic life." Who can fail to admire a man who shows us so well how to love God, life and family to the full?

Finally, we consider family lifestyle. The Holy Family lived a simple lifestyle. Joseph and Mary could only give their Baby a manger-bed. And yet they gave him with it such love and care, and such example of devotion to God that they gave him all that counts most. We need many things in family life, but not as much as most of us want. The desire for much money causes much tension; a simple lifestyle eases it. Jesus said, "Avoid greed in all its forms." Avoid even the greed for action. Over-busy families have no time for love.

Years ago the Wall Street Journal spoke of "Wall Street widows," who rarely see their workaholic husbands. Now the Journal should write of Wall Street Orphans, children who rarely see either their workaholic fathers or mothers.

Parents, recall why you married. Wasn't if for love? Then doesn't the principle of priority require that you put first in your marriage all that keeps love alive and growing? And isn't that what the law of God is always meant to help us do?

"ABC" — Octave of Christmas
Solemnity of Mary, Mother of God,
and Giving of the Name Jesus

Nb 6:22-27
Gal 4:4-7
Lk 2:16-21

KNOWING HIM AND US THROUGH HER

On Christmas we celebrated the birth of the Son; today we celebrate the Mother who brought him and us together. Let our New Year's Resolution be to draw closer to Christ through Mary. But don't keep the resolution like the New Year's party-goer who at midnight proposed a Vodka toast to his resolve to swear off in the New Year!

The Virgin Mother Mary's role helps us understand Jesus and ourselves. We are told that when the shepherds rushed in and saw the Holy Family, "they understood what had been told them concerning this child." What had they been told, and what did they understand? Recall that the angel told them a Savior had been born in David's city, and they should find a sign in the fact that he was lying in swaddling clothes in a manger.

Why was the sight of the Holy Family a sign? What was the sign? What did they understand? There is something here we have to penetrate. What understanding did they come to about the child's meaning? Let us put ourselves in their shoes, and try to find out.

They were poor shepherds, and they saw to their amazement that this Savior was poor like them, and his family was poor. They remembered that the great King David had been born of a poor shepherd family, and when he became king, had concern for the poor. They recalled that when David's son, Solomon, became king he was less concerned for the poor; and when Solomon's son became king he thought of nothing but the royal state into which he had been born, and was merciless to the poor. This child would be like David, and like his parents, Mary and Joseph, who welcomed them as equals, and reverenced their religious experience.

We can go further than the shepherds. In the first reading and the Psalm we hear the blessing, "The Lord let his face shine on you!" The shepherds saw the child's face shining on them as Savior, but we see in his shining face our Lord and our God as well. St. Paul tells us in that second reading that God sent forth his Son born of a woman. The woman who holds him holds her Son and our God.

Her Virgin Motherhood reaches still further. It reaches to us. We are the branches rooted in the life of her Son. By sharing his life we become her children. And so Jesus says to us, "Behold your Mother." One Jewish convert used to envision himself in Mary's spiritual womb until she delivers him into life in heaven. This is what St. Augustine taught as well. For Mary is Mother of Christ and his body the Church.

Prayer through and with Mary helps us to understand more deeply. We commonly and rightly ask our Mother Mary to pray for us. We should also pray as she prayed, and pray with her. Mary teaches us prayer. We are told that "Mary treasured all these things and reflected on them in her heart."

In the rosary we learn from her to do the same. We go over and over the mysteries Mary lived until we are prayerfully steeped in them, so that they change our lives into the likeness of hers. By imitating her prayerfulness we are drawn to imitate her fidelity, her energetic service to Christ and his Church, and her total rejection of sin.

In the claimed visions at Medjugorje, Mary is said to have told the seers that she *needs* our prayers. That is true. Mary has unimaginable power to intercede for us. Still, God requires that we cooperate by praying for the graces he wants to give us. Only by prayer can we open up to all that Mary obtains for us. Christ has already won every grace needed for our salvation, but because we are so wayward, we block those graces and, in God's plan, need the great help of Mary and all the Saints. So Pope John Paul II said that we pray the rosary not just to Mary but with Mary. If we neglect learning to pray, we neglect learning how to be saved. "Ask and you shall receive," Jesus said.

Imitation of Mary helps us to become what we understand. It's not enough to understand the mysteries of our faith. We have to live them, as the shepherds had to learn to live them. Knowledge alone does not save. We have to do the will of the Father as Mary did.

Mary our Mother wants us not only to meditate on the Holy Family, but to become part of the Holy Family by the way we live. If Christ is our life, how can we not be part of the Holy Family? Baptism joined us to the Holy Family as it joined us to the very life of the Holy Trinity. But as a car that never runs rusts out, a life of grace that is never used equivalently rusts out.

The Holy Spirit keeps moving our hearts to cry out, Abba, Father! And he keeps inspiring us to be like the Father by imitating Jesus, who is the Father's Son, and Mary's Son. We can even become like Jesus by imitating Mary, for he surely became what he was through the training and example she gave him when he was a child.

If you don't realize how truly Mary is your Mother in the life of grace, never stop meditating on these mysteries until you do. A flesh-and-blood woman gave us a flesh-and-blood Savior, God in the flesh. He is our resurrection and our life. In this mystery, God has one Son in whom we all live and move and have our being. And that Son is Mary's Son as well. Until we realize that, we are orphaned of our Mother in the life of grace. The poet Gerard Manley Hopkins said she is Maid and Mother to us and him. But only Queen to the Seraphim.

Do you have any doubt Mary is your Mother? Listen to the Second Vatican Council. It tells us that she served Jesus with such love, stood by him with such fidelity even on Calvary, and always helped him with such faith that "she is a mother to us in the order of grace." The Council adds that she continues to pray for us in heaven, so that her maternity will last without interruption until the eternal fulfillment of all the elect.

Joseph gave himself to Mary, and she put Jesus in his arms. Let's take that as a clue on how to prepare for Holy Communion on this Feast when Mary and Joseph named him Jesus. Think of the love with which she must have received the Eucharist from the hand of the Apostle John, and offer her your heart to receive him today. Then imitate the love of her Immaculate Heart as you draw near to his Sacred Heart.

"ABC" — Epiphany

Is 60:1-6
Ep 3:2-3, 5-6
Mt 2:1-12

DOING THE EPIPHANY

Pilgrims from many lands descend daily upon Jerusalem, fulfilling the word of the prophets that the peoples of the world would pour into that Holy City to honor the Lord. Today we celebrate the first Gentiles who went there and found Christ. We celebrate Epiphany, which means the manifestation of the Lord.

This is in a special way your feast and mine. Unless we have Jewish blood in our veins, we are the Gentiles who on this day so many centuries ago first came to faith in Christ. Let us probe our feast in three of its aspects. First, the light of the Gospels has shone upon all the nations; second, we repeat the journey of the wise men to Christ; and third, we *do* the Epiphany.

First, then, the light of the Gospels has shone upon all the nations. The star the wise astrologers followed was only an external sign leading to faith. The true light is the faith within us. Faith is the light that enlightens our hearts with the truth about Christ, the Redeemer God.

The light of faith is the privileged gift of God. Signs and wonders like the star are for unbelievers, not for believers. You may recall how Jesus used to censure his fellow Jews when they kept pressing for signs. They had the faith; they should not have required endless signs. Jesus declared that they would be given only the sign of Jonah. The sign of Jonah was Jonah's exit from the belly of the whale after three days. It would be fulfilled by the resurrection, the exit of Christ from three days in the belly of the earth.

It is this interior light of faith which has gone out to all the nations. It is light from God himself, in accord with the prophecy which Jesus quoted, "They shall all be taught by God." Even as we hear the word of God read or preached, we will not have faith unless we listen to the Holy Spirit confirming it within us. So faith is the true light of God, and can be had only from God, and alone leads to God. This light continues to shine upon all the nations.

Secondly, we repeat the trek, the travel, the following of the star by the three wise men. We travel through life following the light of faith in our minds, and the light of love in our hearts. What the three wise men did is repeated over and over again. Only now what is followed is the interior star of faith. Even the wise men followed the star in the sky only because of the star of faith in their hearts, seen only by the eyes of their mind.

In the second reading, St. Paul, full of excitement, is revealing the secret that was so long hidden. It is the secret that the Chosen People were suddenly given many brothers among the Gentiles. Through the Gospel, we share in the prophets and the promises and the Messiah. We have part with the Jews in Christ, Messiah and Savior, who had been promised, and has come.

Through the Gospel light of faith, we share with the Chosen People the way to salvation. The Gospel is the new star, leading all peoples to the glory of heaven. The Gospel is embedded in the Church, which shines with Gospel light.

In and through the Church, we offer gifts which the wise men's gifts of gold, frankincense and myrrh could only symbolize. We offer to God the sacrifice and food of Christ our life.

Finally, we don't just celebrate the Epiphany, we do the Epiphany. We send the light of the star of our faith out to the whole world, calling all men and women to follow Christ. We have inherited the role of the wise men who gave a shining example of fidelity in following the star of faith. Did you notice that the faith of the wise men, lighted by their own holy yearning, revealed the coming of Christ even to the Jewish people, whose faith had dimmed? Some responded wickedly, as we know. We can be sure others responded with joy, as did the young Jewish shepherds to the angels on Christmas day.

Each of us should be aware that our life is a star of faith to lead others to Christ. The faith has been carried throughout the world, not just by missionaries, but by the movement and migration of many believers. Now, some one billion stars of faith shine around the world, leading others to Christ.

We should examine ourselves today: Does the light of our faith shine bright? Our light will have no brightness unless it shines with love, charity, and good deeds for others. Think of the work of this parish in worship, Christian education, fellowship, donations to serve the needy and feed the hungry. All of these are the light of faith leading others to Christ. If our faith burns bright with love, it continues the Epiphany.

Let us call on our noblest impulses to raise high the light of faith to all. Good soldiers are inspired by ideals of duty, honor, and country. Peoples of all ages have responded to the call of duty to God, father, and motherland. By faith we know the call of our eternal homeland. Do we respond with this sense of duty to Christ, our eternal King?

St. Peter Chrysologus said that the wise men "find, crying in a manger, the one they have followed as he shone in the sky." Jesus combines the highest and the lowest, divinity and humble humanity. Within our own families with their love and need for love and care we find admirable opportunities to exercise our faith.

Make Christian family life glow like the star of faith it was for the wise men at Bethlehem.

Recognize Christ in the Eucharist today. Surely, it is no harder than recognizing him in a crying baby. By the strength the Eucharist gives, resolve to make the starlight of your faith and love burn more brightly. Join the wise men in leading others to Christ, the world's desire.

``C`` — Baptism of the Lord   Is 42:1-4, 6-7
                                                    Ac 10:34-38
                                                    Lk 3:15-16, 21-22

JESUS REVEALED

There are many great rivers coursing through the various heartlands of the world: the Amazon, the Nile, the Niagara. Yet it is the little Jordan River, which could be swallowed up by any of them, that is memorialized in song and hymn and canticle. The Jordan is no mere memory. It just keeps flowing out of the lower reaches of the Sea of Galilee. But it is called to mind above all for the feast we celebrate today. Jesus went down into its waters and consecrated them with his sacred body. And if you go to the Jordan, you are likely to find Christians baptizing the newly converted into Christ.

In this season, the mysteries of Christ are rushing past us and we do our best to enter into them. These post-Christmas Masses presuppose our yearning for Jesus, and are meant to help us know him more deeply, love him more ardently, and follow him more closely.

The baptism of Jesus is a kind of third epiphany which illumines the meaning of his life, and the meaning of our own baptism and life.

First, his baptism is a kind of "third epiphany." Recall that "epiphany" means the revelation of the person of Jesus to the people. Though we don't call it that, the disclosure to the shepherds that the newborn Jesus is their Savior and Lord was an epiphany. We reserve the word Epiphany to the disclosure of the Lord's coming to us, the Gentiles, through the guidance of the star.

In this, the third "epiphany," it is not angels or a star, it is the divine Trinity itself who reveal the identity of Jesus. The Holy Trinity reveal that this man who is being baptized is the Son of God, the Servant of God, and the Savior of the world.

Secondly, then, his baptism reveals the meaning of his life. The baptism of Jesus first strikes us as a problem. What was he doing getting baptized along with sinners of every stripe? We are told clearly by the Scriptures that Jesus shared our human nature and our temptations, but we are told just as clearly that he never sinned. Why, then, was he baptized?

The answer is a profound and illuminating one, expressed in a number of ways. He was baptized to wash away our sins. He was baptizing the people into himself. Water in the Scriptures often symbolizes the people of the world. Jesus is washing the waters of the world with his body so they may wash us free of our sins. He is generating the sacrament of baptism, which will be the source of his mystical body the Church. St. Gregory of Nazianzus says of Jesus that "He who is spirit and flesh comes to begin a new creation through the Spirit and water." So this is the feast which looks forward to the baptism of us all. Christ is entering the waters to be united with his people as their divine Bridegroom through the mystery of baptism.

This sacred moment of his baptism is the first time in the history of the world in which there is a public manifestation that there are three persons in the one God. All three are active here.

Why this revelation of the most blessed Trinity? Because it is the Father's desire to show how pleased he is with his divine Son. And so we have the Father's voice from heaven, expressing his good pleasure. And we have Jesus himself, manifest in his human body; and we have the descent of the Holy Spirit, who rests on Jesus to anoint him in his role as Suffering Servant. The identity of Jesus, and the purpose and meaning of his life are being revealed. He will take upon his body our sins, wash them away in his blood, and redeem us for himself.

Here, then, is that Suffering Servant, so holy and so good, whose coming Isaiah foretold. And here is the Spirit of God resting upon him, as Isaiah said he would.

This, his baptism and meaning, calls us to reflect on the meaning of our own baptism and life. So many people never seem to settle on the meaning and purpose of their lives. But we have been told. By baptism into Jesus, we are begotten again as children of God. Life with God is our destiny.

That is not all. If Jesus Christ himself, who is only begotten Son of God, is also Servant of God as a human being, certainly we, the adopted children of God, are called to be his servants! We share in Jesus' sonship, and his mission. But there is more. St. Peter says the Holy Spirit anointed Jesus in power. Are we aware that the Holy Spirit has also anointed us with the power to carry out the works of the Lord? St. Gregory says that God ''wants you to become a living force for all mankind, lights shining in the world.''

Certainly, many followers of Christ become such a light. Some years ago, *Good Housekeeping* magazine polled Americans on the people they admire most. The first woman named was Mother Teresa. Three of the first four men chosen were Christian religious leaders: Jerry Falwell, Billy Graham, and Pope John Paul II.

We have a call to great joy. Through our baptism, we have been united with the Son of God, and adopted into his family. We are sons and daughters of the Holy Trinity. The divine family is revealing itself to us, as families do at every birth, and every engagement and wedding. From baptism on, we travel through life as disciples, pilgrims and apostles with Jesus. We have work to do

in the world. What have we done for Christ? What are we doing?
What will we do for Christ, our Lord and Savior?

"C" — Second Sunday of the Year   Is 62:1-5
                                                                1 Cor 12:4-11
                                                                   Jn 2:1-12

SURPRISES AT CANA OF GALILEE

The Bridegroom of the Church made Cana dear to us all by
blessing a wedding there with his presence, and providing miraculous wine for the guests. Meanings literal and mystical abound in
the event.

The little town of Cana in Galilee is perched on a mountain
side, but it has never slipped off in two thousand years. Marriages
are meant to have a less precarious perch, but too many have fallen
and broken. Why? Perhaps we can learn by reflecting on marriage,
and the Cana event, and the symbolism of the wine. For in these
things God is surely teaching us about marriage, and also about the
religious mystery of our covenant with him.

Three incisive questions will help our reflection: Why is
marriage such a sacred bond? What is the relationship between
marriage and religion? How does the divine teaching on marriage
illuminate the liturgy of the Eucharist?

First, why is marriage such a sacred bond? The Book of
Genesis tells us. It was created by the Creator of man and woman as
the covenant of their perpetual love, and their companionship of
joy, and the haven of the children sprung from their love.

Marriage and its enduring qualities have lost the esteem of a
secular world, with tragic consequences. The very week one priest
was preparing a Cana homily, he got a phone call asking for

prayers. A ten year old boy torn by the separation of his parents had just committed suicide. The perpetuity of marriage cannot be violated without inviting such sorrow and grief.

No one wishes to blame spouses who fail. The corrosive and confused values of our culture sweep many over the brink. We see all around us the problems of marriage.

What we seek is help and solutions. And they lie in reflecting on marriage as God made it, and gaining such a vision of its beauty and goodness that couples will endure the sorrows that come rather than opt for the grief of divorce.

St. Paul casts light on the way when he says that "there are different gifts but the same Spirit." If father and mother and children look into their lives and their gifts, they will realize each has his own service of love to give. They will better see the nature of the sacred bond of marriage and family and preserve it.

What is the relationship between marriage and religion? The wedded man and woman and their fruitfulness are a loving oneness manifesting God to the world, and first of all to their own. Psychological studies show how much children learn about God through their parents. Loving parents wake their children to faith in God; parents who fail undermine trust in him. Our Christian faith teaches that family bodies forth the mystery of the divine Trinity. Mysterious our Creator is, but when by love the members of family are one, the light of God the Holy Trinity bursts through.

Marriage is also, as Isaiah describes, an image of the bond between God and his people. The good marriage manifests undying love and joy and ongoing devotion, forgiveness and perpetual renewal, a caring and taking care of one another. So too does God love and take care of and delight in his people. Couples who forgive when a partner fails make us hope God will forgive us when we fail.

We Christians are taught that marriage is an image of Christ and his Church. We learn to say, "Christ and his bride the Church are like that loving couple I know." How blessed the couple who can say that of their own marriage, and the children who can say it of their family. The young St. Therese of Lisieux used to meditate on her relationship to Jesus in the light of her married sister's love. How sad for us all when broken marriages as it were deny Christ's enduring love for his Church.

This Christ-Church quality of marriage is given it by the sacrament of matrimony. A sacrament is a sign instituted by Christ to give grace. It is a visible religious mystery. The sacrament of matrimony takes a Christian man and woman, and makes them show forth something profoundly beyond themselves and greater than themselves. It makes their marriage participate in and share the blessing of that greater reality.

That greater reality is the God-man and his mystical body, of which the couple are both a part and an image. As an image, they show forth what is to come, and what they themselves await. And so Christian marriage will find the fulfillment of what it signifies only in the eternal riches of heaven. The ideal marriage, then, really is something *out of this world*. The Christian couple await a higher fulfillment beyond time. For the couple who think to find it all on earth, marriage is a mirage, and can only lead to bitterness and worse. Is it not this false expectation which is the ruin of many a marriage?

What can show the greatness of marriage better than these truths, and the fact that in God's plan all of us in the whole world were meant to be born of marriage? Again, there is an image here, for all are meant to be reborn into eternal life from Christ and his bride the Church. Marriage for the family, and the Church for the family of nations, are the great sources of life, and the guardians of its sanctity.

Third, how does Christian marriage light up the mystery of the Mass? The Mass is a kind of marriage feast between the God-man and his bride-people, the Church. As husband and wife make endless sacrifices of love for one another, Christ perpetually renews in the Mass his saving Calvary sacrifice. He gives us the wine of his blood to fill us with joy, and nourishes us on his risen body, to raise us to immortality.

At Cana, Mary showed us not only the power of her prayer, but her concern for marriage in its every detail. She is eager to help each family, and the family of the Church. Who can propose a better help to families than meditation on her holy family at Nazareth, and appeal to her and her divine Son in every family need?

"C" — Third Sunday of the Year

Ne 8:2-4, 5-6, 8-10
1 Cor 12:12-30
Lk 1:1-4; 4:14-21

WINNING TO SUNDAY JOY

Can we not learn the way to devotion and joy at our Sunday worship by imitating our religious forefathers from Abraham to Jesus and on to his Saints? That is our purpose today.

St. Luke records that Jesus entered the Nazareth synagogue on the Sabbath "as he was in the habit of doing." As a faithful Jewish "son of the Law," Jesus revered the commandment, "Keep holy the Sabbath day." He did it with joy and gladness, for every act of worship is a momentary going home to God.

We try to imitate Jesus. Church law states that "Sunday is the day on which the paschal mystery is celebrated in light of the apostolic tradition." It reminds us of our serious obligation to participate in Sunday Mass, and "to abstain from those labors and business concerns which impede the worship to be rendered to God, the joy which is proper to the Lord's Day, or the proper relaxation of mind and body." Here the spirit of Sunday is highlighted. It is the day God invites us to share his rest as a pledge and foretaste of eternity.

Worship should be joyous, but won't be without a struggle. The Jewish people learned that when they returned from exile in pagan lands where they had neglected their faith. Ezra the priest assembled them, and read and interpreted the Scripture from dawn to midday. When he began, all the people gave their happy "Amen," as was right. But when he read the Scripture with its laws and requirements they broke into weeping. Then Ezra reminded them of their chosen status and calling and privilege, and told them the day was holy to the Lord, and their strength was to be found in joy.

We too have to keep examining our attitude toward worship and the word of God, and its explanation in the homily. How, we might ask, should we conduct ourselves at Sunday worship? What attitude should we have toward the Scriptural readings and the homily which explains them? How do we respond to the Sunday obligation?

Certainly we know it is fitting to go with joy to our Sunday meeting with Christ, as the shepherds hastened to Bethlehem. It is right to attend Mass with deep devotion, as Mary stood on Calvary. Worship of God is meant to be a joy. But we have to work our way to joy, as Mary went from Good Friday to Easter.

The attitude we owe to hearing the Scripture is reverence. But it is not strange if we have a certain anxiety too. We know how precariously perched we are on the stilts of our virtues, walking through the minefields of our passions and sins. We dread to hear of obligations we may have ducked.

Surely, we expect and want the priest's homily to interpret the Scriptures faithfully and with practical applications, even though it may ruin some of our plans for a life of pleasantries. Are we not in the position of the Ethiopian who read the Scriptures, but said to Philip, "How can I understand unless someone instructs me?" The instructions don't always please us, but let's have at least the virtue of King Herod, who, though troubled by John the Baptist, still wanted to hear him. But unlike Herod, we should not lop off the priest's head!

Any who don't experience joy and consolation at Mass should examine their attitude toward the Sunday obligation. Some don't want to be at Mass. At the least pretext, they miss Mass. When they go, they can't wait to get in and get out. They shop around to find the fastest Mass; they get upset with priests who take the time to give a good homily. They put pressure on pastors to be more concerned about keeping the liturgy short than keeping it fitting. Can you imagine any disciple at the foot of the cross saying to Jesus, "Die and get your work of redemption over with, so I can get about my other business"? Since the Mass is Calvary renewed, is a similar attitude toward it less disrespectful?

We all need the inspiration of those who fell in love with the Mass. Young St. Maria Goretti walked a 15-mile round trip to get to Mass; St. Maximilian Kolbe persisted in offering Mass when in such bad health he needed support at the altar to keep from falling. Think of the devotion of our Lady at Mass. She knew the value of the Sacrifice of the Mass because she was standing at the feet of Jesus when he offered it in a bloody manner. She saw the love for us all with which he offered it.

When we go home from Sunday Mass with the intention of savoring its joys throughout the day of rest and relaxation, we will soon find that in coming weeks we will go to Mass with eager anticipation. Sunday is a unity. When we live the whole day in a godly spirit, it will reflect on our way of attending Mass. We will worship together rejoicing, for eternal life is ours in Jesus Christ, the risen Savior and Lord.

A fitting conclusion to these thoughts is the poem, "Sunday Joy," which invites us to ponder the meaning of our day of rest.

> O God, you made a day of rest
> When earth and sky you gave its frame,
> As promise of that future blest
> Awaiting all who love your name.
>
> You made a newer day more blest

When Christ immortal death destroyed,
To start our week with leisured rest
And keep our hearts with love employed.

Now Sunday's hymns to heaven ring,
As we by Holy Spirit led,
Do offer Christ our Victim King,
And break with joy our Father's Bread.

And so with angels we rejoice
As weekly we our sacred best
Devote to you in gifts most choice
Until on high we find our rest.

"ABC" — The Presentation

Ml 3:1-4
Heb 2:14-18
Lk 2:22-40

THE GOD-HERO IS RECOGNIZED

Someone has said that when you can't sleep you shouldn't count the sheep; you should talk to the Shepherd. How many times old Simeon would have loved to do that. But until the hour recounted in today's Gospel the Shepherd had not yet come.

To appreciate all that is going on in this Feast of the Presentation is not easy. I resort to a comparison with one of the most loved story lines of all time, that of the hero suddenly coming on the scene to save the girl in distress. Coming suddenly onto the scene in today's Gospel, coming to our rescue, is the God-hero promised by Isaiah. He is not easily recognized as the hero, for he comes as an infant. We need Simeon's help.

We also need to reflect on how this Hero comes to fulfill all of God's promises. God punished Satan who deceived our first parents, but promised them a redeemer for the human race. This Savior would pay the debt of sin of anyone who believed in him.

God freed his people in Egypt from slavery to the Egyptians. The Egyptians were sinners, and Pharaoh has been compared to Satan. It was just to punish them. But his people were sinners too. How justify not punishing them along with the Egyptians? The fact is, God would have spared the Egyptians too if they had turned from their sins and believed in him as his people had believed. He told his people to mark their doorposts with the blood of the paschal lamb who died in their stead. Thus when the angel of death came to slay the firstborn of each Egyptian family, he passed by the homes of God's people where the lamb's blood was on the doorpost.

But this was only a stopgap measure. A lamb's blood can't take the place of human blood. The lamb was a temporary substitute. It was a promise that a human lamb, innocent and holy, would come and die to take away the sins of his people. He would be their true Hero and Savior. Until he came each newborn son had to be redeemed by a lamb who would die in his stead.

And so the newborn Jesus had to be redeemed by a lamb too, in accord with the Law. That is the meaning of the Presentation. Mary and Joseph brought Jesus to the temple to be redeemed by sacrificing a lamb in his stead. But they were so poor they couldn't afford a lamb. They substituted a couple of pigeons. That was allowed in the case of the poor.

In that hour the Holy Spirit inspired the old man Simeon and old Anna to see the truth: this Child was not to be redeemed at all. He was the Redeemer. He was the human lamb for which all the other lambs had substituted until he came. He was the Lamb who would die to take away the sins of the world. He is the light of life for all peoples. He is the Innocent Victim who would pay the price of redemption for all God intended to save from their just punishment. Jesus made it possible for God to be merciful in saving some without being unjust in condemning others. The Hero had come on the scene in the disguise of an infant. The girl he was to rescue was his bride the Church. That is why this is such a joyous mystery. It is, as you will recall, the fourth joyful mystery of the rosary.

It began when the Holy Family came to fulfill God's law by worshipping together. To see a family worshipping together is inspiring, but here there was more than simple inspiration. Through their worship the presence of the Savior was revealed.

We are meant to repeat and share the lovely mystery we recall. How can we who worship at Mass discover the Savior as did Simeon and Anna? By acting as they did. Like them we come into the Temple of God to pray and worship and long for the Savior. Like Simeon and Anna we dwell on our sins and need of a Savior. As they used to do, we listen to the Scriptures. We hear how they met the Holy Family. And suddenly at the consecration Jesus is in our midst. By faith we recognize him as the Savior of the world.

Not all recognized the Savior then, nor do all now. Even at Mass some complain they get nothing from it. They come with too little faith and too little longing to be freed of sin.

How can we experience liberation as Simeon did? He uses the image of a slave being freed from bondage. Only if we confess that we are slaves to sin can we hope to share his experience. By faith we see in the Mass what he only foresaw: the Mass is the Last Supper, Calvary and the Resurrection brought into our midst in the person of Jesus our Lord and Savior. Jesus offers his temptations, sufferings and death to free us from ours. St. Bernard said, "I may have sinned gravely," but adds, "What sin is there so deadly that it cannot be pardoned by the death of Christ?" Isn't that Simeon's experience? It should be ours too.

How take the Savior into our arms like Simeon? We can do even better. We simply respond to our Redeemer's own invitation to us: "Take and eat. This is my body." The Church calls us to this. In the Opening Prayer we asked the Father that his Savior-Son entering the Temple may free us from sin and admit us into his presence. In the Mass and Holy Communion he does that beyond measure.

Since we share in the joy of Simeon and Anna, like them we should spread the Good News. Note how much the worship and word of Simeon and Anna helped both their fellow believers and us. By fully participating in word and song and prayer at Mass we help one another find the presence of the divine Hero. By great interior recollection and piety and every outward mark of respect and devotion we proclaim to all around us the presence of our Savior. By coming eagerly, coming early, and going home without haste, we give powerful witness to Christ.

The Holy Family went home too. They went to the work of salvation awaiting them. Jesus would foretell his passion; Mary's was foretold by Simeon. The lance which would pierce his Heart would transpierce her soul.

Their suffering led to resurrection and glory. Ours will too. Consider the touching parallel between the Presentation and the Assumption. Mary lovingly presented her Son to the Father in the Temple in Jerusalem. In the Assumption, the Son lovingly presented his Mother to the Father in the Temple of Heaven. Our turn will come as well. Again and again we present the Son to the Father in the Holy Sacrifice. How happy will be the day when the Son presents us to the Father in the Temple that will be our home forever.

"C" — Fourth Sunday of the Year

Jr 1:4-5, 17-19
1 Cor 12:31 - 13:13
Lk 4:21-30

ANGRY WITH GOD

To reach the town of Nazareth in Galilee you climb a steep mountain. Once there, you can be shown "The Mount of Precipitation," cited as the place where Jesus' fellow townsmen intended to murder him by hurling him down headlong. These were ordinary people he knew and loved, neighbors when he was a growing boy. He visited their sick, attended their weddings, sorrowed at their funerals, had fun at their festivals. He helped build their houses when they married, made their furniture and baby cribs, and fashioned their ploughs.

How could they turn on him so? Asking that question is asking to look into the dark depths of the human heart — not just theirs but ours. Still, it is necessary to ask, and urgent to look, for this angry turning against God and his word has never ceased. It may go on in us.

Jesus entered their synagogue and preached. They had hardly praised him when they vented their murderous rage. Why? Because their praise was dishonest. They marvelled at him and at the same time said, "Isn't this Joseph's son?" Judging by what happened next, would we be wrong in interpreting their thoughts this way: "He's just a country hick like us. Who does he think he is? Is he going to tell me what to do or think? Never!"

What lies behind this? What, except the wrong response to a key question: Do we believe there is such a thing as a vocation from God? Does or doesn't God choose and appoint human beings to speak for him? Not simply those in the past or far away, given some aura by time, distance, and imagination, but pimply kids like the boy down the block who returns an ordained priest and tells us things we have no intention of tolerating.

Jesus preached to them the word of God that is the "food of salvation and the fountain of life." But his harsh words didn't sound like salvation to them! Even if he was quoting God's word, how dare he remind them that Elijah was sent to a pagan widow to work his miracle, and Elisha cured none of the many Jewish lepers, but a foreign dog of a non-believer? And did he have the gall to pretend he could work miracles for them, if only they weren't deficient in faith? Toss this upstart off the nearest cliff, and good riddance!

What were they saying? "We will not listen to our alleged shortcomings from you. And never dare tell us we reject God's spokesmen!" They expressed these sentiments by attempted murder.

This same drama plays itself out in all times and places, including our own lives. Jesus comes to us in many guises, to be accepted or rejected. Like the Nazarenes, we may reject him unawares. Today is meant to be a moment of truth for us.

Jesus speaks to us in the Mass, the Scriptures, the priest, the bishops, the Pope, and one another. He speaks to us in our hearts and in our lives. It is the faith of the Church that "Christ is always present in his Church, especially in the actions of the liturgy. He is present in the sacrifice of the Mass, in the person of the minister, and most of all under the eucharistic species." And "He is present in his word, for it is he himself who speaks when the holy Scriptures are read in the Church."

Do we have listening hearts, or are we "Nazarenes"? We certainly see much Nazarene-like anger in the Church. The response of many Catholics to Church teaching is far from the "Amen" of acceptance that is the mark of listening faith. We see a plague of dissent amounting to crisis.

Rejection didn't begin with Christ, and has not yet ended. Jeremiah found his experience as God's spokesman so bitter he complained to God that God had seduced him as a naive youth into undertaking so awful a role. He barely escaped with his life.

St. Augustine had the experience of preaching an unwelcome word. He wrote to his flock, "However unwelcome I am, I dare to say: 'You wish to stray, you wish to be lost; but I do not want this.' " Why? He explains that it is because he is a shepherd, and God grows angry with unfaithful shepherds. And so he asks, "Shall I fear you rather than him? *Remember, we must all present ourselves before the judgment seat of Christ.*"

As we meditate on the rage of the Nazarenes, we should examine our attitude toward our own pastors. They are often crushed between their responsibility to God, and the rebuff by many whom they are charged to guide. They are anxious they will be rejected or unfaithful, and anxious for the souls of those who won't listen. Is it a triumph for anyone but Satan when, in their weakness, pastors yield, tell their flock what they want to hear, and become their sheep instead of their shepherds? Is it good when the word of God ceases to be preached? We all have shepherds in the place of Christ. The people have the priests, and the priests the bishops, and the bishops the Pope. We all have to listen.

Today we are called to cultivate listening hearts. We pray to be rich in faith, and beg God to stir up vocations, and give us pastors courageous enough to speak his word. We pray to be rich in hope, looking to what is promised. We pray to be rich in a love quick to catch God's voice, and swift to obey it.

How do we develop a listening heart? There is one secret that can be briefly expressed. The listening heart goes the way which St. Paul says surpasses all others, the way of love. Like Jesus, it is patient, kind and forbearing. It is without jealously, snobbishness, selfishness, anger, brooding. Even in anger, true love never wants to hurt or destroy, only to guard and protect truth and honor and righteousness. Jesus loved those fellow townsmen who tried to kill him. He went his way to die for their salvation, and no doubt many of them in the end became members of his body, the Church. We are all members of one body. Whatever their differences, pastors and people, husbands and wives, parents and children, friends and co-workers should hear one another with listening hearts, and pray that in time we become one mind and one heart in the one Spirit of God. Nothing less becomes us as the people who have as our very pulse the beating Heart of the Savior of the world.

"C" — Fifth Sunday of the Year   Is 6:1-2, 3-8
                                                  1 Cor 15:1-11
                                                  Lk 5:1-11

DISCOVERING I'M CALLED

The young among us are not likely to recall the great magnetism of President John F. Kennedy, which extended far beyond our shores. When he was assassinated, a Filipino woman said, "I felt as though a member of my family had died."

The magnetism of the Son of God reaches across the ocean of time itself. His winning call went to Peter and Paul and will go out to others to the end of time. And so we have questions to ask. Am I called? What is the call like? To what am I called?

Am I called? Every decent human being feels called to do good. The Christian feels a call to do God's work and will. All who have listening hearts will discover their call. Jesus said, "Whoever wishes to come after me must deny himself, take up his cross, and follow me." It's as though he said, "My brothers and sisters, we're all in this Gospel enterprise together. One for all and all for one, we carry on the prayers and works of spreading the kingdom, and share its sufferings and joys."

Obviously, not all are called to leave everything, as Peter did, and as those do who become priests, brothers and sisters. But all are called to the prayer and the work, and so we should be listening for the call in our hearts.

The call is there, but we must tune it in. We can compare the call to the TV signals in our homes. They are present, but we won't receive any unless we turn on our set, and unless we tune it, we won't get the one we want.

What is the call like? We know how to tune in a TV set, but do we know how to tune in God's call? How does it feel to experience the call? Are there any guidelines to keep us from following a will-o'-the-wisp? Fortunately, there are. First, there are examples of calls proved out by those who had them, like Isaiah's and Peter's and Paul's. Then there are principles to guide us in hearing our call and making a right decision.

One priest described his call. Even as a boy, he felt an attraction to the priesthood. He also felt sinful and unworthy, as did Isaiah and Peter, and drew back, as they almost did. He went to work in industry, but found no peace. He would take a job and get involved in it, but after some months, start thinking, "Good Lord, don't tell me I'm going to be doing this the rest of my life!" Each time that theme song started, he went to another job. Finally, he found the solution in the realization, "I am a sinner. So are all men. No one is worthy of so sacred a call. But if called, we should respond." And he did. When he entered the distant city where he was to study for the priesthood, he had the sense, "I have come home." From then on, that sense remained, no matter where his vocation took him.

When we find our call, and find ourselves in the service of God, we have come home. That's what the call feels like.

There are three ways of hearing and responding to a call. The first is when the call of God is so attractive it draws like an irresistible magnet, as when Jesus said to Matthew, "Follow me," and Matthew got right up, left all, and followed. The second is when a person is buffeted by various attractions, one day to the priesthood, the next to marriage, and so on back and forth, until the issue is settled by prayer and penance. The third is when a person sits down calmly and prayerfully, and reasons out the meaning of his life and what he should do with it, and what he thinks would please God, and tries to make a decision in accord with his best lights. When he comes to what he thinks is the right decision, he offers it to God, and if he finds a lasting sweetness and peace and rest, he knows it pleases God and he has "come home." If not, he keeps searching.

A help to making a decision in that third way is simply to ask ourselves questions like these: What is the purpose of every life? What does my life call me to do as a Christian? If I were asked to advise another person like myself, what would I suggest? What would the Virgin Mary do in my shoes? When I'm lying on my deathbed, about to go home to God, what will I wish I decided at this moment?

Each of us, then, has the question, "To what am I called?" If we are already in a permanent state, whether of marriage or the priesthood or the religious life, the answer, in part, is that we are to offer our service within that context. For holiness is found in being faithful to the duties of the state of life we have chosen, since that is what pleases God. Certainly, we don't please God by abandoning our vows.

The Church needs priests, sisters and brothers. It also needs the tremendous potential of the laity, and is coming alive to involving the whole people of God in the work of God. The people of God preach the Gospel most often through works of charity. They are hearing things like, "The Eucharist is incomplete everywhere in the world as long as there is hunger anywhere in the world. What are you doing to feed the hungry?"

"What have I done for Christ?" a Christian should ask. "What am I doing for Christ? What should I do for Christ? Can I do anything to see that people have jobs? Or to provide affordable housing? To stop abortion? To help the homeless and the street kids who sell their bodies to survive? To bring people together in the parish, and the place where I work? To influence the political process for family-oriented legislation? To teach Christian doctrine, and the moral and religious values that lead to eternal life, and prevent many of the ills of society? What needs do I see around me that I can relieve, if only a little?"

Generally, it all begins with prayer. We say daily the Morning Offering, "O Jesus, through the Immaculate Heart of Mary, I offer you all my thoughts, works, joys and sufferings of this day, for all the intentions of your Sacred Heart." We pray the Our Father,

"Thy kingdom come, thy will be done on earth, as it is in heaven." Then some need around us hits us in the face, and we hear in our listening hearts the words of God to Isaiah, "Who will go, and whom shall I send?" Generous Isaiah said, "Here I am, Lord. Send me!" What will you and I say?

"C" — Sixth Sunday of the Year

Jr 17:5-8
1 Cor 15:12, 16-20
Lk 6:17:20-26

THE WEALTH OF THE POOR AND POVERTY OF THE RICH

"Blessed are you poor." Isn't it thought-provoking that even some atheists don't mock that statement? They see in it a profound truth that makes one think.

But do any take it seriously in their own life? Quite a few. Young men and women continuously leave all the world offers and take the vow of poverty to more surely possess God.

"Woe to you rich!" Do any take *that* seriously? Some do, like the young son of a wealthy mother who left behind his promised inheritance to follow Jesus more closely. We all take this teaching seriously to the extent that we won't rob or kill or break the other commandments to get rich. And married couples sacrifice much to have and bring up their children.

Why are the poor called blessed, and the rich pronounced to be in a dangerous state? The rich are in danger because they are tempted to become inordinately attached to their wealth. They are in danger of loving their wealth more than their God; the poor are not. The poor are almost compelled to turn to God and God to them, and what greater blessing is there than that?

Wealth is certainly not evil; it's only our hearts that make it dangerous. Jesus had wealthy friends who were generous, not greedy. They were "poor in spirit," that is, they put God above all possessions, and were ready to sacrifice all for God.

If the poor are blessed, why does the Church urge us to relieve their poverty? For many reasons. Let's consider two. First, the same Christ who pronounced them blessed commanded us to show them mercy. Second, poverty is a limited blessing. It brings a blessing only to poor people who don't turn bitter or violent or hateful. The blessing of poverty lies not in having nothing, but in the way it makes many poor people turn to God. And their experience of suffering often makes them feel compassion for others who are in pain or in need.

Sometimes the poverty of the poor makes them suffer horribly. Not only do they have nothing on earth, but they feel that God doesn't love them, that they have nothing in heaven either. By giving them help on earth, we also restore to them their trust in the love of their heavenly Father.

In God's plan for the human race, we are to relieve one another's poverty. God created enough for all. The right to private property must always be limited by the needs of all. It's ancient Catholic wisdom that not to share with the hungry is to kill them.

For a century the Church has been interpreting this beatitude to fit the conditions of the modern world. It sees poverty today to be a result of armaments and war, mismanagement and greed. It teaches nations and individuals to share what they have with the deprived.

Vatican II said the Church is a sign of the unity of the whole human race. The Church can't remain silent when rich nations refuse to help poor ones, and wealthy people the poor around them. Poverty is so bad that ten out of every hundred children in the world die before their first birthday. Many people go hungry much of their lives. Does anyone think Christ wants that? "Love one another," he said, "as I have loved you."

Pope John Paul II said that the griefs and anxieties of the poor are the griefs and anxieties of all the followers of Christ. "Christians have the moral obligation," he said, "to take into consideration in personal decisions and decisions of government this relationship of universality" that calls us to heed the poverty and underdevelopment of so many millions of people.

The Pope pointed to the new vision of the oneness of all on planet earth. We're linked to a common destiny. Unless we work together, we can't elude anguish, fear and escapist phenomena like drugs, or solve the worldwide ecological problems.

The Pope said that people too attached to wealth never really learn what it means to be human; and people with too little are too deprived to have the chance to live humanly.

Our true nature is to possess not just things, but God. God is big enough to go around, and so are the material goods he gave us. We need only overcome greed and mismanagement. Christ and his beatitudes lead the way, if only we will follow.

We must give up the all-consuming desire for profit at any cost, and the desire for the power to manipulate others. When we break the commandments, we wound ourselves and others.

What can we do, then? First, we can realize that the world, like a building made of bricks, takes its shape from each of us and the other five billion like us. It's the sum of the way we live as individuals and families and nations, and the way we use our resources. When you or I change for the better, the world changes for the better. That's the only way it will change. We can each begin a trend of one. The old saying is still true: "It's better to light one candle than curse the darkness."

Christ is calling us to grow poor in spirit. It means avoiding all excess; it means making our politics and our vote express our faith-vision of the oneness of all God's children. We think in terms of the common good and shun all self-centeredness. We see that true freedom lies in possessing the truth and the holiness that avoids the slavery of sin. "If you remain in my word," Jesus said, "you will truly be my disciples, and you will know the truth, and the truth will set you free.'' This freedom is the contagious kind that spreads far and wide.

In today's Opening Prayer we reminded God that he promised to remain forever with those who do what is just and right. Surely we believe that and want to win his divine presence.

We know where to get the strength. It comes from the Bread of Life. Pope John Paul II said that ''All of us who take part in the Eucharist are called to discover, through this sacrament, the profound meaning of our actions in the world in favor of development and peace.''

Christ's sacrificial death, which the Eucharist celebrates, is transforming the world. By uniting our hearts to his Sacred Heart and our lives to his holy life we become the agents of that transformation. When the well-to-do help the poor, they gain the blessing of poverty of spirit which the poor have, and the poor the advantages of the wealthy, to the glory of God.

''C'' — Seventh Sunday of the Year   1 S 26:2, 7-9, 12-13, 22-23
                                                        1 Cor 15:45-59
                                                        Lk 6:27-38

HEARTS THAT KNOW ONLY PEACE

In the late Eighties, in Jesus' homeland, the Palestinian uprising provoked events that clash and harmonize with today's Gospel. A Jewish father with his kids in his car saw a spark in the dark woods. Fearing a Palestinian with a bomb, he fired his pistol. The fire was returned. His year-old boy was killed. Soldiers rushed out. He had been firing at his own troops.

Three months later a Palestinian shot and killed an Israeli

soldier. The Israeli's wife donated his heart to a Palestinian await-ing a heart transplant. Soon the dead soldier's heart was beating in his "enemy's" chest.

"Love your enemies, do good to those who hate you." Never think this is unreal, or beyond us. It goes on in this poor old world, even among those who don't have faith in Christ to sustain them. Will they leave us behind? Will they shame us?

Today's Mass lights up our high calling with word and exam-ple. Help us, we asked the Father in the Opening Prayer, to be like your Son in word and deed.

Help us, we ask now, to be like his forefather David, who spared King Saul's life, though Saul was out to murder him. Help us, as St. Paul urges us, to overcome the wild earthly nature we inherited from the first Adam. Help us live by the spiritual nature given us at baptism by the Son of God, the last Adam. Heavenly Father, help us to fight and overcome our evil passions and live as Jesus lived, in your likeness. Inspire us with eagerness for noble deeds.

In the Psalm we confess our heavenly Father doesn't deal with us according to our sins. Him we must imitate, even toward our enemies. We are to put enmity from us as far as the east is from the west. The love and forgiveness we're called to is not natural but supernatural. If we don't get that message we'll fight God's word and be at enmity with God as all sinners are.

The readings call us to the work of peace, peace in our hearts, peace in our neighborhood, peace in our world. Little things are important, but the Church today is also calling us to big things, to universal concern. The Pope called this "the age of the Church." The Church has matured in itself and its members, and is finding its true stature and place in the world community.

The Church guides us not as an expert in sociology but as an "expert in humanity." It teaches not ideology but theology. But it does condemn certain ideologies which destroy peace.

Marxism is evil because it is atheistic. It denies God's existence and makes the state supreme. From this many other evils follow. It deprives individuals of freedom and incentive to be productive according to their own lights. In the effort to level out the possession of goods, it only levels down, and poverty spreads.

War is no answer to the quest for peace. It plunders resources and kills those it means to save. "War never again!" cried Pope Paul VI to the United Nations. Terrorism is no solution. It preys on and slaughters the innocent, thus using an evil means that can never achieve what terrorists intend.

Capitalism has proved beneficial only when infused with safeguards to protect the many from the greedy and the power mongers. But unless the hearts of people are converted every system becomes corrupt and none yields its promise.

Peace begins with me and with you. We are the living building blocks of society. Nothing can give us peace but our own hearts and consciences. God's word teaches that, and so does common sense. "What causes wars, and what causes fighting among you?" the Letter of James asks pointedly. "Is it not your passions that are at war in your members? You desire and do not have." Passions between two cause fistfights and murders, but the passions of many together cause wars and nuclear explosions.

That is why the beatitude of poverty of spirit (which we considered last week) is the foundation of both personal peace and world peace. Haven't we yet found that Jesus the Son of God knows what he is talking about? When we are no longer grasping, and are actively concerned for the good of all, we become peaceable and peace makers. Then we are the true children of God. The first order of promoting peace is to cultivate it in ourselves, with our family, and among all our acquaintances.

The second step is to contribute to peace in our society. Here, attitudes and politics are the means. We need human and Christian attitudes toward ethnic and racial groups. People can't help being black or white or copper colored or of a certain ethnic origin. To hold it against them is both unjust and irrational. The heart of the

Jew beat contentedly in the chest of the Palestinian, knowing nothing about ethnic origins. If we are fair to all, we will use our politics to vote that fairness into our laws and leadership.

The third step we take is to contribute to international peace. The new name for peace, said Pope Paul VI, is development, the development of nations. When nations develop, individuals develop. When people have a sufficiency for their needs, and a chance to cultivate their talents and services, most do contribute to the peace all desire. Peace is the tranquillity of right order. It requires a fair distribution of earth's goods.

But all of this will fail unless we remember God and infuse our cultures with the spirit of faith and religion. "You have made us for yourself alone," said St. Augustine, "and we are restless until we rest in thee." When we let non-believers give shape to our culture and our government we end up with the turmoil of horrors like legal abortion.

We don't demand that all citizens share our beliefs. We only demand that our society be built on the foundations of the moral law which is as fundamental as human nature itself. It can be read in the heart by all people of good will. We also insist on the freedom to preach the Gospel. The very Gospel we believe in commands us to spread the word of salvation. God desires that all peoples be saved and come to a knowledge of the truth.

So we end in prayer, praying to you, heavenly Father, that our quest for peace may be inspired by the example of the love we touch in this celebration of our Lord's self-giving. May it bring us and all whom we influence to the eternal life he promised.

"C" — Eighth Sunday of the Year   Si 27:4-7
                                                    1 Cor 15:54-58
                                                    Lk 6:39-45

THE POWER AND GLORY OF THE TONGUE

One priest likes to tell the story of what he learned from an old, infirm priest he used to visit years ago. Once they were watching a cops-and-robbers program on TV. A woman of loose morals in the story was treated with contempt by the cops, but the old priest just kept repeating, "Poor thing, poor thing." What a lesson in the use of the tongue that old priest gave!

"Each one," Jesus says, "speaks from his heart's abundance." Today's readings say wise things about the tongue. Can I give a whole homily on the tongue? It's such a small thing. Yes, but it seems to be all muscle and taste buds — and what tastes it has! It craves the sweet and the bitter, love and hate, truth and lies. Does anything on earth do more to bring peace or destroy it in home and nation and world than the earth's five billion wagging tongues?

God gave only Ten Commandments, and yet devoted two to the tongue. "You shall not take the name of the Lord your God in vain," and "You shall not bear false witness against your neighbor." The Bible mentions the tongue more than 150 times. The tongue wins resurrection or forfeits it, merits heaven or hell.

"Death and life are in the power of the tongue," says the Bible. The tongue glorifies and curses God and man; it saves and destroys children and grownups, marriages and nations. Cemeteries house many bodies put there by traitors' tongues; wars have been provoked by the wild tongues of leaders, and peace recovered by the golden tongues of statesmen; divorce courts are filled by the bitter tongues of spouses. Christians use the tongue to receive the sacred body of Christ one moment, and to rail at someone who delays them in the parking lot the next. Martyrs have had their tongue torn out for using it to glorify God, and others gain applause for using theirs to tell dirty stories.

St. James marvels at the power of the tongue. He compares it to the small bit that governs powerful horses, and the little rudder that gives direction to mighty ships, and the touch of fire that sets a whole forest ablaze. "From the same mouth," he says, "come blessing and cursing. This need not be, my brothers."

One homily can hardly enumerate the virtues and vices the tongue can practice. When the devil tells a lie, Jesus says, "he is in character, for he is a liar and the father of lies." So let's begin with honesty. Honesty is the link that binds us, as lies divide us. The Second Vatican Council said that we should hold honesty in high esteem as one of the social virtues "without which no true Christian life can exist." It tells us we should practice honesty in all our dealings so we "will attract all to the love of the true and the good and finally to the Church and to Christ." It tells us that "honesty compels us to declare openly our conviction that there is but one true religion, the religion of Christianity," and that we hope all will come to it.

Honesty is a must in family life. Once we begin doubting one another, how can we live in peace and trust? Don't we all appreciate the "honest John" we can always rely on? Family life built on honesty is built on rock, and family life lacking it is built on quicksand and earthquake.

But if lies offend against honesty, so does an excess of honesty. People sometimes commend themselves for honesty who are only gross and brutal and even destructive of the character of another. Slander is the telling evil lies of another; detraction is the sin of telling another's sins without necessity. It is not only the priest-confessor who must keep secrets; we're all bound to keep quiet about the sins of others unless duty-bound to bring them up. To gossip or intend harm is not honesty but sin.

Finding the balance between praise and criticism in family life isn't easy. Parents have the duty of correcting children, but St. Paul warns against nagging them. It only discourages them. To constantly put children down is to break their morale. Let me suggest a good norm. After you criticize once, praise once before you criticize again. And when did you last say to spouse or child or dear one, "I love you"?

It's strange how little we use the tongue to praise others. Are we afraid of inflating egos? Praise usually has the opposite effect. When friends fail to praise us, we think they're either blind or unloving. When they do praise us, we so appreciate it we're likely to bring up one of our faults to show we're not really that good — yet we're inspired by the praise to become better. Between husband and wife, a compliment a day is more important than a vitamin a day. But give only honest praise. Some people praise not to give honor but to gain influence. Genuine praise is served up with delicacy and truth; baloney is praise cut out of thin air with a butcher knife.

In a democracy we freely express our minds, but excessive criticism of public officials, pastors and teachers only does harm to their influence and embitters us. And it makes us forget gratitude is a duty too. Let's recall the lives of the Saints. So many of them spoke only good of others. Do we ever hear St. Peter criticize others? He was too conscious of his own faults.

Use of the tongue is so tricky I'm fortunate if I can get through this homily without offending someone, and if I offend I apologize. It's easier to talk about the faults of the tongue than to avoid them. Jesus gives the reason: "Each man speaks from his heart's abundance." St. James says that anyone who doesn't fall short in speech is perfect, and "able to bridle his whole body also." So we needn't be disheartened or give up on ourselves or others; we patiently try to grow in all the virtues.

One boy had his mouth washed out for using bad language, but it didn't cure him. He stopped only when he realized he was taking dirt into his mouth, and didn't want to do that.

Let us close with a look at the holiness of speech, above all for a Christian. St. John writes that "In the beginning was the Word, and the Word was with God, and the Word was God." God is pure Spirit, and words have a special relationship to God the Son, who is even called "the Word." Before a word is sounded by our tongue, it is first conceived in our mind and heart as a spiritual reality akin to God the Son. So we want all our words to be pure and honest and truthful to image the Son of God.

Today when we receive the sacred body of Christ on our tongues, let's promise him we'll dedicate our tongues to good words, because they honor him, the Word of the Father.

"C" — First Sunday of Lent

Dt 6:4-10
Rm 10:8-13
Lk 4:1-13

WHO WINS THE VICTORY?

A girl of six saw her family fall apart. After the divorce her father was gone. She lived with her mother in a poor flat where she could hear the huge sewer rats gnawing their way in through the floorboards. In school she worked hard and did poorly. "I wasn't interested in the capital of Iowa," she said; "I was interested in surviving." In her time, divorce was rare and she felt like an outcast. "If there is a God," she said, "then why am I so different, why don't I have a family?"

She developed a serious stomach illness, and had no money for doctors. Her mother heard of a stigmatic in the city who had been cured of cancer, and sent her for a blessing. She went, without any conscious faith, and got a prayer card, a novena to the Little Flower. On the ninth day she was cured. Then she knew there was a God, a God who loved her, a God who cared. She grew up, and is known to millions as Mother Angelica, the Sister who founded a TV network to teach others of the God who loves us.

She shared, as we all do, in the temptations of Jesus. We don't like to think Jesus was tempted. We prefer to think he was like us in all things but temptation. The Scriptures won't have it. He was like us in all things but sin.

Why resist the fact he was tempted? Because we prefer to believe he was too holy to be tempted. In doing that, we're saying he was too holy to be human. But he proved that not even God is too holy to be human. So here's another reason we prefer to believe he wasn't tempted: If he wasn't tempted, we could use the excuse, "Lord, you were too good to have my troubles, so you don't understand."

We can't be honest and hold to that subterfuge. Jesus was tempted more violently than any of us. Satan brought all his biggest guns to bear against Jesus, and let fire. He aimed at Jesus' "weak spot," his love for us. What Satan was really saying is, "Make it easy for them, or they won't follow and be saved. Give them bread by miracle, work miracles they can't disbelieve, and be so magnificent they will follow you in hordes." What Satan was really doing is inviting Jesus to serve himself, to seize power and glory and lord it over us instead of living a life of example for us.

Jesus resisted the temptation to give us an easy way, as we have to resist every false way. Because he was tempted and won out, he shows us the way, and is our way. "If he were not tempted," St. Augustine says, "he could not teach you how to triumph over temptation."

Lent is the holy season we go into the desert with Jesus. We pray, do penance, and uncover the deceits into which we have fallen. I say deceits, for temptation often attacks faith. When we want something that is wrong, few of us are so bad as to fly right in the face of God and seize it. No, we argue and convince ourselves that what we want is not really wrong. That was what Satan tried to lead Jesus to do, and lends us a hand to do.

That's why Lent calls us to see the whole history of our faith. We say with each of the Jewish people, ''My father was a wandering Aramean.'' We recall how Abraham, our father in faith, was chosen by God, and fathered the people from whom Jesus the Messiah was born, through the maternity of the Virgin Mary.

We see this approach to Lent in the way the Church prepares converts. In the new Rite of Christian Initiation of Adults, catechumens are marched into Lent for solemn reflection, conversion, and preparation for the initiation rites of Holy Week. The Church examines them, and judges if they are worthy to share in the mysteries of Christ's death and resurrection.

We, who were long since baptized, judge ourselves. Do we remain worthy? Long ago we began answering God's call, but his call never ends. We remain ever in need of a deeper conversion. The sin of catechumens will be washed away by baptism. We must seek the Sacrament of Reconciliation to wash away ours.

On the first Sunday of Lent, the Church puts before us Jesus in his temptation. Jesus is our agenda for Lent. St. John of the Cross says Jesus is ''a rich mine with many pockets containing treasures — however deep we dig we will never find their end.'' We will not even recognize many temptations unless we know Jesus.

St. Jerome said that ''ignorance of Scripture is ignorance of Christ.'' To dig into the pockets of the treasures of Christ is to dig into the Scriptures, especially the Gospels. There we find the God-man, and love him for all he is — for all that he is that we will never be, and for all that he is that we are, and for all that he is that we hope to become. Lent is the time to read and ponder Scripture at least a few minutes each day.

The most privileged of entries into the treasures of Christ is the Mass. St. Leonard of Port Maurice illustrates the value the Mass has to atone for our sins by the story of a seaman aboard ship in a terrible storm. He took in his arms a child, offered the little innocent to God, and begged God for love of that child to forgo the death of the sinners who deserved it. The sea fell into a calm. How much more, St. Leonard asks, will God accept as atonement the divine Victim offered at Mass? Lent is the time for daily Mass.

Offering that Victim calms the storms of our passions. Offering it devoutly, says St. Augustine, keeps us from mortal sin and removes venial sins. It stirs us to the service of others, without which no Christian walks Christ's way, and no Lent is complete. It moves us to draw others to know the Christ we love. We cannot all preach Christ on TV like Mother Angelica, but we can support those who do, and also speak to others with our own mouths, as Jesus did.

To overcome temptation, Jesus fasted, prayed, meditated on Scripture, and used it as his invincible weapon. Lent is the time to lay hold of sinlessness with him. We were baptized into him, given his life, fed on his body, harnessed to his load, and led forward to share in his dying and rising, in both liturgy and life. It only remains to be faithful to the end. "Who wins the victory?" Christ asks. "I will share my throne with him."

"C" — Second Sunday of Lent

Gn 15:5-12, 17-18
Ph 3:17 - 4:1
Lk 9:28-36

NO CROSS, NO CROWN

The Grace Kelly story, which has fascinated millions, is like a modern parable. A brick-layer's daughter, Grace aspired to be a movie actress. One can imagine her critics jeering, "She has her feet off the ground, nose in the air, and head in the clouds." For as the Jewish saying goes, "God hates our sins, but men hate our virtues." And it is a virtue to aspire to goals of high worth. In fact, a fault of many Christians is their failure to see themselves in the stirring role of sons and daughters of the great King, called to noble deeds and eternal glory.

Grace persevered in her aspiration and went beyond. She became an actress, received an Oscar, won a prince, and became a princess. But not without the cross. She sacrificed her career for marriage and motherhood. Nor did her suffering end there. On her tenth wedding anniversary this Catholic woman said that anyone who survives ten years of marriage deserves a prize.

As Christians, we are in danger of letting suffering deter us, and criticism convince us that faith in the resurrection reduces us to fools hopelessly reaching for the stars. Even our Lenten meditation on our sins can take the heart out of us, can attack our sense of self-worth. Jesus too knew discouragement; and so the Father sent into his life a profoundly reassuring experience meant for both him and us. Let us consider it.

Surging up from a plain a few miles from Nazareth towers a cone-shaped mountain call Tabor. Tradition identifies it as the Mount where Jesus was transfigured.

There Moses and Elijah came to Jesus. Their presence summons up all Jewish religious history back to Abraham. God promised Abraham descendants who could no more be counted than the stars. To seal the promise, or covenant, God told Abraham to offer sacrifice. In those days, men sealed a covenant with God by splitting an animal in half and walking between the halves as a way of saying they would rather be torn to pieces than break the agreement. In the case of God and Abraham, a flaming torch appeared and passed between the pieces. God was promising Abraham that rather than break his agreement, he would be torn to pieces. And in a sense, he was, in Jesus.

What, exactly, is the meaning of the transfiguration? To grasp it, we have to consider why Moses and Elijah came to Jesus there. They stood for the law and the prophets. They were reminding him of the covenant and prophecy he must fulfill. He must be torn to pieces rather than go back on the promise to Abraham; he must atone for sin as the law demands, and fulfill the suffering that the prophecies foretold. We could say they were mankind's spokesmen pleading with Jesus not to fail us.

And we know Jesus accepted. At the Last Supper he gave us the New Covenant, his commitment to be slain by the splitting apart of his body and blood on the cross. In that hour he made the commitment on Tabor, his human body shone out blindingly. The Father was giving his Son a promise of the resurrection that would follow for him and for all who endured his cross.

But why did Jesus go up Tabor and pray at this particular time? If we look into Jesus' circumstances just before he went up, we find out why. He is being rejected. The religious leaders are opposing him, the synagogues refusing him, and the cities so hostile he has taken to preaching in the wilderness. His life is in danger. His disciples are worried about him, and Jesus is worried about them. Their faith was weak. They knew so little. They had confessed him to be the Savior, but when would they clearly realize he was God become man? If they did not, how could they stand when he fell in death?

So he rushed up Tabor, fell on his knees, and prayed. ''Father,'' did he not cry, ''must you yourself not give witness you are my Father and I your Son if you want them to believe so terrible a mystery?'' And down from the sky thundered the Father's voice in the ears of the disciples, ''This is my Son, my Chosen One. Listen to him.'' Thus the Father answered the human needs which drove his Son up Tabor to pray.

And so the Father charges us to hear his Son reveal the wisdom of God, the meaning of life, and the promise of eternity. By listening, obeying and following, we enter into life.

Resurrection *will* be ours if we too accept the scriptural prophecies of necessary suffering. St. Paul warns all who are enemies of the cross of Christ that they will end in disaster. Anyone set on this world abandons Christ. Despite Tabor, the disciples abandoned him and ran. But when they saw him whom they loved risen, they learned not to fear the cross, for lovers of the Conqueror of death can bear anything. St. Teresa of Avila said that if we keep our eyes on Jesus to stir our love, and he gives us the gift of awakening to love of him, "all will become easy for us and we shall accomplish great things quickly and without effort."

Salvation is by faith, as Abraham learned; but as St. Paul found out, fidelity demands we bear the cross with Christ. And as Jesus revealed so marvelously, his Eucharistic body already brings us here on earth a taste and share of the life to come.

If we can grasp it, the Mass is our way of standing with the disciples on Tabor. We hear in faith the word of the Father; we see by faith the glory of the Son; we experience in Holy Communion the flood of the Holy Spirit's love that makes us taste, like Jesus on Tabor, the glory of the life awaiting us.

We have to ponder that experience in personal prayer. If Jesus had to pray, surely we must pray! Praying over Scripture, we confirm our identity as children of God, ask and receive God's forgiveness, feel our call to noble deeds, and refuse to think we are too small for greatness. Jesus prayed, and we must pray. By prayer we conquer, as did he. It is no accident that Paul described the results of our prayer in the very word used of Jesus on Tabor. He wrote, "All of us, gazing with unveiled face on the glory of the Lord, are being *transfigured* into the same image from glory to glory." Tabor is for us too.

"C" — Third Sunday of Lent

Ex 3:1-8, 13-15
1 Cor 10:1-6, 10-12
Lk 13:1-9

HISTORY IN GOD'S HANDS — AND OURS

God is the Lord of history, but some doubt it, and then doubt there is a God. One man was asked why he had lost his faith. He said he had been a soldier, and had seen some of his buddies slain along with their loved chaplain.

Christians who know their religious history are not likely to be so easily shaken in faith. The Lenten liturgy carries us back to our roots in God. The Easter liturgy will sweep us forward to God in Jesus' resurrection. The readings for the Third Sunday of Lent give us a capsulized history of salvation. It shows history is controlled by God. In God's hands, creation is ripening like wheat in a field. We too grow and ripen by cooperation with God's grace. The young grow in body and soul; the old continue to grow spiritually, even as their bodies fail. Lent is a special time for pulling up the weeds that stifle our growth in Christ.

Like the young soldier, Moses saw injustice against his people at the hands of the Egyptians. His effort to help backfired. He ran for his life. Did he then doubt the existence of God? We're not told. We're only told that God appeared to him in the burning bush, and enlisted him to free his people.

At the burning bush God intimately revealed himself, his being, and his proper name. ''I AM,'' he told Moses. ''I AM WHO AM.'' In Hebrew, it is written as ''Yahweh.'' Yahweh is the unchanging, eternal God who IS in past, present, and forever.

Fortunately and touchingly, God gave himself a second name, ''the God of Abraham, the God of Isaac, the God of Jacob. This is my name forever.'' God has rolled up his sleeves and entered history to save his people. He takes history into his hands. He shapes it like putty to produce his people's salvation.

Through Moses he freed his people from slavery; through the prophets he worked to free them from sin, and through the faithful of all ages, from oppression and injustice. Then he sent his Son to free all who accept him from sin and death.

Despite this progress, sin and suffering continue. Like the soldier who fell from faith, many fall away from God because of the evils around us.

To strengthen us against unbelief, Jesus connected sin and

suffering, but in a complicated way. He referred to eighteen people killed by a falling tower, and said they were no greater sinners than the rest. He added that all would come to the same end unless they reformed. Then he told the parable of the farmer who wanted a fig tree chopped down because it wasn't producing. But his employee begged for time to hoe and fertilize the soil around the tree. If that didn't work, it would be chopped down.

St. Paul takes seriously this teaching of Jesus and all Scripture. He sees in the Chosen People of old our own hopes and aspirations. He sees in their many failures and punishments a grim warning for us. God's trees must bear good fruit, or they will be cut down. Though God is tender and loving to the repentant, the unrepentant must experience his justice.

Moses himself had to be taught reverence. He was learned in Egyptian lore, but not in the ways of God. On first witnessing a mysterious religious event, he reacted in an irreverent way which could be put thus: "That's a strange fire. I'm going to stroll over and have a better look." He had to be warned by God, "Don't come any nearer." Only then did his reverence awaken.

We need to find a delicate balance between love and reverence for God. Profound love dares to approach God intimately. Sensitive reverence knows we dare not approach him until we have first repented and found forgiveness.

Moses, on realizing God was present, reverently hid his face, for to see God was to die. That is the very lesson of Lent. Lent is the time for prayer and penance and a good confession to do their work in us. They pare away the dead branches, and fertilize our hearts with grace until we bring forth the good things of the trees of God. Then we can approach him intimately.

That is the way it worked with Moses. As time passed, and his love for God overwhelmed him, he threw caution to the wind, and begged of God, "Show me your face." If he went up in a burst of flame, it would be worth it to see for one moment the face of the Beloved.

Moses also learned beyond doubt that God is God of history. He sees and hears the oppressed and does something about it. "I have witnessed the affliction of my people in Egypt," God says to Moses, "and have heard their cry of complaint against their slave drivers." And he adds, "I have come down to rescue them." Even a cry from an oppressed unbeliever is heard by this God of the universe, who is responsible for justice in his creation.

Sin and suffering are interconnected; sometimes the sinner suffers, and sometimes his victims. Were the people killed by the falling tower the sinners? Or workmen who put it up sloppily? Or did the contractor cheat on the quality of the materials?

Sorting out sin and punishment is beyond us, but we know sin brings suffering, and we know God is just. Instead of asking why God allows suffering, we should ask, "Do *I* allow suffering by doing nothing? Am I working to heal it?" Christians who fail to work are dead cells in the body of Christ.

God's inexhaustible mercy is our hope, but we don't ask mercy for ourselves and punishment for others. Like the employee of the parable, we beg time for all; and we do what we can to help and encourage others to produce good deeds, the way the employee worked on the tree to make it bear fruit.

Lent is a time to lend a hand to God and his world. God has given partial control of history into our hands. Lent is a time to straighten out the affairs of earth, and grow closer to the God of heaven. In the prayer of need, we cry out to the God of history; and in the prayer of love, we go beyond history into the presence of I AM WHO AM. Both are prayers of Lent.

"C" — Fourth Sunday of Lent   Jos 5:9, 10-12
                                                        2 Cor 5:17-21
                                                        Lk 15:1-3, 11-32

COMING HOME

They tell the story of Napoleon visiting a prison, and finding
all professing their innocence but one man, who confessed his
guilt. Napoleon called a guard and said, "Free this man! Get him
out of here before he corrupts all these innocent people!"

In the parable of the prodigal son, Jesus tells of a sinner who
admits what he is: "I have sinned," he says to his father, "against
God and against you." There is no fakery, no excuses. What a
breath of fresh air! But before we look at the repentant son, let's
take a look at the parable. Jesus did not call it the parable of the
prodigal son, nor would he. The word prodigal means "recklessly
extravagant," and the parable is really about a father recklessly
extravagant with forgiveness. He is so extravagant that many
would call him a fool. But Jesus would call him our heavenly
Father. With such a father, no wonder the son had the courage to be
truly repentant.

To bring out how repentant he was, let me revise the parable.
Here is the son coming home. He sees his father at the top of the
hill, and thinks, "I suppose the old boy has been out here every day
for a year waiting for the sight of me." The father comes running to
meet him, and the son says, "Dad, I guess you're grateful I'm
home, aren't you? But look, no sentimentality, or talk about
repentance. You have to expect a young buck to sow his wild oats. I
have schemes to earn my own way, but you'll have to put up the
shekels. If you're short, dig into my brother's share. I'm sure he
hasn't spent a red cent. How is he, anyway? As dull as ever?"
Would any of us like that kind of parable? Our Lord told it the way
it ought to be. We should be most sorry for our sins for the sake of
the Father's tender love.

When God led his people into Israel, he said, "Today I have removed the reproach of Egypt from you." He is telling them he let them fall into slavery in Egypt as a result of their sins. Now he has forgiven and rescued them, and led them into the promised land, a symbol of heaven. That's what repentance is, coming home to the Father. This Fourth Sunday of Lent is about coming home.

St. Paul says, "In Christ's name, be reconciled to God!" For that is what Christ came to do — lead us back to the Father. We should all aspire to be like the son of the parable. Jesus says he "came to his senses." Sin is senseless, but at last he escaped back to good sense. We too are called to shun fakery and false excuses, and listen sensibly to God and his Church.

One young woman used to "shack up" with her boyfriend on Saturday night, then go to Holy Communion on Sunday morning. Since the law of the Church requires confession before Communion after serious sin, her mother said to her, "Don't you think that's wrong?" The girl retorted, "Why? I love him." Contrast that with the honest repentance in the parable: "I have sinned against heaven." God makes the laws, not us.

God also set the way to repentance and forgiveness. The moment we fall into sin through weakness, we can make an act of contrition, and find forgiveness. If our sin is mortal, we need an act of perfect contrition: that is, one in which my primary motive of sorrow is that I have offended God. We also work for the removal of sin by prayer, penance, and Holy communion, and by giving to the poor.

But let us remember: The Church teaches that we have a responsibility to receive the sacrament of reconciliation after serious sin before receiving Holy Communion. Putting off such a confession is a mistake, and putting it off for more than a year is forbidden, because it keeps us from receiving our Lord.

Our Lord himself gave us the sacrament of penance after his resurrection. He breathed on his Apostles and said, "Receive the Holy Spirit. Whose sins you forgive are forgiven them, and whose

sins you retain are retained.'' St. John Chrysostom said that this
wonderful authority is one which ''God has not given to angels or
archangels.''

This sacrament is one of the most wonderful gifts of God. No
one knows this better than a priest, who experiences it from both
sides of the confessional. The story of the prodigal son is a figure of
confession. One who goes to confession goes to the Father. The Old
Testament story of Naaman the Syrian is another figure of this
sacrament. He was a leper who visited a Jewish prophet with healing
powers. The prophet told him to wash seven times in the Jordan.
Naaman was outraged. There were two better rivers back home! His
servants brought him to his senses by pointing out that if he had been
told to do something difficult, he would do it. So Naaman washed in
the Jordan, and his flesh became pure as a little child's. The grace of
confession is more powerful than the Jordan. What other tribunal is
there where anyone can confess his crimes and walk out a free man?
It is the sacrament of peace. How we should thank God for it!

Jesus said, ''If I do not wash you, you can have no part in
me.'' He gave us baptism to save us from the shipwreck of Adam
and, to save us from drowning in our own shipwreck, he gave us
confession. It is not only for grievous sins, but for lesser sins as
well. Holy Communion will remove lesser sins, but consider this:
If you were going to a distinguished friend's house for dinner,
would you go in need of a bath? Shouldn't we give our Lord the joy
of seeing us clothed in the fresh graces he can admire?

Pope Pius XII praised frequent confession. It brings self-
knowledge, humility, victory over bad habits, purification of conscience, strength of will, and growth in holiness. And there's a
bonus he didn't mention: It teaches us to be more loving and
forgiving, and reconciled with everyone.

In the light of the parable of the prodigal Father, we ought to
resolve to be honest about wrongdoing, make no excuses, confess
our sins, come home to the Father and the Church of his Son, draw
close to Christ and grow in his likeness.

"C" — Fifth Sunday of Lent   Is 43:16-21
                                              Ph 3:8-14
                                              Jn 8:1-11

THE PRODIGAL DAUGHTER

Last week the prodigal son stood before our eyes; this week it is the prodigal daughter. Both were threatened by death: the son by starvation, the daughter by stoning. Last week the Father rescued the sinner; this week, the Son does the rescuing.

Others besides the prodigals are on trial. When someone we love is in trouble, we are on trial. In this case, Jesus is on trial. And what of us? When we see a sinner on trial, we should recognize ourselves. For the issue is not some particular sin, but the fate of a sinner, and that we all face.

An adulteress is publicly paraded to Jesus, and he must decide her fate. If we step back to gain perspective on this event, we discover a classical drama common in our literature. A hero comes upon a "damsel in distress." Will he rescue her?

Will Jesus prove to be a real man, a hero? The real man is said to have three qualities: fearlessness, self-assurance, and independent action. Gary Cooper, in many a film, illustrated these qualities. But in one of his late films, he fell in love with a woman who abhorred violence, and the issue was raised: How does the real man come to the rescue without use of violence? That issue has never been satisfactorily resolved, and so this event is all the more absorbing. This real man, who himself rejected violence, faced a challenge few could meet.

Let us not miss the fact that Jesus is on trial. Just as no one cared for the prodigal son but the Father, no one cares for this woman but the Son. Theologians and Pharisees are using her as bait to trap him. They know Jesus stands for mercy and justice. They confront him with the Mosaic law that an adulteress be stoned, and ask: "What do you say?" The quiet descends. If he says, "Stone her,'' his mercy fails; if he says, ''Don't stone her,'' his justice fails. They have sprung the trap.

Calmly, Jesus writes on the ground, as if to say, ''Why all the fuss?'' Then he speaks. We talk about ''the fastest gun in the West.'' When it came to debate, Jesus was the fastest gun in Jerusalem. Out of the trap he comes with the words, ''Let him who is without sin cast the first stone.''

The theologians understood. Moses gave the law, intending that the innocent judge the guilty. Judges who punish others for crimes they themselves commit with impunity are hypocrites, not ministers of justice.

Jesus writes again. What did he write? It has been suggested he wrote the sins of the judges. Whether it was his writing or his words, something began to work on the accusers' consciences. The bystanders drifted away. Without violence to others or to his own convictions, he had rescued the woman in distress.

He stood alone with her. Until now, had she not considered herself a brave lover? Isn't that the way of it? Now she looked up, looked into the eyes of God, into the heart of Christ, and passed from her world into his. From his world, she looked back at herself, and found a sinner. In love's name, she had betrayed married love. Danger was gone; defiance gave way to grief and guilt and perhaps despair. And then his words sounded in her ears, ''Neither do I condemn you. Go, and sin no more.'' Her heart soared into forgiveness and hope. She walked into the new world of redemption he had originated, sensing that she carried something of him with her as a new power for true love.

In her we have the meaning of Lent: our renewal in Christ. Lent is the time to discover that we are the wayward son or daughter of God, each in his or her own degree, small or great. In these Gospel events, the Lord speaks to each of us. Looking into Christ's eyes as this woman did, we will find love, and respond. We may even learn to say with St. Paul, ''I have accounted all else as rubbish that Christ may be my wealth.''

That kind of love of Christ frees us from everything, frees us for everything to which Christ calls. It's hard to understand Christians who don't understand that. Young women entering the religious life tell of their family saying, "Why are you doing that? You're throwing your life away!" Is a girl who, attracted by the vocational call, throws herself into the arms of Christ, throwing her life away? If Christ appeared to any believer and said, "I want you to leave everything and follow me," could any believer think it was folly to do it? He or she might be too attached to this world to say yes, but surely there would be the realization of how unwise it was to say no.

Listen to St. Paul again. To him, even a lifetime of virtue without Christ is trash compared to what a lifelong sinner gains when he finds and is baptized into Christ. "I have accounted all else as rubbish," Paul says, "not having any justice of my own based on the observance of the law. The justice I possess is that which comes through faith in Christ." Paul would far rather be like the woman taken in adultery, but claimed now by Christ, than be like any of her accusers, however righteous, who had no faith in Christ. "I wish to know Christ," Paul says, "and the power flowing from his resurrection."

Let us see Christ and Paul as opposite sides of a coin. Did Christ stand before the adulteress as a superior being before an inferior? No! He stood as a man before an equal in distress. And Paul did not shrink before the greatness of Christ. He sped to him as one who had learned what every child knows, that love obliterates all inequalities and soars beyond all differences, until there is naught but friend with friend. Love is a godly bridge over-arching highs and lows, where friends and lovers meet.

Love is what we need to have the kindness of Christ. If the parable of the prodigal son teaches fathers and mothers what untiring forgiveness is, Jesus' care for the prodigal woman tells his brothers and sisters what true virtue is. To despise a brother who has failed the test of virtue is to expose our own moral bankruptcy.

Love without understanding is a mirage, and justice without mercy is savagery. Lent summons us to leave sin and savagery behind, and climb Christ's bridge of love.

"C" — Palm Sunday

Is 50:4-7
Ph 2:6-11
Lk 22:14 - 23:56

RECOVERING THE PURPOSE
OF SUFFERING

Sometimes we tune our ears to hear only the "Good News" which the scriptural readings proclaim. Today's readings force us to face up and ask another question: What is the *bad news* they contain — the news we all have a tendency to bracket, shun, and ignore?

Christ did not hesitate to preach to his Apostles the "bad" news along with the good. He foretold the bad news clearly, and dealt with resistance to it sternly.

Even children see the bad news in the Gospels, and if we deal with it evasively they resist the whole Gospel. Once in preaching a mission to children a priest sensed both inattention and resistance. Thereupon he asked this question: *Was Christ a success or a failure?* Quiet descended. A boy of about eighth grade vintage answered boldly: "He was a failure. The people didn't believe in Him. They killed Him. His men ran away." The decibel level fell to zero. The priest had an audience. The bad news was out in the open, and they wanted to know what he was going to do about it.

The hallmark of Christianity is that it comes to grips with bad news — with evil and suffering — and overcomes it. The ancient Greeks were defeated by evil. Even their gods were in the hands of the fates. The gods, who issued decrees, were in turn subject to decrees. The Greeks were fatalists.

In our day the Oriental pantheists fail in their confrontation with evil. They deny there is a creation, and claim we are all a part of God, so we all must be good. To condemn evil and suffering would be blasphemy. There is no exit.

Christianity overcomes sin and suffering, but not all Christians do. The majority of Americans are Christians, yet Americans commonly respond to bad news with tactics of evasion. They employ drink, drugs and death.

Drink: Alcohol dissolves families, careers, the will to live, and life itself. *Drugs*: Ours is a pain-killing culture that uses tranquillizers by the truckload — and kills the energies of life along with its pain. *Death*: Most people who use violence to solve problems kill not themselves but others. The violent solution has multiplied. According to one report from New York City, homicide was the leading cause of death among males. In recent years in the U.S., over one million unborn children were slaughtered annually. Projections from one poll indicate some one-third of Americans would kill for money.

Perhaps today's worst escape is the sin of denying sin. Consider the Judases of our day. They are theologizers. They dogmatize their betrayal. They evade the burdens of faith and morals by reinterpreting them in ways traitorous to the Revelation. They run from their moment of confrontation.

Christianity does not run. Its answer to sin and suffering is Jesus in today's Gospel. We have to chew through the hard and bitter shell of the Gospel bad news today before we taste its sweet kernel of Good News.

Jesus confronts sin and suffering in today's Gospel. He does not run. He *sets his face like flint* and goes his way. He dreaded his hour of suffering, but he also looked to it with longing, and advanced upon it with decision because he knew its meaning. We need to know it with him, or we will run away in our hour. The three readings carry us with him into his final hour, and help us to find its meaning.

The first reading is the third song of the Servant of Yahweh. He prefigures Christ. He meekly submits to the outrage of violence and injustice not out of weakness but out of flinty strength. He submits because his "open ears" hear God calling him to submit. The other servant songs (not in today's reading) find the meaning of his ordeal in the mystery of vicarious suffering. Paul formulates the mystery boldly: God made the sinless Christ "to be sin" to take away our sin.

The second reading is the great *kenosis* hymn. Christ emptied himself. Though God by nature, he humbled himself to share our nature. He became man, and descended into suffering and death. For his *obedience* God exalted him to the highest glory.

Here is light cast upon the meaning of sin and suffering. They *are* evils, but God has a plan. The moral evil of sin must be fought at any price. The physical evil of suffering must be endured when that is necessitated by God's purposes. God is more powerful than both sin and suffering, and will do away with both for those who love him.

The Gospel reading begins with the Last Supper. The Last Supper explains the Passion which follows: "This is my body to be given for you . . . This is the new covenant in my blood, which will be shed for you." Eucharist is not only banquet but covenant and sacrifice. Christ *is* our covenant. His sacrifice is offered not only liturgically; it was offered historically, in outpoured blood, on Calvary. Only he who enters by deep meditation into the Passion enters profoundly into the Mass.

Christianity does more than explain suffering. It gives suffering the meaning it explains. Suffering is unredemptive except in Christ. What else is the meaning of the teaching of Scripture and the Church that "fallen man cannot redeem himself." Christ has redeemed our suffering along with us. Now our suffering can and must help redeem us: "Anyone who does not take up his cross and follow me cannot be my disciple.'' Doctrines of atonement and love are present in this teaching.

Those who run from every suffering multiply suffering in their own lives by sin, and multiply it in the lives of others by fleeing the sacrifices that are the price of serving others. The Christian who stands and suffers when need be stands with Christ in the work of serving and redeeming the world. We can see this plainly now in some respects, but we will see it fully only when we look back into history from the vantage point of our own personal resurrection.

"C" — Easter Vigil   Gn 1:1-2; Gn 22:1-18; Ex 14:15-15:1; Ezk 36:16-28
                                                                        Rm 6:3-11
                                                                        Lk 24:1-12

PASSING OVER WITH THE LORD

This holy night, this Easter Vigil, is a solemn memorial of the whole mystery of our redemption. It is steeped in revelation and symbols, and alive with fresh-flowing graces. In it we recall the prophecies, promises and events that prepared for Christ's coming. We look back in sorrow to his death on Good Friday, and we look with hope and desire to the liturgical moment when he, the now-risen Lord, will come among us here.

We began by striking new fire and lighting the Easter candle to signify the new life of Christ on Easter morning. Our candles were lit from his, to express the flowing of his risen life and the light of his wisdom among us. In the Easter Proclamation we recounted with exultation the victory of Christ over sin and death in events past, present, and to come.

In the liturgy of the word we reviewed how God saved his

people through the course of history in various ways that prefigured his Son's redemptive work.

God created man and woman and found his creation very good. He tested Abraham by calling him to sacrifice his son, but spared the boy at the last. For it was only God the Father's own Son whose sacrifice could bring salvation. It was in the saving death-resurrection of Jesus that Abraham became the father of many nations.

God led his people out of slavery by the hand of Moses. He drowned their enemies in the sea. Just so, he led us through the waters of baptism, as the prophet Ezekiel promised. In those waters he drowned all the deceits of Satan, who schemes to make us the slave of sin and death that he is. By baptizing us into Christ, God freed us from both sin and everlasting death, as St. Paul makes clear in the reading we just heard.

In the Gospel the women find the tomb empty, and are at a loss what to think. The angels appear to them and explain that Jesus has risen as he foretold. They tell the Apostles. Seeing the empty tomb, Peter is filled with amazement.

What do we do now? We play our own role in the Easter mystery. We baptize the men and women whom faith calls to share with us our new life and membership in the Church, the body of Christ. We rejoice that on this holy night we the Church, the spouse of Christ, bring forth new members in him, new sons and daughters of God the Father.

They will be anointed with the Holy Spirit as we were, anointed into Christ's priestly, prophetic and kingly mission. They will share in Christ's resurrection, and their whole lives will be channeled into the new purpose and destiny that we too have shared.

Then we will all renew our baptismal vows. We will be reminded that we are still in the battle against Satan. We still have our hardships, sufferings and sorrows. We must bear them bravely as Christ did. Only when we have won all our battles can we fully pass over from death to life everlasting and join Jesus in the house of the Father. We must be faithful to the end.

In this awareness our burdens are seen as passing things. They are lessened by the light shining in from the home port, and cannot overpower us. Carrying our cross with Jesus, we can carry it more bravely, inspired by him to noble deeds.

After our baptismal promises are renewed, we will go on with the Mass, the mystery of redemption. Through the Mass we enter most deeply into the Easter glory. At the consecration Christ will come among us in his risen body as he came to his disciples on the first Easter.

We are in the position of the women who came to the tomb. They did not yet see the risen Jesus; they were told of his resurrection by angels; nor did the Apostles yet see him; Peter heard the women's report and saw the empty tomb. From what they saw and were told they were called to believe.

With the eyes of the body we will see only the bread and wine, and hear Jesus' words of consecration repeated; but with the eyes of faith we will recognize the Easter sacrament. ''Take and eat. This is my body,'' Jesus said, and we believe.

With faith in his resurrection, we no longer search for the living among the dead; nor do we search for life among dead things. Materialism, money and all ways of life that are not on the road to God are dead ways.

Like the women carrying the news to the others, we seek refreshment in these mysteries to carry the Gospel message to one another and to unbelievers by the way we live it. We look to Jesus to know how. We see him serving and teaching and praying. We see him loving all and giving all. What can we name of all he has that he did not share with us all? If we name his Father, we hear him called by Jesus, ''my Father and your Father.'' If we appeal to his Holy Spirit, we recall Jesus promising him to us as another Advocate; if we look at his Mother, we hear Jesus say, ''Behold your Mother.'' If we recall his power over all things, and his divine riches, we remember he said, "Ask and you shall receive." If we ponder the way we should live, we hear him declare, "I am the Way."

On this holy night when we are so close to how Jesus has loved and served and given to us, let us take hold of our inexpressible closeness to him and pour out our hearts to him. Is it not clear that neither life nor death nor devils nor deceivers nor things present nor things to come can ever separate us from him if only we resist for love? If anyone is in distress in any way, surrender to his love. If there is distress of conscience, cry out your sorrow in a word of contrition. All will be forgiven; if in anguish about life's sorrows, cast your cares on him. Trust that by his grace all things will work for your good, as they did for him by the Father's loving care.

Soon now, fed by the bread of heaven, we will share with the first disciples the joy of Jesus risen. We recall his pierced heart, which poured out the water and blood of our baptism and Eucharist, and we nourish our souls with them.

We remember his everlasting love, and pour out our love to him in return. In the Eucharistic mystery above all we experience that this is the day the Lord has made, and we rejoice and are glad in it.

"ABC" — Easter Sunday, Morning Mass

Ac 10:34, 37-43
Col 3:1-4 or 1 Cor 5:6-8
Jn 20:1-9

THE NECESSARY RESURRECTION

In this spring season, with new life sprouting everywhere, we rejoice in the resurrection. We praise the day God the Father rained down the graces of new life upon the tomb and the body of his Son, and the God-man rose from the dead.

Padre Pio, the mystic who had the five wounds of Christ, was once asked to explain the Mass. "My children," he said, "how can I explain the Mass to you? The Mass is infinite, like Jesus." How can we explain the resurrection, when it manifests the power of God Almighty? The resurrection of Christ, said St. Augustine, was God's supreme and wholly marvelous work.

We are much like John that first Easter morning. He rushed to the tomb, saw it empty, and believed. We heard the word, and we believed. But like John, we long to see Jesus. We long to see the glory of his risen body.

We can recall Jesus' transfiguration, when his face shone like the sun, and his garments were like light. And we can say, "That was only a preview!" His risen body is so much more glorious, it is beyond the power of the human eye to see without the help of grace. Its splendor and nobility are so great that if we multiplied a hundredfold the grace and favor of the most noble human body we have ever seen, it would not begin to approach the glory and the beauty of his risen body — or even of ours, when we rise from the dead. We long to smell the fragrance of sanctity his body gives off, and see the power and agility with which it passes through walls and is instantaneously present wherever he pleases. But it is not the time. St. Paul tells us the risen body is beyond description. It must remain a mystery until we are raised from the dead and see not only Jesus' glorious body, but our own. It is God's will and purpose that we walk by faith.

What we can do is reflect on the meaning of the resurrection for Jesus and for ourselves. Let us begin by saying that a Christian without faith in the resurrection is like a cut flower. It looks pretty for a time, but after a while it wilts and fades and decays, and has to be thrown out. Christian faith has at the very center of its meaning Jesus' resurrection and our own.

What was the meaning of the resurrection for Jesus? Did you ever think about it? Jesus didn't need a human body and soul. He is the eternal Son of God. He remains that; he never ceased being that. But he did raise the human body he took to save us. Why? Because he was born of Mary to join us and be one of us, and he'll never take that back. He will be our human companion as well as our divine companion for all eternity.

And so the first meaning of the resurrection for Jesus is the joy of his ascending to the Father in his human nature, body and soul. If we imagine that meeting, we might hear Jesus say, "Look, Father, here I am! We won! I went down to rescue humanity, our creation. And here I am back, the first of them, the first human being risen immortal, the first of our new creation. Delight and rejoice with me. My brothers and sisters will be following me one by one, until finally I go back and gather them all, all who have been faithful."

If Jesus took great joy in returning victorious in his risen body to his Father, he took a similar joy in one other return. He is the only lover who was able to return to his lifeless beloved, take her in his arms, and breathe into her not just the breath of life, but the breath of immortality. That beloved of his is our Church and ourselves.

Now what is the meaning of the resurrection for us? What first comes to mind is, "Hooray! We're going to live forever!" That is our faith.

But, taken in proper order, what should come first is our joy for Jesus. If we love him, how happy we should be for him. His sufferings are all over and ended. He is radiant with joy, and we are joyful for him. He himself said at the Last Supper, "If you truly loved me, you would rejoice because I am going to the Father." So you see, joy is a religious duty today. Because I love Jesus, I put aside all my own troubles and sorrows, and forget them as best I can. I concentrate on Jesus, and rejoice in him. I invite all of you to do that. Do you love Jesus? Rejoice for him. They used to have a saying, "Don't rain on my parade." Don't rain on Jesus' parade. Rejoice for him.

Further, we rejoice for ourselves. We'll join him, if we're even reasonably faithful. We'll share that glory which we can't even describe.

In fact, we rejoice because we're already sharing in his life. We began to participate by baptism. So our minds and hearts should be turned to the things above, as St. Paul tells us in the second reading. But what Paul has in mind may surprize you. He is not talking only about life with God in heaven. He is referring to our life with God right now. He is talking about the virtues and actions here on earth that make us like Jesus: heartfelt mercy, humility, kindness and patience. These virtues and gifts help us to live a heavenly life, in its beginnings, here on earth. So this call to have our mind on heavenly things is not a call to abandon earth. It's a call to live here on earth as Jesus did, aware that by living as he lived, we will join him one day in the heavenly realm.

Today we can't see the glorious risen Jesus as we long to, but we do have a better gift. If I, personally, were given the choice between seeing Jesus risen as the Apostles did, or receiving him in the Eucharist, I would choose receiving him, my resurrection and my life. That is the greater gift, and the Father, in his wisdom, has made that better choice for us.

So today it is our joy to Easter with the risen Jesus, in mystery, in the Mass and the Eucharist. "This is the day the Lord has made. Let us rejoice and be glad."

"C" — Second Sunday of Easter

Ac 5:12-16
Rv 1:9-11, 12-13, 17-19
Jn 20:19-31

PROPAGATING THE RESURRECTION

Jesus returns to his Apostles on the first Easter evening. What was his mission? To increase their faith? That, and much more.

Jesus was returning in possession of a *good* no man ever

possessed before: immortality of the body. Philosophers say that *the good diffuses itself,* and we have all seen that principle operative throughout nature. The sun radiates its light; scents diffuse; plants and animals disseminate themselves in billions of seeds. Dedicated parents, educators, scientists, writers and artists passionately communicate their life, knowledge, discoveries, insights and vision. In accord with this self-giving impulse of love, Jesus was communicating his new-won good.

What was Jesus' mission? He was propagating the resurrection with a passionate devotion unparalleled in history. "I came that they may have life," he had said and now he was doing it.

The Apostles were in a locked room. Abruptly Jesus was there without the doors opening. The risen body, Paul wrote, is a *spiritual body.* Paul is contrasting the natural body given life by a soul with the risen body given life by the Spirit, a divine principle. Paul is describing a *divinized* body. In his letter to the Romans he says, "The Spirit will give life to your mortal bodies."

Christ's divinity has now completed the Incarnation by bestowing divine qualities on his risen body. It passes through solid objects. That is nothing. The powers of a divinized body are unimaginable.

Jesus gives the greeting of peace: *Shalom!* He shows his hand and side. The Apostles see for themselves that it is the body of the Crucified. Jesus is communicating not only faith but *facts.* These men are appointed to support the foundations of Christianity. They need the *facts* to which they will witness.

"The Apostles rejoiced." The joy bursting into their lives is necessary to authenticate them as witnesses of the resurrection. "Shalom!" Jesus repeats the greeting which was heard on all the street corners of Jerusalem before he was born, and is still heard there to this day. But that morning he gave it a new meaning. He gave it to them in power: "As the Father has sent me, so I send you." Their mission is to communicate biblical peace, the peace of restored relationship with God, and therefore of life and goodness and all good things.

The Son of God is propagating the resurrection, carrying out the mission which he received in eternity, in the Godhead, when the divine Father fathered him. The Apostles now share his mission. We all share it. We are sent by him as he was sent by the Father. We are an extension of the Incarnation. We are by grace what Jesus is by nature.

Jesus breathes on them: "Receive the Holy Spirit." This is the true giving of the Holy Spirit. The Holy Spirit comes on them as he will come on the whole Church publicly at Pentecost.

In sharing the Spirit of Jesus, the Apostles are given a share in his sonship and the power needed for their mission: "If you forgive men's sins, they are forgiven them." By forgiving sins they have a power for peace the world had never known.

John does not here mention baptism, which saves us from the primal shipwreck of Adam. He treated of baptism in chapter 3, and he knows that Matthew and Mark record the baptismal mandate in their resurrection accounts. John confines himself to the sacrament of reconciliation, which snatches us from our own private shipwrecks.

Jesus has now communicated his mission. Peter describes its nature in the Acts of the Apostles. He states that Judas' place among the Twelve must be filled by one who walked with Jesus. The chosen one, he says, "should be named *as witness with us to his resurrection.*" Giving witness to the resurrection is the heart of the apostolic and priestly mission. Henceforth the Church had to communicate what was seen and done on that first Easter eve.

The mission of the ten was soon in action. Thomas returned, and proved difficult. Men want resurrection so desperately they are deathly afraid of deluding themselves.

Thomas rejected the apostolic witnesses. On what grounds? Witnesses must be truthful and possessed of the facts. Thomas passed over their truthfulness and scorned their gullible souls. If he saw Jesus, he would demand contact, not mere sight.

Fortunately for Thomas and us, Jesus came. When confronted

with the evidence seen by the ten, Thomas went further than they: ''My Lord and my God!'' he cried. Thus originated the first public act of faith in Christ's divinity.

Jesus withheld praise from Thomas and reserved it for us. Mutual faith among men is necessary for human society. Only by faith in human witness can a historic religion be passed on. Of course, that witness is confirmed by the Holy Spirit in our hearts, as Jesus taught. But if we were all like Thomas in his hour of obstinacy, we would be demanding that Christ be born and suffer and die and rise in every age and place, so we could see for ourselves.

Unbelief often has nothing to do with the facts. It is rooted in vacillation, jealousy, pseudo-sophistication, stubbornness, desolation, depression, disappointment, adolescent anti-authoritarianism, and many other psychological states and ills that are not the fault of the evidence. The trouble is not with our evidence but with ourselves. The resurrection is not in the eyes of the beholder. It is in Jesus Christ.

How can we grow in faith? A man with a great reputation for sanctity was asked that question. His answer: Read Scripture. Spend time before the Blessed Sacrament.

Jesus Christ is still propagating the resurrection. Indeed he *is* the Resurrection. Those who spend time with him in any and every way they can will find themselves becoming more and more the visible partners in his joyous work of propagating life.

''C'' — Third Sunday of Easter

Ac 5:27-32, 40-41
Rv 5:11-14
Jn 21:1-19

OUR MYSTERIOUS RELATIONSHIP TO JESUS

The Good News today is that seven disciples see the risen Lord with their own eyes on the shore of a familiar lake. All well and good, but is there any bad news? In the realism of our revealed religion, there usually is. The bad news is that the disciples have trouble recognizing the Lord even staring straight at him. When they beached their boat and joined the man on the shore, they somehow at the same time saw him as a stranger and recognized him for who he is. "Not one of the disciples," we are told, "presumed to inquire, 'Who are you?', for they knew it was the Lord."

Now, this is bad news, news that troubles us because it probably means trouble for us. What is going on here? If the risen Jesus had not already identified himself beyond doubt to the Apostles, this present difficulty would really worry us. After all, the disciples are our historic link to the resurrection.

The problem is acute. On seeing face to face a person as well known as Jesus was to the disciples, we don't have any need for doubts or questions. *It is he or it isn't!* Yet here are the disciples staring at Jesus and their eyes are not able to say, "It's definitely Jesus." "They knew it was the Lord," but apparently only because of his familiar behavior, and the immense catch of fish he had engineered, and the voice of their hearts and of the Spirit, and of whatever else. This manner of identification leaves us uneasy. What explains it? Let's search for an explanation in the total event.

Jesus, the stranger on the shore, guides the fishermen to a net full of fish, and John recognizes him. Jesus invites them to breakfast. They "know" their chance companion is Jesus yet, strangely, their eyes can't prove it. This kind of experience is only too familiar to us! Jesus comes as our companion in the bread of life, and we "know" it, but only by faith.

Jesus is present to them, and almost a stranger to their eyes. Again we look to our own experience. The Gospels teach us that Jesus is in us and in every stranger on the shores of our lives.

Why could not the disciples recognize Jesus with their eyes when he appeared? Well, to begin with, John does not tell us that Jesus appeared," but that he "revealed himself." If we look at the other times the risen Jesus revealed himself as reported by John, we find the same mysterious principle of recognition at work.

Mary Magdalene, to whom he was the "Teacher" who had taught her true love, recognized him by his voice calling her name. The Apostles, who had so often heard him identify himself as Son of Man, recognized him by his body wounds. The two disciples on the road to Emmaus, who had failed to recognize the Messiah in the broken body on the cross, recognized him in the bread of fellowship. Finally, on the Sea of Galilee, Jesus is revealed as one who is in their midst as *any man*. He is preparing them to make the transition to pure faith. He is in our midst in each member of his mystical body who serves us, or needs our service or fellowship or love or food.

The very difficulty of recognizing the risen Jesus is a witness to his resurrection. His body has undergone mysterious change. It is his body, risen from the tomb with its five wounds, but it is a mysterious body. Our five senses can't apprehend it in their normal way. Mark reports that, to two disciples, he came "completely changed in appearance." Luke says of the two on the road to Emmaus that "their eyes were kept from recognizing him." By what? Apparently, by lack of faith, as though bodily eyes now needed the support of the eye of faith, as in the Eucharist. Both eye and faith had to be helped by his actions, whether a familiar word, or breaking of bread, or a manifestation of his power by passing through walls.

We now reach the final and most fundamental reason for the recognitional difficulty. The Son of Man was and remains mysterious, as is stressed by both the beginning and end of the Gospels. Just when we think we have penned him in one of the cages of our categories, he breaks free in some new surprise.

He is more human than any of us, yet too mysterious for us not to realize that he is more than human. He is the slain and risen man of the first reading, but also the slain and risen *lamb* of the second reading. He is the Final Adam, immortal and eternal. He *is* the resurrection, and he is eternity.

And if we can't cage him in our categories, how will we ever grasp him in our relationships? Each time we think our understanding has circumnavigated him, and our relationships imprisoned him, we come to a rude awakening. Far more real is the fictional cry of Mary Magdalene in *Jesus Christ, Superstar*: "I don't know how to love him!" None of us does.

Jesus questions Peter about his love three times. In the New Testament Greek, Jesus twice uses the word for a more noble, reverential form of love than the one with which Peter responds. Finally, Jesus switches to Peter's word, accepting the ardent natural affection which is all Peter presently knows how to give.

How to love Jesus the God-man is a mystery which must be taught. Jesus revealed that the way is by baptism and Eucharist and serving love guided by faith and the Church. One great help is devotion to the Sacred Heart of Jesus, which opens to us a loving knowledge of him as both man and God.

Only heaven will teach us the rest. "There," the Council of Trent declares, "the veils will be removed," and the faithful "will partake of the same Bread of Angels that they now receive under the sacred species." Then we will see and recognize Jesus not only with the eye of faith and of love, but with the eyes of our risen bodies as well. That is what we will plead for in the Prayer over the Gifts, and it is what our hearts await with eager longing.

"C" — Fourth Sunday of Easter

Ac 13:14, 43-52
Rv 7:9, 14-17
Jn 10:27-30

VOCATION — HEARING
THE GOOD SHEPHERD'S CALL

Have you ever been so busy when the phone rang that you felt put upon and didn't answer? Something similar takes place in our life with God. Our hearts grow busy, the Good Shepherd rings us by the call of the heart, and we pretend not to hear. Or we may be so preoccupied with material things that we really don't hear.

The Good Shepherd calls each one of us personally to the way of eternal life, by the call of the heart. He also calls us through others. He calls some as priests and religious. These are the things the readings prompt us to reflect on today.

First, then, he calls us to his way of life, so that like him we may return to the Father. In that second reading we have figurative expressions of the happiness awaiting us which words can't express. Jesus put it simply: "Enter into your master's joy." Who can imagine the joy of God which we'll share in our Father's house? All of our sins will have been washed away in the blood of the Lamb through this Holy Sacrifice. We'll have at last the snow-white purity of Christ, there in the brilliance of God where nothing remains of shadow or sorrow or sin.

We have seen the magnetic beauty and nobility of some human faces; we have stood in the lovely quiet of the rising sun, and the glory of its setting. We have tasted of life and tasted of love. All of these are but the prelude to joy. Imagine looking on the face of Life and the face of Love, Love who has loved me and will love me forever. Once we have the companionship of God, nothing can tempt us or draw us away.

The Good Shepherd calls us to follow him to the Father's house. Once St. Thomas complained that he didn't know the way, but Jesus said, "I am the way, and the truth, and the life." We long for life with him, but if we long too much for earthly things, the line is busy. His call of the heart doesn't get through. But if we are his we will listen, for he says, "My sheep hear my voice and they follow me." Understanding this, then, we're called today to examine our hearts. Are we treasuring too much things which, though they may seem important in the day and the hour, are as nothing compared with this call home?

There is a further complication: the Good Shepherd's voice comes to us in many guises and through many people. It comes through our parents and our teachers. They have the call to be the Good Shepherd's helper, to be his voice guiding us.

The Good Shepherd calls us too through the voice of the Church, through which the Pope, bishops, priests, brothers and sisters speak of God's call and way. There is a crisis in priestly and religious vocations, and this Sunday compels us to attend to it.

The priest is an extension of the Good Shepherd's phone line. He speaks God's word; he is God's ambassador. What if an ambassador of the president threw the president's message away and made up his own? He could be prosecuted and imprisoned. So too, the priest must speak the word of Christ and the Church. In the first reading Paul and Barnabas speak bravely the word of Christ even in the face of persecution and danger to their lives.

The bishops insist on this fidelity to the word of Christ. In the document, "Human Life in Our Day," they addressed the issue of dissent in the Church, and concluded by saying, "Even responsible dissent does not excuse one from faithful presentation of the authentic doctrine of the Church when one is performing a pastoral ministry in her name."

When Christ calls men to the priesthood and women and men to the religious life by the call of the heart, we say they have a *vocation*, a *calling* to the work of Christ. Not only the word the priest speaks, but the sacrifice he offers is Christ's. What if a man said from the altar, I'm not an ordained priest; I'll offer Mass by my own power? None of us who have the faith would have him. Only Christ can change bread and wine into his body and blood in the Holy Sacrifice. The priest knows that and knows that by ordination Christ has promised to do it through him.

Pope John Paul II spoke on this point to 23 young men about to be ordained. He compared the priest with himself, the Vicar of Christ. He said that if "the title *Vicar of Christ* is so demanding . . . there is another title which is still more powerful and which refers to each one of you as priests. This title tells us that we must act *in persona Christi.* It is much stronger to say *in the person of Christ* than (to say) *Vicar of Christ.* There is more identification, sameness, intimacy. This refers to each one of us as a priest or as a future priest . . . a fascinating mystery and a tremendous mystery.''

The root of this mystery is that there is only one Mediator between God and the human race, Christ the Son of God, the Good Shepherd. The priest at the altar or pulpit is only the voice of Christ. Christ himself performs the powerful deeds, and his Holy Spirit touches the hearts of those who listen.

The role of religious sisters and brothers is of equal importance, as one of the popes said. Their work of serving, caring, teaching and loving and their evangelical form of life inspire the whole Church. Through their work in schools especially, sisters and brothers have been the spiritual parents of uncounted future priests and religious, sharing in the role of Mary, the Mother of priests and of St. Joseph, the guardian of the Church.

Today we pray that men and women will hear and answer the call of the Good Shepherd. The Church needs them; the world needs them; we all need them. Their call is to share all the concerns in the Heart of the Good Shepherd, and to walk and work day and night with him, dedicating their whole lives to speaking his word and doing his deed.

Let's pray for priests like St. John Vianney, the Curé of Ars. He was not brilliant, but he was faithful. Almost ejected from the seminary for his poor academic record, he managed to hold fast to the call of Christ and was ordained. He spent many hours in faithful and heartfelt preaching, and untold hours hearing confessions. People came to his little village from all over France. Many brilliant priests of his day are forgotten, but the Curé still stands as a model for priests. Let that tell us what the core role of priest and sister and brother is: to be a faithful ambassador living the life of Christ and speaking his word to the people of God. Surely we need such vocations, and must be aware of it as we join here for the Holy Sacrifice today. So let us pray from the heart for vocations here and now.

LOVE'S WAY OF LIFE

Love has its disappointments. A father read a survey claiming that children are more attached to TV than to their fathers. To his loving little girl he confidently put the question, "If you had to choose between me and the TV set, which would you choose?" After the proper reflection she answered, "That would depend on what's on."

One day the presiding priest at a wedding ceremony listened as the beautiful bride and very presentable bridegroom pledged their faithfulness to one another. Love was in the air. But in the apartment where he slept that night, the last thing he heard before he fell asleep, and the first thing he heard in the morning was the bickering and shouting of a couple in the apartment above him. How that made him think! Wasn't love in the air at their wedding too? What had happened since?

Among the ancients, Diogenes was said to walk the streets with a lamp looking for an honest man. Perhaps we should hire a street walker with a flashlight to cry out, "Where is the killer of love?" It might make everyone think, and some reform.

"We kill the things we love," said one writer trenchantly. Selfishness and loss of self-control do kill love. But the true lover does not kill love; he is ready to die for love.

Today Jesus calls us to a love like his; he calls us to a love like our heavenly Father's; and his call to love is a call to action.

Jesus calls us to love as he loved. "Such as my love has been for you," he says, "so your love must be for one another." It is fitting to stir up our love in this Easter season, because Easter is a call to joy, and love is its source.

What is love? Is it a feeling? A mood? It is those things, and far more; it is an indefinable mystery and a way of life. When we speak of love we are speaking of a share in the mystery of God who is love.

To love is to wish another well. If love runs deep, it includes vehement affection and ready service. Love is a union of wills, the desire to do what the beloved wishes, so long as it is not wrong. That is why we always speak of doing God's will, for his will is never wrong. Love is compassion: When you suffer I hurt until I relieve your pain. Love is apostolic. It flows into deeds. Love is a missionary. It spreads God's Good News abroad, as we see Paul doing in the first reading.

We see these qualities of love in the life of Jesus. He loves as Son, Brother, Bridegroom, Father and Savior. He gave and never counted the cost, even the cost of suffering and death. He calls our love to the qualities of his. It is a call that asks more than all laws can demand, a call to live in his likeness, to live by his life, and enter his resurrection.

We can be helped to respond if we seriously ask the questions, "How would he live my loves? How would he act in the face of the ingratitude, the indifference, the meanness that I experience?" If we really want the answers, we need only read the Gospels. He faced all these things too. His loved triumphed over them all, for love is more powerful.

Jesus calls us to love like God the Father. Jesus summarized his Sermon on the Mount by saying, "Be perfect, just as your heavenly Father is perfect." It's strange how we're so concerned about whether God loves us! He does! His love is perfect. We need only be concerned about loving like God.

Today's psalm tells us of the qualities of God's love. His love is gracious, merciful, slow to anger. Does that make you think of the couple the priest heard bickering and shouting? God's love is of great kindness, good to all, and compassionate to all. Is your love good to all? Or is it narrowed down to those most deserving, as if it were a paycheck issued to those who have earned it? God's love is good to all. Christ died for all. Our love must be that way too — not just yours; mine; I ask myself the questions which I'm asking you. If my love doesn't go out to all, what am I going to do about it?

Christ's love is kingly. Did you ever ask if your love is kingly? It's an interesting question. There is a kingliness to love. It has a grandeur about it which tells us when someone is truly in love. A true lover's love radiates to all like the sun.

God's love is of enduring dominion. Ours will be too if it's true love. It triumphs over all things, even time. In the second reading, God's love calls us to love's fulfillment in the heavenly Jerusalem where he personally will wipe every tear from our eyes. Is your love concerned for the eternal salvation of those you love? Are you earnest to have resurrection and eternal life for them even as God is?

Jesus' call to love is a call to action. If we live in him we'll produce many good deeds, he said, as a branch of a fruit tree produces much fruit. Paul's missionary journeys were deeds of love. Love is a missionary. It goes about doing good, giving the best it has, especially the faith and the love of God.

The Church is God's family of love, and it surely shows this giving quality. We tire of its calls to give, give, give, but let us remember that this is just another way of putting Jesus' call to love into action. The Church gives to us from the cradle to the grave. Who of us can repay the Church for what it does for us? Only by active love are we truly practicing and witnessing Catholics.

St. Paul tells us that love is enduring. "We must undergo many trials," he says, "if we are to enter into the reign of God," that is, the reign of love. Think of all our Blessed Mother had to endure in a lifetime of mothering Christ and his Church.

Our actions of love need always the guidance of God's truth, or they won't be actions from a love like Jesus' own. If not guided by truth, love is blind, as the saying goes, and you know what can happen to love when it's blind. We're capable of terrible things in the name of love. True love has the best eyes there are, eyes like Jesus' own, eyes that look only to the good things to be done.

As we turn now to the Holy Sacrifice, we recall that it commemorates Jesus' own Heart loving us to the end. The Mass has the power to bring us to new purpose and a new life, the life of a love like his. How can we really live it? By willing it. Take a moment now to resolve to love like Jesus.

"C" — Sixth Sunday of Easter

Ac 15:1-2, 22-29
Rv 21:10-14, 22-23
Jn 14:23-29

WALKING WITH GOD

"Whoever loves me will keep my word, and my Father will love him, and we will come to him and make our dwelling with him." Our calling is to walk with God by prayer, so of prayer I'll speak.

St. Benedict used to visit his sister, St. Scholastica, once a year at her convent. On one visit, after the hour grew late in talk of God and sacred things, Benedict spoke of leaving. His sister begged him to stay longer, but he felt he must return to his monastery. She bent her head in prayer, and a terrible storm broke out. "What have you done?" he cried. She explained that since he wouldn't listen to her request, she asked God and he listened. "So now go off if you can," she concluded.

He stayed through the storm and the night. They gave their hearts to God and one another in blessed conversation. Three days later, in his own monastery, St. Benedict saw his sister's soul leave her body like a dove and fly up to heaven. He knew then that he had refused to prolong their last meeting, but God had not, for she asked out of love, and God is love.

Now a practical question. Here is Jesus talking of a profound mysticism, of God living with us. Is that teaching for everyone, or just for monks and nuns like St. Benedict and his saintly sister? The answer is clear in Jesus' own words: "If *anyone* loves me," he said, "it is for him or her."

Walking with God is for each of us. Don't you like companionship with your best friend? Isn't God our best friend, or at least willing to be if we allow it? Walking with God is a theme in the Bible from Adam to Moses to Mary to us. God walked in the Garden with Adam and Eve; he promised Abraham and Moses, "I will be with you;" and the angel said to Mary, "The Lord is with you." Jesus says the same to us. We too can walk with God.

The Psalmist speaks of how God knew him in his mother's womb, and adds, "If I take the wings of the morning and dwell in the uttermost parts of the sea, even there thy hand shall lead me, and thy right hand shall hold me."

How do we practice this walking with God? Words are clumsy but the practice is simple. It need not follow the four steps I'll now give, but they can be helpful. Here are the steps: Recollection, Attention, Intention, and Companionship.

Recollection comes first. We can't be a good companion without it. Haven't you been with a person, even at a dinner, who hardly seems aware of your presence? He's too busy following every little distraction in the room. That distracted person can be ourselves. If we can't even be with those bodily present to our senses, how can we be with God?

I overcome distraction by really wanting to be with God. I practice recollection by putting all else out of my mind and becoming aware of myself. If not present to myself I can't be present to anyone. The poet, George Herbert, says any one can love except the busied man. He is so distracted by things and projects he can't have a deep relationship with a person.

Attention comes next. We want to attend to God who is present to us. A beautiful way to do it is to memorize Jesus' promise of presence in today's Gospel. We repeat his words, and add, "Lord, I believe your revelation about your presence. I believe your promise to be with me, because you love me."

If you're not used to praying much, at this point you may experience the *absence* of God. Your very effort to feel God's presence may make you feel his absence. Don't worry about it! Just say, "I don't feel your presence; I feel as if you were absent. But that's only a feeling. I believe what you said. I know you're present with me, and I want to enjoy your presence."

Just keep doing that day after day, and the day will come when you sense God's presence. Then you can say, "See, I told you I believed. I knew all the time you are here." That is why this prayer is *called* The Prayer of Faith. As the days and weeks go by you have a sense you're not alone anymore. Like Jesus you can say, "I am not alone, because the Father is with me."

A woman who was taught this practice by a priest wrote to him several months later that she had awakened one night and felt God's presence without any effort at all.

A man who practiced this prayer was making a journey one day all alone when suddenly he was surprized by an intense feeling of God's presence. "I'll never be alone again!" he said to himself, so strongly did he feel that God was always present.

Intention is the step that follows attention. We say, "Jesus, you said if we loved you we'd keep your word. I'm going to keep it just as you kept the Father's word and did all he wanted of you. Inspire me by your Spirit so I can live your life and do your deeds."

Companionship is the fourth step: You simply enjoy the presence of God. As I said, the four steps blend into one if you practice them, and are done much more quickly than I could describe them. On your job, when you walk to the water fountain to get a drink, you recall yourself, turn your heart to God, offer him yourself, and enjoy his presence with a burst of love before you go back to work. As your walking with God deepens, you'll turn to him many times a day, as a good friend should. You will be one of those the Bible says walk with God.

This is the way to prepare for the Ascension, and for your own ascension and eternal life with God. The resurrection has been calling us to this joy of life with God now. The Ascension is reminding us it'll go on forever. Faith and this prayer of faith are the beginning of heaven's vision of God, the vision that brings all happiness.

In heaven there are no churches, as we heard in the second reading. God himself is our Temple. We'll see him and be united with him. This prayer of faith, this practice of the presence of God, is a growth of God's presence that began in baptism. It will increase until it becomes perfect in heaven. It is the very heart of prayer and the spiritual life. It is a prayer of love. It is given us by the Holy Spirit, present with the Father and the Son. It was Mary's prayer. She wants it to be ours.

It can change your life. In that change all whom you love will be blessed, and the Church will be blessed. Walk with God. And let us not forget that in the Eucharist we will enjoy today we have the fullest presence of God until the beatific vision.

"C" — Ascension

Ac 1:1-11
Ep 1:17-23
Lk 24:46-53

WHAT JESUS AND WE ARE DOING

A Christian heard a gathering of atheists scorning the notion that there is a God who created man from the mud of the earth. Addressing them, he admitted creation was a mystery to him too, then added, ''But this I know: One night God stooped down and picked up the dirtiest piece of mud in this city, breathed upon it by his Spirit, and changed a gambling, drinking, thieving wretch into a peace-loving man of God. I was that man!''

God turned earth's clay into man, turned the living clay of humanity into the body of his Son in the womb of the Virgin Mary, raised his body to life on Easter, and at the Ascension welcomed him home at last.

What does the Ascension mean to Jesus, what does he do in heaven, and where does that leave us?

What does the Ascension mean to Jesus? It means his work and suffering as mortal man are over. He carries home to the Father the first body and soul to enter glory. He and the Father embrace in the Holy Spirit with love beyond imagining. The Spirit prepares his Pentecost shower of blessings for the whole earth as if God's love can no longer be contained in heaven.

What was begun in Eden has been completed in Jesus. It is spreading to us. Jesus is first citizen of heavenly Jerusalem. Jesus risen and ascended is the New Creation founded beyond time and space, suffering and sorrow. In his human body and soul he lifts humanity to a share in his own divinity. In him, our humanness is forever glorified. By him, the path to eternal life has been blazoned. The Ascension is the signal that Jesus has completed the work commissioned by the Father.

What does Jesus do in heaven? He drinks from the torrent of life. He enjoys what eye has not seen, nor ear heard, nor man imagined. He celebrates victory with the Father, in the Holy Spirit, in the company of Our Lady and the angels and the souls of all the victorious who await only their risen bodies.

Jesus had no self-centeredness on earth; he certainly has none in heaven. He is praising and thanking the Father. And, as the Letter to the Hebrews says, he is standing before God the Father interceding for us. He can no more forget us than his own Heart. If St. Therese of Lisieux said she would spend her time in heaven doing good on earth, how much more Jesus? ''I am with you all days,'' he said, "even to the end of the world.''

He is with his body the Church, with us everywhere we go in creation. He is present pouring out his graces in his word and sacraments. He is with us in the Eucharist here at Mass, as he is with the Father in heaven. He is in each of us, doing his work through us now. He is loving with our hearts, planning great things with our minds, serving with our hands. When he was a mortal man, his body was in one place. Now he is the new man. His spiritual body is no prisoner of time or space. He makes himself present to whomever he wills in any time at any place. That is made plain in the mystery of the Eucharist.

Where does that leave us? At the Ascension the two angels said to his followers, "Why do you stand here looking up at the skies?'' It's as if they said, "He promised to return. But do you suppose he meant you to stand here waiting for him? Don't you realize that the less you do the longer you'll wait? You wait by carrying out the mission he assigned you.''

"Christ has died, Christ has risen, Christ will come again.'' When? When all is ready. In the early Church some people seemed inclined to sit about awaiting him, but St. Paul said that if a man won't work he shouldn't eat either. We're to live and work in a human way like Christ. His fellow townsmen could say of him, "Is he not the carpenter, the son of Mary?'' He worked with his hands, preached the Good News, spread the kingdom of God. He went about doing good. We, as other Christs, imitate him in all these things, as the first disciples did. They were often in the Temple, praying, worshipping and preaching the Good News.

The Second Coming of Jesus will signal the end of mortal life and the beginning of eternity for all. But first, the work of the body of Christ must be finished. How many generations will that take? We don't know. We do know that our personal going to the Father needn't await his return, except for the resurrection of our bodies. For now, we each love and work for family and for friend and for all as he did, and prepare to return to him one by one, at the hour of our death.

In the meantime, we make daily visits to heaven. What is prayer but visits to heaven while on earth? The Eucharist is that and even more. Jesus is present to us while he remains present to the Father, so while with him we're with the Father too.

We're also led down at times into the dark pit of suffering. Jesus' Gospel is the Gospel of the Cross. It was through his wounds, especially the wound of his Heart, that he poured life and grace into the world. The mystery of salvation is that he continues to pour his graces out through wounds, our wounds, especially the wound of broken hearts.

We have the Gospel of the Cross even on this joyful feast. Jesus mentions the prophecy, now fulfilled, of his suffering and rising. He adds that we must all do penance for the remission of sin. To suffer for love of Christ is to share his victory.

The Gospel of the Cross is not bad news. It's part of the Good News. Sin brought suffering, but in Jesus suffering brings the remission of sin. In Jesus, suffering lifts us beyond Eden to heaven. Those who escape heavy suffering in this life are not as blessed as those who share it gladly. It unites us more to Christ in mortal life and in eternal life. It's really prophesied of us all that we must suffer and rise from the dead. It's our share with Jesus in the work that saves us and the world with us. But be aware that the suffering of Jesus was not self-inflicted. It was the suffering none can escape who live a life of fidelity, love and service for the good of all as the Father wills.

Where does the ascension leave us, then? It leaves us other Christs, following his way of life in the sure hope of arriving where he is in the glory of the Father.

"C" — Seventh Sunday of Easter

Ac 7:55-60
Rv 22:12-14, 16-17, 20
Jn 17:20-26

OUR FAMILY IN HEAVEN AND ON EARTH

Have you seen those places where earth and sea and sky seem no longer separate? The Florida Keys is such a place. As you look out across the water, the pure white sands embrace the boundless ocean, an ocean so blue it unites with the sky far away, blending heaven and earth into one.

That oneness of heaven and earth is the theme suggested by today's readings in this post-Ascension season. Let us reflect on it. First, God and each of us has two families, one in heaven and one on earth. Second, we can cement the bond of family life only by blending earthly and heavenly life. Third, our earthly family is destined to blend into our family in heaven.

First, God and each of us has two families, one in heaven and one on earth. Sometimes this Sunday falls on Mother's Day. It is a lovely blend of feasts, for we recognize in our mother the heart of our family on earth, as we recognize in God the heart of our family in heaven.

Neither to our mothers nor to God can we give as much as we have received. The gift to God and family which suggests itself today is the gift of family unity. What brings a parent more grief than rancor in the home? Or more joy than family peace and unity? Today we're called to cast out all rancor, bitterness, and division, and make this the first day of the rest of our lives.

On earth we are also members of a larger family, the family of Christ, the Church. There, too, we seek the unity of love and truth. We work for it both within the Church and, through the ecumenical movement, with all the separated Churches. Does not Jesus himself pray in today's Gospel that all may be one? This unity is the passion of the Heart of God for humankind.

Secondly, we can cement the bond of family life only if we blend earthly and heavenly life. This is the only way, as society around us with its lost religious values certainly makes evident. Doesn't Jesus clearly pray to the Father, "that they all may be one in us"? St. Gregory of Nyssa comments on Jesus' words. He says the followers of Jesus "were no longer to be divided in their judgment of what was right and good, for they were all to be united to the one supreme Good." Only if we center ourselves on the teachings of the God-man and his Church can we be one in mind and heart in our family of origin, and the family of the Church, and if you want to go on, the family of man.

Only if we cultivate love and unity in family life will there be peace in families or in the Church or on earth. Family life is God's own creation and gift to us. There is nothing like family. We know we can experience bitterness and disappointment in family, but we know that it is still our best hope here on earth. In its finest mood family life reflects the life of heaven's own family. God made husband and wife and family in the image and likeness of God, with their love and lifegiving. Children give life to their parents too by making life a joy.

Family life shows forth the mystery of the divine Trinity. It expresses what love is, what giving is, what happiness should be and can be. The home is the place where we go beyond external unity to share mind and heart. We share values, possessions, concerns and confidences. This is true intimacy. Family life is intimate life. I know the way the world uses the word intimacy, but let us remember here and now that the word has first of all a spiritual and psychological meaning before it has a physical, bodily meaning. The word *intimate* comes from an old Latin word (*interus*) which means inward, interior. Intimacy is the spiritual journey into one another's mind and heart to share all that we hold most dear, all that we believe most truly, all that we love most firmly. Intimacy is that wonderful sense of being known, accepted and loved, and of knowing, accepting and loving.

St. Ignatius of Loyola used to love to speak about familiarity with God, intimacy with God. God is pure spirit, and this makes the point that intimacy is first of all a spiritual relationship. Without it, intimacy fails. We can cultivate this warm familiarity at home by deeper sharing of our concerns, our needs, our faith, our prayer together. Even between husband and wife, spiritual intimacy long precedes that special gift of bodily intimacy which God has given to spouses. Their bodily intimacy is a celebration of their spiritual intimacy.

What is more beautiful than faithfully lived family life? People are always out for novelty, but nothing is newer and rarer and happier than family life well lived. If you want true newness, search out family togetherness.

Thirdly, our earthly family is destined to blend into our family in heaven. We have just celebrated the Ascension. God has his Son, Jesus, at home now. He has his daughter, Mary, at home through her Assumption. He longs to gather all of us home and to be Father and Mother of us all.

If you paid careful attention, you saw that in the readings. In the first reading, St. Stephen sees his home in heaven opening, and he goes there. In the second reading, our Lord Jesus says that he will return for us so that we can go up through the gate of heaven and eat of the tree of life. He wants all of us at home, and wants us to want it too. So he gives us the prayer, "Come, Lord Jesus!" In the Gospel Jesus tells the Father of his desire to have us with him. Just as our earthly parents want us around them, our God wants us gathered around the divine Trinity. Then we will experience what family life can really be.

In the meantime the Lord continues to live with us, and in his person our two families are already in union. But we pray for the fullness of that union. There is a great mystery here which Jesus brings out when he prays to the Father "that their unity may be complete. So shall the world know that you sent me, and that you love them as you love me." Can you believe that the Father loves us as he loves Jesus? It seems impossible, but here is an insight: The Father looks down, and through baptism and the Eucharist he sees only one life, the life which Jesus has shared with you and me. We are one with him and in him. Even when he looks at us the Father sees only Jesus.

In this Mass and Eucharist we cement that oneness with Jesus. We say to him, "Come, Lord Jesus! Live among us. Make our family on earth one with our family in heaven. Help us make earthly life a preparation to join you in our Father's home."

"ABC" — Vigil of Pentecost

Jl 3:1-5
Rm 8:22-27
Jn 7:37-39

THE NECESSARY HOLY SPIRIT

In each homily we priests try to show the meaning for us here and now of what God is saying to us. What, then, is the meaning of this feast of the Holy Spirit for our daily lives?

Well, have you ever had that experience of having important things to do, and just not having the spirit to do them, so they were put off or even left undone? Have you seen a marriage falling apart and finally ending in disaster because the couple just didn't seem to have the spirit to try to save their marriage? Have you observed the spirit of death in the air in this country? — the readiness to slaughter the unborn innocents to escape burdens, and to spread the doctrine of euthanasia, that is, to peddle the doctrine of death to the older members of the nation?

These disorders of the spirit should make it evident to us how much we need the Spirit of God. The Spirit of God is God, is love, truth, mercy, joy, goodness. He is the Spirit of peace and of all good things, and he comes with a power to help us that we can't even dream of. The planets, the stars and the sun are to him less than a pocketful of marbles to a little child.

This Feast is God and his Church telling us the Holy Spirit's help is available to us, if only we open our hearts to him. What will he help us do? For examples, I refer to the readings.

In the first reading, the prophet Joel prophesies this event of the coming of the Holy Spirit. He said the Spirit would be given to everyone, men and women and slaves alike. Old people tend to get cynical and give up their dreams, but Joel tells us that the Spirit will make the old dream their dreams. Joel also warns that a "great and terrible day" is coming, that is, the Day of Judgment. How can we be saved? Joel says, pray! Pray, and the spirit of repentance and grace will be given you.

What other gifts does the Spirit give? In the second reading, Paul says the whole of creation is groaning under its burdens, looking for salvation. We can see a new meaning in that today, with the pollution of the water and air, the corruption of so many resources, the poisoning and dying out of animal species, and all the other environmental problems. All nature is groaning under the corruption that sin and its greed and selfishness bring into the world. God has solutions for these problems by the wisdom of the Spirit. Paul says that we, too, are groaning for the redemption of our bodies. Biologists tell us that from the moment of birth we begin to die. We groan for that immortality which God promised. We thirst for it.

Where do we fill that thirst? In the Gospel Jesus says, Do you thirst? Drink of this stream of living water! So if we go to him, we can drink of that living water which is the Holy Spirit of eternal life that pours out from him.

There are so many other problems, too, for which we need help. The turmoil in the world — those struggles, divisions, racial tensions — what do we do about them? How do we solve these problems? In the Opening Prayer we made this petition:

"Almighty and ever-living God, you fulfilled your Easter promise by sending us your Holy Spirit. May that Spirit unite the races and nations on earth to proclaim your glory." God the Spirit can produce that unity. We see it at times in the world and its communities. In 1990 we saw the spirit of freedom and brotherhood bursting out in communist countries, and only hoped it would continue. It was a transformation amazing to the world, surely the work of the Spirit of God and, many would hold, of the prayers of Our Lady of Fatima.

If we see this much happening, how much more could happen if we really got serious about asking for God's Spirit? The Spirit is the "payload" of Christ's work of death and resurrection. He is the fulfillment of the promise of Easter. As the Second Divine Person came to do the redeeming work, the Third Divine Person is coming to do the sanctifying and healing work which Jesus won for us.

Does not family life need help? Whenever there is need for help in family life, the greatest need is always for more love. This Spirit *is* love. As the substance of our body is flesh, the substance of the Holy Spirit is *Love*, the mystery of love, that is, God. Do you think he can't help fathers and mothers, sons and daughters, brothers and sisters to imitate, to feel and live the love of the Holy Family of Nazareth, and the love of the Divine Family of the Trinity? He can, and it's what he came for, to give us this gift and infinitely more.

One most important gift is this, to draw closer to the Heart of our Redeemer. This feast has an inseparable relationship to the Feast of the Sacred Heart. In today's Gospel, you heard Jesus say rivers of living water would flow out from his body. He was the last Adam, hanging on the cross. When his side was pierced and his Heart was opened, blood and water and his Divine Spirit poured forth. That Spirit is what we're to drink of. The water gave us new birth in baptism; the water of his blood gives us heavenly nourishment; and the water of his Holy Spirit gives us love, the life of love, and with that every good thing. It also gives us that relationship to

Christ which makes us the Church, the bride of Christ, more closely united with him than any human bride and bridegroom ever can be.

To foster this union, we must face up to sin and fight it off. That spirit of death in the world which I mentioned always involves a denial of sin. That is the road to final disaster. Jesus called the Spirit "the Spirit of truth." He leads us along the way of truth that rejects false answers.

The Mother of Jesus was most full of the Holy Spirit. Let us cry to her today to teach us to open our hearts to the Spirit as she learned to do. Let us not neglect either, to remember her advice concerning her Son: "Do whatever he tells you."

Every trade has its trade secrets. Let me give you a trade secret of the spiritual life, a great one. If you want the gift of the Spirit, *go to the Source!* That is, today, when you receive the Bread of Angels, drink of the Spirit, that river of living water. Drink it from the Heart of the Redeemer, the wellspring from which it comes forth.

"ABC" — Pentecost

Ac 2:1-11
1 Cor 12:3-7, 12-13
Jn 20:19-23

LIFE IN THE SPIRIT

On Pentecost love came down with the roar of passion and the eloquence of flaming tongues. It could alarm us if we're not at home with love. It could frighten us out of our wits if we're not one of those who knows that love won't harm a flea, though it has the power to move mountains.

Psychologists who researched love came up with interesting

data. The data showed that loving people promote harmony, responsibility and commitment. They don't feel compelled to have a handle on power; they're at peace in the hands of fate. Their values make them look for intimate friendships and thoughts of love. Their caring for others without worrying about what they get out of it improves their own health of body and psyche.

This is the Feast of Love. It's the flowering of the crop of Easter and the Ascension. The word Pentecost means *the fiftieth day*, that is, fifty days from Easter. It is the day when Jesus' Last Supper promise is fulfilled. It was then he promised us another Guide, the Holy Spirit, to recall his teachings to us in all circumstances, and fill us with the holiness to live them. Jesus revealed to us the Father's truth; the Holy Spirit guides us to live the life of love and the truth about love.

Today we're called anew to life in the Spirit. From the first the Holy Spirit sanctified the Church and guided it to teach faith and morals and to hand these on through the generations.

The pastors of the Church instruct us in that teaching. Still, each of us needs the personal guidance of the Holy Spirit too, to open our hearts to the teaching, and apply it to our lives day by day. Life is a long journey. The road is always branching. Which fork is the right one for me? Often we can't know without the Holy Spirit's help. We don't know the future. God does. The Spirit uses that knowledge to guide us if we will listen. I will try to say some helpful things about listening.

First, though, let's look at the goal of life. The goal of life is God; the experience of life is to be attracted to a lot of lesser goals, like ease and pleasure, money and power. We won't be ready to listen to the Holy Spirit if we don't hold firmly to the goal of love of God and one another. So life involves setting priorities.

Now we are ready to consider how to listen to the Holy Spirit when making our choices. The first step is to set out all the choices clearly. St. Ignatius of Loyola gives us great help here. He was a master decision maker who was taught by God a very helpful way to make decisions. Ignatius describes three sets of circumstances in which we have to make decisions. The first is when God gives us so much light and draws us by so much love we know at once which way to go. St. Matthew illustrates that. Jesus called him to follow; he was so drawn he left his tax business then and there, got up and followed, and never turned back.

The second set of circumstances is when a person carefully considers the alternatives before him, and clearly sees what is best for him. Still, he may have to fight some selfish impulses in himself to make the right decision. Let's illustrate this by a boy and girl who fall deeply in love. On their dates they find they share the same values and goals, and are firm in their will to do nothing that displeases God. They think about marriage, are free to marry in the Church, and are drawn to it. But he or she or both also want to be free of marriage responsibilities. A battle begins within their hearts.

So they begin to pray. Prayer is essential to good decisions. We pray for God's help, look for the Holy Spirit's guidance, and ask to be freed of our resistance to the right decision. Jesus himself spent the whole night in prayer before he made the decision of selecting the Twelve Apostles.

Our couple pray, and soon they realize that the resistance they feel is just the old self-centeredness. They see clearly that if they marry they will help one another on the journey to God, and live a life of love together. And so he proposes, she says *yes*, and soon they set the wedding date. A good decision has been made with the help of the Holy Spirit.

St. Ignatius also proposes a third set of circumstances for making a decision. It's the most common case. Let's illustrate it with a young man or woman who is seriously thinking about the way to spend his or her life. Will it be a religious vocation, or marriage, or the single life in the world? The person calmly considers the alternatives. He wants to choose the way most pleasing to God and most certain to embrace the purpose for which God created him. If he feels enslaved to one choice which he's not at all sure is the right one, he puts off the decision. He prays and does other spiritual exercises to grow in the freedom to make a real choice. Not until then does he proceed.

Then he considers each choice. Which one will more surely help him to live a life of faith and love? Which will help him give the greatest glory to God, like Jesus Christ? He begs God for the great-heartedness to give his all in the right decision. He takes pen and paper. He writes out the advantages and disadvantages of each choice in view of the true meaning of life. When he comes to what looks like the best choice, he offers it to God in prayer and asks if it pleases him. If he finds peace and joy when he makes his offer, he decides it is the right one.

If that peace and joy don't come, he takes the next step: he imagines someone else in his shoes, and asks what advice he would give him; and he pictures himself dying, and going before God, and asks what decision he will wish he made then. With the help of these added ways, he should find peace and joy at last in offering God the best decision he can make.

In daily life we can also have the Holy Spirit's help to guide and choose through our thoughts, feelings, impulses and moods. We set out to become more conscious of them the moment they arise. We try to understand and assess them. We decide which to cultivate and which to allow to wilt by withdrawing from them the sunlight of our attention and the good soil of our wills. We learn to pull the plug on worries, fears, dreads and desires, and replace them with peace and joy. When the tree of love grows tall, the weeds in its shade die. Today the Holy Spirit is announcing his intention of helping us to find love and true life. Let's all invite him into our hearts now and always.

Pr 8:22-31
Rm 5:1-5
Jn 16:12-15

THE TRINITY: FAITH'S FAMILY MODEL

A man once attended a showing by local artists. One lovely work depicted a family scene with parents, children, and even the family dog gathered by the fireplace. Their faces and postures spoke volumes of their togetherness and love. The man described afterward how he yearned to meet the artist who revealed his own heart in capturing so well the essence of family life.

Today we celebrate the mystery of God, the most Holy Trinity, the Most Holy Family. They too have revealed their heart to us in their majestic and glorious works, as today's psalm says so eloquently. And where have they revealed themselves more admirably in their created works than in family life?

But that comparison of God to an artist is inadequate; let me take another. We honor George Washington as the Father of our country. We know him by his works and his labors to establish a country with laws of fairness, equity and freedom. We are grateful to him for the citizenship that we hold through his works. In a far more profound way, it is in the great works which God has done for us that we come to know and love God.

But the comparison with Washington is inadequate for another reason. None of us has ever met him. But we have met God in Christ his Son, who comes to us in mystery.

On this great feast of the Holy Trinity, what is more fitting than to reflect on how God revealed himself as Father, Son and Holy Spirit? We confess the mystery in the Nicene Creed each Sunday, but how did we learn about it? Not by gazing at his creation!

None knew God had a Son, though God gave a hint of it in the creation account. He said, "Let *us* make man in our image and likeness." And in the first reading today we had the account of God's Wisdom, whom today we call the Word of God. But who suspected before Christ came that Wisdom was a second Person in God? Who suspected God had a Son, the "first-born of his ways"?

The Son of God became known to us only when God gave us his Son to be our Son. We learned of him only when the Father sent the angel to say to Our Lady, "The Holy Spirit will come upon you, and the power of the Most High will overshadow you. Therefore the child to be born will be called holy, the Son of God."

Pope John Paul II said, "Mary of Nazareth is the first believer of the New Covenant to experience the one God in three Persons, the source of all Life, all Light, all Love." We can see more deeply into that truth if we recall that her family was not just an image of God; her family included the God it imaged. Her Son was not just a man in the divine image; he was the God who made the image. He was true God and true man.

Jesus' divine Sonship was further confirmed for us at his baptism when the voice from heaven said, "This is my beloved Son, with whom I am well pleased." And after many months of preaching the Gospel, Jesus, who was struggling as a human being to reveal himself, went up a mountain to prayer. And there the Apostles, who were still unaware of his divine identity, heard the voice from heaven, "This is my beloved Son, with whom I am well pleased. Listen to him." So we learned God had a Son only when God gave his Son to us to become a man, share our human life, and work our redemption.

And how did we learn of the Holy Spirit, the third person of the Blessed Trinity? We learned when he descended on the Virgin Mary to make her the Virgin Mother of Jesus. And when he descended on Jesus at his baptism. Even these events did not make it very clear that the Holy Spirit is the third Person of the divine Trinity. Jesus began to make it clear at the Last Supper, from which today's Gospel reading comes. He promised he and the Father would send us another Intercessor, the Holy Spirit, the Spirit of truth, who would imprint the Gospel in our hearts.

On Pentecost the Holy Spirit roared into the world in power. In the form of fiery tongues symbolizing the eloquence of love and of truth, he descended upon the Apostles. And from that moment the Holy Spirit carried the Church of Christ forward in the boldness of truth and the ardor of love, to spread salvation to the whole world.

Let us not miss the lesson: It was in the actions of giving themselves to us and calling us to be their children and part of their family that the Trinity revealed themselves to us.

Do you think enough about the fact that as we grow up and learn about our own family life, we are learning something of the mystery of the Trinity? After all, God made us in his image and likeness. And more, through the prophets and the coming of Christ, God took us up into a higher participation in his divine nature. He gave us rebirth through water and the Holy Spirit, and made us share in the Sonship of Christ, made us his children, his sons and daughters in the very life of Christ.

We learn of the mystery of God by our family life and by our life in Christ. By the very graces that he gives us to live like him, Christ is revealing himself to us. The Holy Trinity gave us the highest and noblest calling, that of growing up as sons and daughters of God.

It is not an easy calling; it is a noble and a high calling. It leads us through many straits and dangers, temptations and difficulties. Paul says in that second reading that we boast of these troubles. Affliction makes for endurance, endurance for tested virtue, and tested virtue for hope, and hope leads us home to the Trinity.

The world will always teach us the shoddy, the easy way, the way that sells out our birthright. But God our good Father, and Christ our true Brother, call us to love and live in the Spirit of truth. They call us to labor and grow and serve, to reveal ourselves to one another by giving self, as they did. If you've ever asked yourself bitterly why people don't seem to know you, perhaps its because you haven't given enough. In the revelation, we hear God saying to us, "I am your Father. You must live like my Son. Don't be afraid. The Spirit of strength, of truth and of love is with you, and you will never lack what you need to be faithful. Don't listen to the world; listen to me, for I have created you, and I have given you rebirth. Live through my graces the life that I have shared with you, and you will live one day in my home, with my Holy Family, Father, Son and Holy Spirit."

"C" — Corpus Christi

Gn 14:18-20
1 Cor 11:23-26
Lk 9:11-17

SACRAMENT OF THE HEART OF JESUS

Food is a gift of God we all enjoy. We take pleasure in all kinds, colors and sizes, in servings from snacks to feasts. Jesus too enjoyed food, whether his mother's home cooking, or his meals with friends. He liked to compare heaven with banquets, and he was present at many himself. But he alone was able and willing to give his own body and blood for the banquet of the world.

We celebrate that gift today. It is the feast of his love. It calls us to consider with love what faith tells us about it. We'll look at the Eucharist as the mystery of his love for us even to death; we'll reflect on reception of Holy Communion as the experience of our redemption; and we'll rejoice in the Eucharist as the mystery of the love of the Heart of Jesus.

First, then, the Eucharist is the mystery of Christ's passion, death and resurrection. It is the sacrament Christ created to capture the substance of his work on earth for us. Though he was in the form of God he came, as St. Paul said, in human likeness, and obediently died on the cross. The night before, he instituted the Eucharist as a way we could offer his sacrifice of the cross till the end of time for our salvation.

This Feast of the Body and Blood of Christ often falls on Father's Day. Pause on that thought. All parenting is modeled after God the Father. It is the nobility of fatherhood to give, guide, and cherish life. Perhaps Jesus gave the most resplendent tribute to fatherhood when he said, "Call no man on earth your father; you have but one Father in heaven." Be sure Jesus meant to take nothing from the honor we owe our fathers, for the third commandment says, "Honor your father and your mother."

What then did he mean? Surely he meant that the role of fatherhood is a task so monumental, so impossible, that while a human father can begin it, only God can complete it. Perhaps he was implying that we should not be too demanding of our fathers; we should be forever grateful to them for doing their best; we should honor them all our days; but we must look to God himself to complete the work they began.

Jesus does complete it in the Eucharist, by his own fatherhood. Jesus said at the Last Supper, "Whoever has seen me has seen the Father." As Son of God, Jesus is the perfect likeness of the Father, and sharer in all his powers. Again at the Last Supper he said, "My children, I will be with you only a little while longer." Should he not call us his children, since in the sacrament of the Eucharist he gives us immortal life? In the Church we call Jesus "the Father of the world to come."

The most generous of fathers, Jesus at the Last Supper was as it were giving us everything in sight, so moved was he by his love for us that night before he died. Here I can only mention that he gave us not only his body and blood, but his mystical body. He gave it in telling us to love one another as he loves us. When he fulfilled the Eucharistic mystery on the cross, he gave away the rest. He gave us his Mother, Mary, to be our Mother. He gave his life to give us eternal life. As he hung there, his side was pierced, and blood and water flowed out, all part of this mystery of the Eucharist. He was the new Adam, and from his side and his heart we the Church were being born in the water of baptism and blood of the Eucharist. The Eucharist is clearly the mystery of his love for us even to death.

Secondly, we reflect on the reception of Holy Communion as the experience of our redemption. The other sacraments give us the grace of Christ; this gives us Christ himself with all his graces. We receive the Resurrection and the Life. We "taste and see that the Lord is good." Communion is meant to give in a spiritual way what other food gives in a physical way: spiritual pleasure, growth, healing, health, and all food's other benefits. This is the bread of angels. We should experience some of the delight the heavenly Father takes in the presence of his Son.

If we don't, we should examine ourselves. Do we pray too little? Then we'll be too distracted. We'll be like a man who invites a guest to his house, and when the guest comes, he finds the host absent, or so involved in other affairs he might as well be absent. We have to do our part to experience Jesus present. We need a good conscience and a pure life. If we do not examine our conscience, we won't even know; if we do and find fault, we confess our sins in the sacrament of penance. If we find mortal sin, we must not receive until we have confessed. Then we will be spiritually healthy enough to find the taste of this divine food.

Finally, the Eucharist is the sacrament of the love of the Heart of Jesus. It is the most personal of all the sacraments. Christ comes to each of us as if each one were the only one he loved. He comes under the separate signs of his body and blood, to remind us that he died for love of us as the full measure of his devotion. By those signs he also appeals to us for a full return of love and service to him and his people.

In coming this way to each person, he exalts our dignity beyond all measure. If the President paid you a personal visit, you'd be proud to tell others of it. Here God himself comes to you to tell you of his love for you, and to give you his love and his very self. How could he better honor us and tell us how much we mean to him? We are beyond all price, and so he poured out his priceless blood for love of us. But to give himself personally this way seems like an even greater love. There are heroes who have died to serve others but who, if they had lived, would not give themselves for a lifetime to those they served.

We all know something of the mystery of love. It involves a mutual giving. The Eucharist is a giving no one else can achieve. It goes beyond human powers to give. None of us can give self so completely to another as Christ gives himself to us in Holy Communion. It can only be called God-giving.

In coming to us body and soul and divinity, our divine Redeemer literally gives his Heart to us. And as Pope Pius XII said of those who receive him, he "longs to speak with them heart to heart, especially after Holy Communion." Don't disappoint him.

They tell the story of a king who visited the home of one of his lowly subjects. To a child there he said, "Wouldn't you like to see my palace? It's the greatest house in the kingdom." And the child responded, "When you're in my home, my home is the greatest in the kingdom." So can we all say to Christ our King.

Solemnity of the Sacred Heart

Ezk 34:11-16
Rm 5:5-11
Lk 15:3-7

THROUGH HIS HEART TO THE TRINITY

Sisters preparing the confirmation class for the bishop's arrival put the bright lights in the front of the class to answer the bishop's questions. The bishop asked, "What is the Trinity?" One child answered in a piping little voice. The bishop said, "I didn't understand you." A voice from the back of the class cried out, "Bishop, you're not supposed to understand. It's a mystery!"

A little boy who learned about the mystery of the Trinity rushed home to tell his father, but his father didn't seem impressed. The child was put out, and said, "Dad, without me you wouldn't be a father!" He reminds us that family life is patterned after the mystery of the Holy Trinity, and we should feel at home with it.

This Feast of the Sacred Heart of Jesus draws us into the Family of the Holy Trinity. That will be our reflection today. We look in spirit at the pierced side of Jesus hanging on the cross. We pray that through our devotion to the Heart of Jesus we may grow to a full love of the most Blessed Trinity.

St. Margaret Mary received many visions of the Heart of Jesus. She also had a vision of the most Blessed Trinity which she called an incomparable favor. The Blessed Three appeared to her. The Father gave her a heavy cross and said, "See, my daughter, I make you the same present which I made to my beloved Son." The divine Son said to her, "I myself will fasten you to the cross as I myself was fastened to it, and will bear you faithful company." The Third Adorable Person told her that, being Love Itself, he would purify and consume her on her cross.

What is the meaning of this for us, except that all of us are called to bear life's sufferings as a privileged share in the atoning work of Jesus our Savior?

Pope Pius XII connected the Sacred Heart Devotion to the Blessed Trinity. He wrote that "essentially this devotion is nothing else than devotion to the human and divine love of the Incarnate Word and to the love which the Heavenly Father and the Holy Spirit have for sinful human beings." In the Gospels Jesus gives three revelations on his Heart: One leads to him, the second to the Holy Spirit, and the third to the Father.

First, he called us to his own Heart. "Take my yoke upon

your shoulders and learn from me," he invited, "for I am gentle and humble of heart." Here he calls us to his love for us. His Heart is a human lover's heart, and a symbol of his divine love. Here, too, the need to share the yoke of his suffering is mentioned. No one can be faithful to love without suffering.

Because his human Heart was just like yours and mine, we understand his love. We know our heart is not just a pumping station. The medical profession calls it a "psychosomatic organ," a body-soul organ. It registers our human emotions. Our hearts melt with love, thunder with fear, beat wildly with anxiety, shrink with coldness, and turn bitter with hatred. Our Lord's Heart was like ours, except that he hated only sin while loving all sinners. Jesus experienced the sensible and spiritual human love which we have, plus the divine love which only God has.

Sometimes our hearts amplify our spiritual love, and we feel them melting with love. At other times, our hearts register nothing. We feel nothing. Yet if our love is true, we go on serving just as if we felt that sensible love all the time. And even if we are afflicted with doubts, we go on believing in the love of others and especially of God. So our sensible love sometimes fails us, but if we are faithful our spiritual love never fails.

Jesus next invited us to the love of the Holy Spirit. He said, "Let anyone who thirsts come to me and drink. Whoever believes in me, as Scripture says, 'Rivers of living water will flow from within him.' He said this in reference to the Spirit that those who came to believe in him were to receive."

To quench our thirst *for* love and our thirst *to* love we drink spiritually from Jesus' pierced Heart. We drink of the river of the outpoured Holy Spirit of love. Pope Pius XII called the Holy Spirit of love the greatest gift of the Heart of Jesus.

Jesus, as he hung on the cross, gave us the call to the love of the Father through his human Heart. The Holy Trinity is present at the crucifixion. The Son is present bodily on the cross. The Holy Spirit is present in the love Jesus is pouring out for the redemption of the whole world. The Father is present in the conversation Jesus holds with him.

When Jesus breathed forth his Spirit and his Heart was pierced, Jesus returned home to the arms of his Father, and opened the way there for all of us. You remember that Jesus called his body the Temple of God. Now on the cross the veil of the Temple, that is, his breast, was opened, and there in his open Heart we see by faith the presence of the Adorable Trinity, the Father, Son and Holy Spirit. They wait for us to enter and pour out our adoring love.

Holy Communion is our meeting with the risen Lord Jesus. When we receive him, we should drink spiritually from his open Heart, drink of the Spirit of Love from its original Source in the world, the River flowing from the side of the Temple that is Christ. If we drink deeply we will never fail to love and be faithful to the adorable Trinity. And we will be faithful to one another, for we are made in their image and likeness.

Let us close with a condensed form of the Act of Reparation for the Feast of the Sacred Heart: "Most sweet Jesus, we are eager to repair by a special act of homage the cruel indifference toward and injury to your loving Heart that is so widespread. Mindful of our share in those indignities, we ask pardon and are ready to atone for both our sins and those of others.

"We resolve to atone for unbecoming ways of dressing and acting, for seduction of the innocent, for violations of Sundays, blasphemies against your Saints, and insults to your Vicar on earth. If we could, we would wash these sins away with our blood.

"Heavenly Father, we offer the atonement Jesus made on the cross, which we renew in the Holy Sacrifice of the Mass, in union with the atonement made by his Virgin Mother and all the Saints. We will try to live and love and believe in atoning ways in accord with the Gospel, especially its call to faithful love. Guide us home to you and your Son and the Holy Spirit, to be happy with you forever. Amen."

GOD: FOR OR AGAINST OUR SUFFERING?

A mother discovered her little child had fallen into the swimming pool. She flew to the phone. She couldn't reach the emergency number. She came screaming out of the house. Her neighbor, a paralyzed war vet in a wheelchair, rushed to her help. He made it part way and crawled the rest. By then someone had dragged the child out of the pool. The war vet gave her artificial respiration. Her life was saved.

Anyone who has worked around a hospital or seen accidents along the highway has witnessed the tremendous drive to come to the rescue when human life is in danger. People rush to save life as though it were their own — as though they sensed the mystery that love makes all life one. In the movie, *Starman,* the extra-terrestrial creature marvels at the human race because when things are at their worst, we are at our best. Urgent dangers tend to mobilize us all.

If dangers mobilize us, what of God? As one man says, "God is at least as good a guy as I am." The readings give us three life crises in which God comes to the rescue. They also portray a crisis of faith preceding the rescue that poses some questions: *Did* God send the prophet Elijah to chastise the woman for her sins? When suffering comes, do we have reason to question God's love? When suffering and death afflict us, what should we do?

Did God send the prophet Elijah to chastise the woman for her sins? Her little boy dies, and she asks the prophet, "Have you come to call attention to my guilt and to kill my son?" It's as if she said, "Letting you into my house called God's attention to me, and he said, 'She's a real sinner. I have to punish her.'"

The widow has a modern counterpart. She came to a priest

with a question. She had been abused in unmentionable ways as a girl and as a wife. Uneducated, poor, hooked on drugs, with an 84-year old dying father in her care, she said, "I don't wants money. I wants to known sumpin. Is this what God wants for me? Do I'se always gots to live this way? God, he hate me or what?"

Since the widow is really asking similar questions, how do you think Elijah felt? He *was* often sent to warn people of God's threatened punishment. Is the widow right?

Take another modern case. It was 5:04 p.m., October 17, 1989. Mass was being celebrated in Berkeley, California. The epistle to the Romans was being read: "The wrath of God is being revealed from heaven against the irreligious and perverse spirit of people who, in this perversity of theirs, hinder the truth." The earthquake interrupted the reading. The chapel rumbled and shook. The aftershock followed. The chapel stood. The Mass went on.

God does punish evil, so how does Elijah feel? Whatever is going on, he feels he must take his case to God. He prays, and in the power of prayer he raises the child. Life goes on, and the widow knows that God and a man of God have come into her life.

In the second reading, Paul recounts his crisis. He had judged Christians as heretics. In the name of God he persecuted the body of Christ. Jesus appeared to him and said, "I am Jesus whom you are persecuting." Here Jesus is rushing to his people's help, saving Paul from his blind zeal, and choosing him to preach to and save the nations.

In the Gospel, the widow of Naim is burying her only son. Did she think God was punishing her? He was immortalizing her! What was Jesus thinking? Was he thinking of his Mother Mary, soon to be weeping when she buried him? Was he thinking of his words, "I have come that they might have life and have it more abundantly"? Whatever his thoughts, he told the widow not to cry, and then took away the reason for her tears.

When suffering comes, do we have reason to question God's love for us? We do not if we have faith. We do not if we believe

God's word that he loves us with an everlasting love, loves us so much he gave his own Son that we may have eternal life.

But at times we should ask, "Is God correcting me?" In Psalm 119:76 the psalmist says, "I know, O Lord, that your ordinances are just, and in your faithfulness you have afflicted me." Isn't that striking? "In your *faithfulness* you have afflicted me." God is a loving Father who is for us even when he allows suffering to enter our lives as a corrective.

But often suffering is simply a call to be Jesus' helper in the work of salvation. Pope John Paul II said that suffering is in the world in order to release love. Our suffering releases the love of others, and theirs releases ours. I began this homily by describing how people forget themselves in heroic ways when others are in great need. The sufferer helps the crucified Christ to release love into the world. We try to grow in love to the point where even little sufferings of others release our love.

When someone's mortal life is in danger most of us are readily mobilized, but do we respond when eternal life is in danger? Aren't many asleep then? Doesn't that explain the shortage of priests and brothers and sisters? Yet who would deny that immortal life is far more important? Here, Jesus set the example. As we rush around to save someone's life, he was, as it were, rushing around to save our eternal lives. We can give no greater aid than helping others to discover eternal life in Christ.

When suffering and death afflict us, what should we do? We should pray and think about these mysteries. Today's readings show us the troubles into which God allows us to fall. They also make known the power and compassion with which he comes to our rescue. And they show how he moves human hearts to rush to our rescue, above all the human Heart of the divine Christ.

Someone might secretly think, "Christ raised the dead of others, but not my dead." How forgetful he would be! We who were baptized into Christ were baptized into his resurrection. In the Eucharist, Christ implants himself, the root of immortality. Death has lost its old meaning. Death is dying. Suffering too is dying. We do our best to help suffering die by our works of love; but we also remember that Christ has won an end to suffering by his work of redemption. In God's eternal home there is no suffering. When we receive Christ in the Eucharist today, can we do better than to thank him for destroying death? Can we refuse to promise to help him destroy suffering as well? The more we help, the more it dawns on us that God doesn't want the suffering that is in the world. We are the army sent to clear it away.

"C" — Eleventh Sunday of the Year

2 S 12:7-10, 13
Gal 2:16, 19-21
Lk 7:36 - 8:3

FORGIVERS AND REPENTERS

"Dad, why are we alive?" an eleven-year-old son asked his father. "What do the nuns say?" his father shot back. "To know, love and serve God," the boy said. "What's the matter," the father said. "Looking for a better answer?"

Fathers' Day sometimes falls on this Sunday. It's a happy conjunction, because today's Scripture readings illustrate the qualities we all hope to find in our father. How can any of us have any peace if our fathers do not have a healing presence and a forgiving heart?

In the readings we have three people restored to peace by the healing presence and forgiving heart of God and his Son. They were rescued from their blunder of trying to find the answer to life's meaning not in God but in sin.

The first reading recounts God's forgiveness of David. God the Father had loved David the shepherd and made him king. He entrusted to David the guidance of his people. David failed God by committing adultery with Bathsheba and trying to cover up his sin by having her soldier husband put in the front lines where he was killed.

God sent his prophet Nathan to confront David with his sins. David confessed and was forgiven. He was also told that the bad example he set would plague him the rest of his life. And in fact David's own son rebelled against him, as David had rebelled against his heavenly Father.

The harm that continues even after sin is forgiven points out to us that it is not enough for a father to be forgiving; he must also try to prevent our sins by training us in discipline. He has to teach us faithfulness, duty, responsibility, loyalty, love. Someone has to be strong enough and loving enough to discipline us patiently, with kindness, devotion, and untiring energy. That role normally falls to the father. Without it, family life would be a shambles. But it must all be done with endless patience. If you fathers would only think about how long it took you to grow up, you might develop the patience you need.

Jesus told us the beautiful parable of the loving father who forgave his prodigal son. While the story is first of all about God the Father, it is surely addressed to all fathers, and to all children. In today's Gospel we see Jesus himself living out the parable. He is the good Father forgiving his prodigal daughter. If Jesus had not projected a healing, forgiving presence, the sinful woman would never have found the courage to come and weep out her broken heart at his feet.

All fathers and mothers need a role model for their demanding task. God the Father and Mother of us all is that model. When you as parents feel despairing about the way your children are behaving, go to God. He will sympathize with you; he has the same experience. We are told in the Book of Genesis that "When the Lord saw how great was man's wickedness on earth . . . he regretted that he had made man on the earth, and his heart was grieved.'' Is it any wonder that the story of God and his people has been called a story of tormented love? The story of many parents and their children is little different. But true love goes on, for it is stronger than trouble.

To complete the picture, we have to look at the role of children as well. That includes us all, for even parents have parents. Our parents can't do their part if we don't do ours. If we want our parents to be forgivers, we must first be repenters. If we want God our Father to forgive us, we must confess our sins.

The readings today give us three roads to repentance. The first is to hear the prophetic word of God calling us to repentance, as David heard Nathan. In hearing God's word today, we are hearing that call. The second road is by the call of our conscience, as the psalmist reports it in today's psalm. There, God speaks directly to our hearts. The third road to repentance lies in looking on Jesus and finding how far we have fallen. The sinful woman who took this road is traditionally identified as St. Mary Magdalene.

She is truly a saint for our times, times in which so many commit the sin of denying sin. What a breath of fresh air she is with no denials, no excuses, only the tears of a broken heart. Jesus doesn't condone her sins; he only explains that she is readily forgiven because she loves greatly and comes with faith.

What was her conversion experience? We can't really say, but we can project what happens in many conversions. First, there is a sense of helplessness, of fouling up the self and the nest; it includes a sense of disintegration, of feeling the life force being spent uselessly; and a sense of alienation, of friendships corrupting, and all that is good receding. In brief, there is a sense of helplessness and hopelessness.

Then the heaven-sent Forgiver appears on the horizon. For Mary Magdalene it was Jesus. She discovered his Heart, wounded by her sins, bleeding out his love for her. If only she had the courage to go to him, she could heal his Heart, and hers would be healed too. In her longing she found that courage, and her tears flowed, and she was forgiven and healed.

She is a Saint for our times because she knew serious sin, as so many do today, and faced up to it. She met her Savior, repented, and became a Saint. What she did, we can do. As children of God our Father, we all feel the call.

If we expect love and forgiveness of God and our human parents, we should expect sorrow and repentance of ourselves. This conversion from our wrong ways is helped by the feeling of thankfulness we should have toward our parents. Whatever their failings, they have given us life, the unpayable gift. The word *thank* comes from the word, *think*. If we think and are mindful of what God our Father and our-human parents have done for us, thankfulness comes, and regret for our ingratitude comes, and that is the road to repentance.

Repentance and forgiveness are in the air in this liturgy. May Mary, our sinless Mother, take us by the hand and lead us along the road of repentance in Christ Jesus our Lord.

"C" — Twelfth Sunday of the Year

Zc 12:10-11
Gal 3:26-29
Lk 9:18-24

DISCOVERING DISCIPLESHIP

In far-off India they tell a great and fabled love story. A nobleman and a beautiful woman fell deeply in love and married. All too soon, death was at her door. She asked her lover to build a memorial to their love. He gathered 20,000 artisans and workers from all over India. And now over three centuries later people from round the world go to gaze at the beautiful Taj Mahal.

Today we hear Christ the divine lover foretell his death and resurrection. We hear him calling us to keep his memory alive until he returns by building his memorial. The living memorial he wants is our discipleship, making up his body the Church.

What we are as disciples overrides all else we are, whether man or woman, rich or poor, as St. Paul makes clear. How can we ever give enough attention to the task? We are invited to reflect on our discipleship along three lines. First, we need to discover that Christ is our Savior. Second, each of us needs to learn of the personal love for him or her burning in Christ's heart. Finally, we have to understand what it means to be his disciple.

First, we need to learn that Christ is our Savior. The disciples were with him for many months before Jesus put the question to them: "Who do you say that I am?" It was Peter who was able to respond, "You are the Messiah, the Savior." But they still didn't really know what it meant. Judas never learned. If he had, would he have crucified the Lord of glory?

Some Christians don't seem to understand the meaning of the word, "Savior." Young people have been heard to ask, "What do I need a Savior for?" Why must they ask? Can't they see the world is full of sin? Can't they see they are sinners with us all? That they desire to be good and do good, and often fail? That they cannot wash away their own sins? That sin can be washed away only by the blood of the Savior hanging on the cross as priest and victim for the world's salvation? That this is true because only God can forgive what offends him, and only the God-man can offer the needed atonement? That denial of God's existence does no good, because even those who deny him are fated to stand before him and be judged? That a just Creator must also be a just Judge who will one day call us all to judgment? That heaven and hell are necessary? But that the just Judge is also the merciful Lord who has offered us a Savior? Those who turn to him in faith, renounce their sins and ask forgiveness won't be judged. They've already been judged, judged worthy of Christ their Savior.

If that's not enough, who doesn't know he will soon die, though he wants life? Who can give or even promises to give him that life except the Savior who said, "I am the resurrection and the life," and proved it by rising from the dead?

How do we learn these things not only with the head but with the heart? We learn the same way the disciples did: by keeping Christ company. By pondering the Scriptures we walk with him; by praying we become his companions. By listening to the Church we hear his teaching. By living in his likeness we discover him in discovering ourselves. If you have any doubts about your behavior just ask yourself, "Would Jesus do it?" He is model and pattern for us all because he is the Savior of the world.

Secondly, we need to learn of the personal love for each of us burning in Christ's Heart. How? Jesus tells us how. As soon as Peter confessed him Savior, he spoke of his suffering and death for us. Since I took that seriously, I know how much he loves me. He didn't just die for a crowd out there! He died for me. And for you. Until you know that, you don't know his love for you.

Some have lived in the Church for decades and then walked out, complaining they never knew Jesus personally. How does that happen? Isn't the Church constantly teaching us, urging us to develop a personal relationship with Jesus? Doesn't the Church give him to us personally, body and blood, in the Eucharist?

To know Jesus' love for me, I must meditate on his suffering for me. So must you. Aren't we here offering the very sacrifice in which he died on Calvary? But all of this is external to us unless we pray personally, and spend time with Jesus as truly as the Apostles walked with him on those roads of Galilee.

The great theologian, St. Thomas Aquinas, wrote a theology book big as a telephone book. Where did he learn so much about Jesus? He tells us. His source was the crucifix. On his knees he studied it. If we don't know Jesus' personal love for us, we're most likely neglecting prayer on his passion, we're neglecting the sorrowful mysteries of the rosary, and the way of the cross. Meditation on the passion is the way of the saints. Go into your room, look at a crucifix, and say to Jesus, "You have loved me and delivered yourself for me." Once you know that, you know his love for you. You know him as the Savior of the pierced Heart.

Finally, we have to learn what it means to be his disciple. He himself told us in solemn words. "Whoever wishes to be my disciple must deny his very self, take up his cross each day, and follow in my steps." What does that mean? It doesn't mean to nail two pieces of wood together. He didn't. It means to bear the cross of the burden of living life faithfully as he did.

To carry the cross is to refuse to commit sin. We sin either to avoid the suffering of doing our duty, or to steal a pleasure that doesn't belong in our lives. God gives us many pleasures, but others he refuses us at least for a time. If we steal them by sin, we betray Christ and refuse to share the cross with him. To be a faithful husband or wife, parent or child, wage earner or worker at home, requires carrying the cross. We have responsibilities towards one another, toward our work, toward the law of God. To break that law is to refuse to carry the cross of Christ, to refuse to love, to sin by lack of love.

To carry the cross is to love on when those who should love us don't; it is to turn the other cheek and continue to be faithful ourselves; it is to say *I am faithful for love, not just because someone is faithful to me. If they are unfaithful, I will continue to be faithful, like Christ.*

In one church, Christ is pictured rising from the dead right from the cross. He has taken his turn on the cross; now its our turn. Looking around, we can see some of our fellow parishioners hanging uncomplaining on the cross. Can we also see ourselves? If so, let's be glad. It means we've learned to be disciples, and can be sure we're on our way to the resurrection with the Lord.

THE WAY OF DISCIPLESHIP

"Let the dead bury their dead; come away and proclaim the kingdom of God." My theme today is these tough words of Jesus. Who is the person whom they address? The person is you. The person is me. Jesus is naming demands only he can make.

I propose we reflect on the pain Jesus must have felt at the action of James and John in today's Gospel; on what Jesus is requiring of all of us, his disciples; and on the practical effects in our lives.

First, consider the pain Jesus felt at the reaction of James and John to the hostile Samaritans. Jesus had been teaching his disciples for years what they must do: love your enemies; turn the other cheek; forgive as you want to be forgiven.

Now, here is Jesus with them on the way to Jerusalem to live out his own doctrine and accept rejection, crucifixion and death. Rather than use violence he would die. They arrive in Samaria. The Samaritans were schismatics and heretics. When they heard that Jesus was to go on to Jerusalem, they rejected him. That's when James and John proposed calling fire from heaven to destroy them.

Jesus blamed and berated them. Had they understood nothing? What a moment of pain for him! To bring it home, imagine teaching your child for years how bad drug addiction is. Then you're shocked to learn he's begun using drugs. Worse yet, what if he thinks he's pleasing you? James and John thought they were pleasing Jesus. They were blind to their blindness.

But we don't recall Jesus' painful experience just to sympathize with him. We recall it to ask, "Do our attitudes and values bitterly disappoint our loving Lord too? Do we have hang-ups toward races, attitudes toward groups, and hostility toward persons that are no different from that of James and John?

This brings us to consider what Jesus is requiring of us all. Whatever it is, can we think it too much? He is our Lord and Friend, Savior and Redeemer. He is more forgiving than he asks us to be; more human, humble, lowly than we; yet also our Creator and God. He is our way, truth and life. If we don't follow him, we can't reach our destiny. If we don't accept his truth we live a lie. If we don't live by his life, we can't live eternal life.

One man whom Jesus called wanted to return and bid his people good-bye. That's what Elisha asked of Elijah. The answer of Jesus was *No*. He is making us realize that God and his work for the kingdom must come first. Putting anything before God is idol worship. I say anything: wife, husband, parents, children, property. We need to give up even our lives rather than give up God by sin.

Perhaps the hardest thing to give up is enemies. Do you recall the story of the woman who heard that President Lincoln had freed a rebel soldier to work on his poor mother's farm? A northern woman who heard of it rushed up to Lincoln and cried, "Mr. President, you don't free your enemy, you destroy him!" "Madam," he replied, "if I make my enemy my friend, don't I destroy my enemy?" Isn't that precisely what Jesus Christ was about? Others may treat us as enemies, but to us they are sisters and brothers in our heavenly Father.

What then are the practical effects of his demands? Perhaps the first thing to treat is what weapons we have against those who consider us their enemies. And some do. If we stand up for moral principles in our society, we're treated as enemies. If we say abortion must stop, we're considered enemies. What weapons do we have then? Our chief weapons are truth, witness and martyrdom. These are the three weapons Jesus used. He spoke the truth; he gave witness to it by living it; and affairs came to such a pass that he went to Jerusalem to die as a martyr to God's own truth.

Perhaps one of the hardest issues to deal with is war. Let me begin with two Christian principles: We fight against evil; we love evildoers. What weapons can we use to fight them if we love them? In their 1983 *Pastoral Letter on War and Peace*, the bishops agreed that a just war can be fought. But then the question: Can the weapons of war become so evil that to use them is to war against Christ? The answer is that nuclear weapons are so destructive that in their opinion a nuclear war cannot be justified. Generals in the American army themselves said that if a nuclear war started it couldn't be controlled because the nuclear explosions would so derange the capacity to send messages that there would be no way to stop the war. So even in conflicts between nations we could come to a time when the only recourse Christians would have is to fight evil as Jesus did, by dying to give witness to the truth of brotherly love. That's what martyrdom is; it's dying at the enemy's hands, in witness to Christ, without raising a hand in violence. That's what we honor when we honor a Christian martyr, or Jesus himself. In Gethsemane when Peter wanted to use a sword, Jesus forbade it, saying he could have legions of angels if he wanted to use force.

I know it's hard, but here is the truth. We have to fight the evil evildoers do; we have to love the evildoers. That is what Jesus did; he died for us when we were sinners. It's what his heavenly Father does; he sends down sun and rain on the farms of the just and the unjust. If we allow evildoers to make us hate, than hatred triumphs over love. But if like Jesus we love to the end, love triumphs over hatred.

This kind of love has everyday applications in our family life and friendships. We should love and forgive the worst of enemies; then how much more should we love and forgive spouses and brothers and sisters and friends! St. Paul says, "If you go on biting and tearing one another to pieces, take care! You will end up in mutual destruction!" How often that happens even between Christian husband and wife. They begin with love and marriage, and end in hatred and divorce courts. If spouses listened to Christ and loved their enemies, how different divorce statistics would be! Surely in most cases they could forgive the faults of their loved mates before they let the wounds fester and become death-dealing to their marriage.

We Christians are to forgive brothers and sisters, parents and children, friends and enemies. Can you imagine Jesus or Mary or Joseph doing otherwise? How else can we go to Jesus in the Eucharist and whisper our love? How else can we be the children and friends of God? How else deserve that noble name, Christian? I resolve to go the way of discipleship. Do you?

"C" — Fourteenth Sunday of the Year
Is 66:10-14
Gal 6:14-18
Lk 10:1-12, 17-20

ATTAINABLE HAPPINESS

Can you imagine the happiness of Christopher Columbus as he went about telling friends, acquaintances, and strangers about the New World he had discovered? Can you picture the joy of our founding fathers as they began to realize their dream of establishing the land of the free?

And yet, what was the joy of Columbus and our founding fathers compared with that of the disciples of Christ? They communicated to the world the Good News of the land of eternal freedom and the kingdom of eternal life.

Their joy is meant to be ours. It is attainable happiness. We prayed in the Opening Prayer to be stirred by the fact that the Son of God has raised a fallen world. Free us from our sins, we begged, and bring us the joy that lasts forever, a joy that has begun. We have inherited the joy of being co-workers with Christ, the joy of boasting in the cross of Christ, and the joy of the assurance of eternal life.

First, we've inherited the joy of being co-workers with Christ. We, the Church of today, have inherited the role of the Apostles and the disciples. We take their place laboring at the side of Christ who said, "I will be with you all days."

In one parish a priest asked a layman on the pastoral team how it was going. The man replied, "Magnificent! Inspiring. I can't describe it!" He was experiencing the joy of the returning seventy-two. He was sharing with them the noblest enterprise this world has ever seen, the work of resurrection and eternal life. He was responding to the call of the Son of God.

Do you think we can fail to find joy in that privileged call if we truly respond to it and experience it as that layman did? We promote faith and justice. We help to raise this fallen world by the grace of Christ. We inspire people to follow Christ to the land of eternal life. We lead them to the Church, of which the Jerusalem in the first reading is a figure, as the Church is a figure of heaven, the eternal Jerusalem. In the Jerusalem of the Church, we are nourished with the sacraments. We grow strong in the grace of Christ. Sin, evil, sickness and injustice are on the way out.

"The things I have done you will do," Jesus promised. We truly are doing his work. That is, we are if we are united with him by grace. "Without me you can do nothing," Jesus said.

The second joy we inherit is the joy of boasting in the cross of Christ. So far, I've described the high side of Christian life. There are also the failures and sufferings. Even the Apostles ran away when things seemed to be falling apart. Yet suffering too can be turned into a boast. You heard Paul's boast. He wanted no other boast but that of the cross of Christ. We know of his burdens, sufferings, stonings and shipwrecks. He endured them all for the love of Christ and the salvation of souls. We too rejoice in the cross because it is the sign of God's great love for us, and of ours for him and one another.

Columbus was proud of the ordeal of his voyage of discovery; our founding fathers were proud of their labors and sufferings to give birth to this great nation. Can we take less pride in the work of restoring a fallen world, and leading the way to life everlasting? Can we even imagine the joy we'll have in heaven when the spiritual battles are over, and we recall the victories we won at the side of Christ? Even if we had the choice, would we want to go up to our heavenly homeland without a story to tell of the wounds we bore and the hardships we endured with Christ?

Certainly we have no love for unnecessary suffering. If we didn't care for our health, how could we do our work? We want no useless hardships. That's not what the cross means. The night before our Lord died, he asked his Father to take away the coming suffering if it wasn't necessary. But it was. We cannot receive the crown of everlasting life without the cross. St. Paul says from experience that all who desire to live a godly life in Christ Jesus will suffer persecution.

What is sin but a running from danger, or a theft of pleasure when we should be busy doing our duty? What good is a soldier who runs from every hardship and flees every danger? The cross is the symbol that the spiritual soldiers of Christ don't run any more than Christ ran. That's what Paul was bragging about. He bragged that God loved him so much he sent his Son to die for us. And he bragged that he loved God and his people so much he was willing to die in turn. Paul would be ashamed to claim Christ's redemptive death for his salvation without helping to shoulder the burden. We should be too.

If we have sinned, we can atone by carrying our cross. Think of the good thief. From the moment he believed, his suffering became part of the redemptive work of Christ. He's the only believer who hung on the cross on Calvary with Christ. Can you imagine how he's bragging about that in heaven? Who wouldn't?

Finally, we're called to rejoice in the assurance of eternal life with God. Did you notice how Jesus pointed this out? He's saying as we do in sports, "Keep your eye on the ball." We're often warned not to get so attached to material things that we neglect spiritual things. Jesus goes much further. He cautions us not to get so involved even in our success with good works that we forget their purpose. Their purpose is eternal life with God for us and for all. Without that, what does anything come to in the end? Jesus, Mary and Joseph are waiting for us at the side of the Father and the Holy Spirit and all the saints. That is our goal in everything. Let's keep it always in mind.

Perhaps the one thing on earth to which we can't become too attached is the Eucharist. It is common to heaven and earth. At times when we receive the Eucharist, we have a foretaste of heaven. We commune with the Heart of our Redeemer pouring out his love for us. If we don't we should examine ourselves. Are we doing our work with Christ? Are we embracing necessary crosses with Christ? Are we thinking with anticipation of the joys awaiting us as Jesus urged us? We're called today to focus on these joys and make them more a part of our lives than ever.

"C" — Fifteenth Sunday of the Year

Dt 30:10-14
Col 1:15-20
Lk 10:25-37

UNRECOGNIZED CALLS TO OUR CALLING

A laborer applying for a dangerous job was filling in a questionnaire that asked who should be informed in case he suffered an accident. He wrote, "Anyone in sight!" Isn't that how we all feel? Isn't it the point of the Good Samaritan parable?

Modern travellers can still walk the ancient road from Jerusalem to Jericho. It remains as wild and forsaken as the landscape of the moon. Life too is like that unless we are neighbors to one another.

The readings prompt three reflections. First, love is our calling. Second, We are all called to be Good Samaritans. Third, we are all wounded healers.

First, love is our calling. We have the call from nature itself. There is a limited form of love even in the animal kingdom. Who has not seen the care an animal lavishes on its offspring? Who has not heard of a dog leaping into fire or water to save its master?

We also have the call to love from God. In the first reading Moses says the law of God is written in our hearts. But because God knows the deceits we use to evade the call of love, he spelled it out with the ten commandments and other laws.

The lawyer who spoke to Jesus knew God's command to love God and neighbor but he wanted an escape clause so he asked, "Who is my neighbor?" Jesus made it clear that every one is our neighbor so we would no longer wrangle over that question.

We all want to love, but not all will pay the cost of loving. We surely all want love. Love's greatness is beyond our imagining. We won't see love in all its sublimity until we see God who is love. But if we grow in love we want it more and more.

Second, we are all called to be Good Samaritans. We are on the road to Jericho daily. What day passes that we don't meet one who needs a word of comfort, a helping hand, a word of caring? When we come on our wounded fellow travelers our love is tested. Love and suffering recognize one another as brother and sister. What is love for but to bring aid and comfort and joy? Love is for use.

The suffering of others does us a service. There is love in us, but it is often chained up by selfishness. When we see another so needy that our hearts go out to him, our love stirs like a sleeping giant and breaks its bonds and goes into action. That is why Pope John Paul II says that suffering is in the world in order to release love. Suffering and need are opportunities to become the lovers God calls us to be.

The compassion and mercy the Good Samaritan showed are the noblest forms of love. What is compassion? If I see you hurting and I hurt too, that is compassion. And what is mercy? If I act as best I can to remove your hurt, that is mercy.

Thirdly, we are all wounded healers. We know our own sins and feel our own inadequacies, and that inclines us to think that we can't be of much help to others. The truth is the very opposite. It seems to be a mystery of life that the wounded are the best healers. Jesus himself is the wounded healer.

Think of how Jesus' very wounds draw us to him for healing. Who that is suffering can't go to Jesus and say, "Lord, you understand"? Who that is tempted can't go to Jesus tempted and say, "You know how hard it is to resist"? What sinner cannot go to Jesus and say, "Because you became a human being, you know how weak we are, and how easily we fall; forgive me"?

We, too, become healers by the very fact that we have been wounded. Who better understand wounds than the wounded? Who understands need better than one who has felt it? Because we have been tempted and sinned we are patient with those tempted and sinning. If we have suffered, sufferers see in our faces that we understand, and that is help already.

We will love all our neighbors if we love God with a passion. For we must love God with a passion. How else can we love him with our whole heart and soul and strength and mind? Love like that is a burning fire. Anyone who is satisfied with the way he is serving God and neighbor doesn't have that burning fire. For that fire of love is like a forest fire which, having consumed all it has reached, thirsts for more. This consuming fire is a share in God, for God is love. God is a consuming fire, but so is love for God a consuming fire.

When we become wounded healers we begin to find God as never before. This is brought out in James Russell Lowell's beautiful story, *The Vision of Sir Launfal.* Sir Launfal is a proud young knight who sets out to find the drinking cup Christ used at the Last

Supper. As he leaves the city, he tosses a coin to a leper at the gate. Years of trial and suffering follow. At last he turns homeward an old man. He has failed to find the Holy Grail, but he has found more than he realizes. When he returns to his city, the leper is still there. The knight's heart is full of pity, but he has no money. He dismounts, sits with the leper, and shares his last crust of dry bread. They were thirsty and had nothing to drink. The knight borrows the leper's bowl and goes for water. Wanting to honor the leper, he presents him the cup first. Before his eyes the leper becomes the Christ, and the drinking cup the one for which he had searched in vain.

Like this knight, we are the good Samaritans. Who is the one we help but Christ? Has he not said, "Whatever you did for one of these least brothers of mine you did for me"?

I will close with a modern parable. A woman is on the way to have an abortion. God's grace calls to her heart and the hearts of all involved as a voice for the unborn one. To quiet her conscience, the mother says, "My body is my own." To quiet his, the father says, "It's not my fault that she wasn't careful." The doctor says, "I'm not doing anything illegal." The priest of the parish says, "I'm too busy with the spiritual cares of my people to get involved in the abortion issue." The politician says, "I have to yield to the greatest pressure group to get reelected." The voters say, "Let the politicians fight it out." But one voter writes to his senator, "As long as you are pro-abortion I'll never vote for you again." He sends a check to Birthright and asks, "Would you recommend a right-to-life organization I can join?" Who would you say is neighbor to the unborn child?

THE HEART OF JESUS
AND THE APOSTLESHIP OF PRAYER

A wife and mother we'll call Joan loved to play tennis, and did it frequently. No one criticized her; it was understandable. But when Joan's values changed, and she began to attend Mass daily, the criticism began: "Aren't you neglecting your family?"

If you like fun and games, criticism is unlikely; if you want to show special attention to the Lord, expect criticism. Martha criticized Mary, and even criticized the Lord for not correcting her. But Jesus corrected Martha, not Mary. "One thing only is required," he responded. Jesus' human heart hungered for love, not a seven-course dinner. If we're not fed with love, none of us is happy. He came with love and the Good News of salvation, and Martha bustled off to the kitchen. Jesus didn't say Martha had neglected him, but he did say Mary had given him the better gift.

God calls us to love him and serve him, but love takes first place. Our love for God needs to be expressed in prayer. Prayer is hospitality toward God. We listen to him and speak to him. Jesus told us to pray always; he never told us to work always.

Our lives are empty and dreary and even suicidal without love. We find life's meaning by finding the heart of God and doing the works of love. Jesus called us to both: "Come to me, all you who labor and are burdened," he said, "and I will give you rest. Take my yoke upon you and learn from me, for I am meek and humble of heart, and you will find rest for yourselves. For my yoke is easy and my burden light." We can picture Jesus the Carpenter fashioning yokes and seeing the draft animals wearing them to pull the plough or the wagon together. Using that image, he is calling us to come to him, love him, and share his yoke to pull with him the load of the work of salvation.

Today I'll describe The Apostleship of Prayer, which teaches us to draw near the heart of Jesus and combine Mary and Martha in ourselves, so that we love and serve in a balanced way.

Jesus called us to his heart by more than words. On the cross he allowed his side to be opened, and blood and water came forth from his heart. It's as though he said, "There, the way to my heart is open now. Enter through prayer and sacrament, and experience for yourself the love for you of which I spoke."

The Fathers of the Church saw in the flowing water and blood the sacraments of baptism and the Eucharist. They saw the new Eve, the Church, being born from the side of the last Adam, the God-man. Despite this, devotion to the heart of our Redeemer grew at a snail's pace. So, about 300 years ago Jesus, like an impatient lover, appeared to St. Margaret Mary and told her to get busy spreading the devotion. She was so fired up she said that if Christians knew how much this devotion pleased Christ, not one would fail to respond to him.

Zealous priests founded the Apostleship of Prayer to spread the devotion around the world. Pope John Paul II called the Apostleship of Prayer "a precious treasure from the Pope's heart and the Heart of Christ."

What is the Apostleship of Prayer? It's also called the League of the Sacred Heart. It's a union of tens of millions of Catholics from little kids to the Holy Father who band together to say and try to live the Daily Offering. Recite the prayer with me now (prayer cards should be in the pews): "O Jesus, through the Immaculate Heart of Mary, I offer you my prayers, works, joys and sufferings of this day in union with the Holy Sacrifice of the Mass throughout the world. I offer them for all the intentions of your Sacred Heart: the salvation of souls, reparation for sin, the reunion of all Christians. I offer them for the intentions of our Bishops and of all our members, and in particular for those recommended by our Holy Father."

By that prayer we give Jesus our loving attention as we begin each day. We offer him all we do that day, as members of his apostolic team. We find love and find life's meaning by serving the Sacred Heart of our Savior. We put to use our baptismal share in his kingship, priesthood and prophetic mission.

First, we share his kingship. Christ became man to restore all creation to the Father. We help him. Parents complete creation and redemption by rearing their children as good citizens of heaven and earth. And all of us, in whatever way we make a living or help to support human life, offer what we do with Christ the carpenter to bring the kingdom of God. We struggle to rule over sin and rule it out of our lives. That is truly a kingly rule.

We put to use our share in his royal priesthood. Christ was priest not just on Calvary. He consecrated his work, rest and recreation to the Father for the world's redemption. We do the same. We put every thought, word and deed on the paten with Christ to be offered to the Father in Masses around the world.

We offer it all in the spirit of atonement and reparation as Jesus offered it. What is reparation? It's a profound word, but basically it means *to repair*. Sin broke God's world. We repair it with Jesus. Pope John Paul II explained that "the true meaning of reparation demanded by the Heart of the Savior" is to learn from the Heart of Christ "the true and only meaning of life," and on the ruins of hatred and violence to build the "civilization of love, the kingdom of the Heart of Christ." In all of this, we are also sharing the prophetic ministry of Christ, for his prophetic actions spoke louder than words, and so will ours.

To sum up: The heart of our religion is the Incarnation: God became man. The heart of the Incarnation is the Heart of Jesus. There we the Church have our life and our home. We offer all to Jesus through the Immaculate Heart of Mary, his loving Mother and ours; we love the Church as his creation and her teachings as his own, so we pray specially for the intention of his Vicar on earth, the Holy Father, who knows the Church's needs.

I now invite you to join the Apostleship of Prayer. There are no dues, signatures, meetings, or obligations under sin. If you're willing to say the Daily Offering and try to live it, and recite at least a decade of the rosary in honor of Our Lady, you may join. Just stand now and repeat after me the following words of consecration: "Lord Jesus Christ — I wish to become a member — of the Apostleship of Prayer — I promise to make, and with your help to live — the Daily Offering." I now admit you as perpetual members of the Apostleship of Prayer, the League of the Sacred Heart.

"C" — Seventeenth Sunday of the Year

Gn 18:20-32
Col 2:12-14
Lk 11:1-13

FRIENDS IN HIGH PLACES

Back in February, 1976, severe draught plagued the San Francisco farm area. The bishop ordered a prayer for rain beginning at the Sunday Masses. Reporters called the bishop's office to ask if he were serious about expecting rain through prayer. A spokesman said yes, and added that the prayers would be answered. Late Tuesday the National Weather Service predicted "possible light showers" within a few days. Late Wednesday night a tremendous downpour came, and more rain the next day. Reporters returned for more information, and one said, "The archbishop must have some powerful friends up there."

"Ask and you shall receive." We all have friends in high places, the highest places of all. Abraham knew that. We heard his classic prayer of petition in the first reading. He prayed that the sinful people of Sodom be spared. His prayer is an example of charity. His prayer is persistent and daring. He's afraid of angering God with his bargaining, but bargain he did.

But let us dare to push on further. What if Abraham had been still bolder, and gone on to ask that Sodom be spared if two just people could be found there? Might not Sodom have escaped the fire from heaven, and be standing to this day? We don't know the answer to that question, but we do know the whole world has been offered salvation through the life of one just man, Jesus Christ.

"Ask and you shall receive," Jesus promises. This is a stunning revelation. Holy men and women of old would have heard it with cries of praise and tears of joy. The wonder is that the promise is addressed not just to holy people, but to all. It's a new truth based on what Jesus did for us. He paid the charge against us by nailing it to the cross, as St. Paul says in that second reading. By baptism he gave us a new birth and a new identity. Now we pray not as mere creatures, but as children of God. Parents listen when their children ask. God is the best of parents. God loves us so much he wants our good more than we do. He gives not because we are good but because we are his children.

Now we take up the most difficult question about the prayer of petition. "Ask and you shall receive," Jesus said. But we've asked and not received, haven't we? So we don't believe him, do we? But doubting the word of God is folly. What we should do is try to understand his word better so we will believe.

What limits of common sense should we put on his promise? They tell the story of the little girl who asked for a bike and didn't get it. Her friends mocked her and told her God didn't answer her prayer. But she denied that. "He answered it," she retorted. "He said *No*." James and John would agree with her. When they asked Jesus for the highest places next to him, he said, "To sit at my right hand or left is not mine to give, but is for those for whom it has been prepared." So it would be mere foolishness, not prayer, if we all asked for the first place in heaven. But what about asking for forgiveness, something we all need? About that Jesus said, "If you do not forgive others, neither will your Father forgive your transgressions." Clearly, then, his promise must be understood reasonably, according to his other teachings. Let's look into them, for they will encourage rather than discourage our prayer of petition.

Jesus invokes our good sense to understand his promise. He says, ''What father among you will give his son a snake if he asks for a fish, or hand him a scorpion if he asks for an egg?'' If your children ask for something that's good for them, won't you give it if you can? But if your baby asks for a red hot poker, would you hand it to him? Of course not! That's the crucial issue here. We don't know what's good for us. Before asking anything we should pray over what we want to ask for. Then, if we think it is good for us, we pray the way Jesus did when he faced torture and death. Let me summarize his prayer: He said, *Father, you can do anything. Take this suffering away. Yet not what I want but what you want.* Isn't that the perfect prayer of petition? It trusts, it believes, it seeks guidance even in asking. The Father answered by sending an angel to strengthen him to go on.

If your little child cried for a red hot poker, you might distract him by giving him something better for him. That, I believe, is what the Father always does. He never refuses us. Rather, he gives us something else, something better. Prayer of petition is never a waste. St. James says, ''You do not possess because you do not ask.'' It's a tragedy we are not always asking God for things. Our loving Father wants to be asked. How much richer we'd all be in what counts if we asked for something every day. How much poorer the world is because we don't ask!

But on the other hand, James goes on, ''You ask but do not receive, because you ask wrongly, to spend it on your passions.'' He adds, ''Do you not know that to be a lover of the world means enmity with God?'' Should we ask for wealth when so many don't even have food and shelter? Should we ask for millions when Jesus warned us how hard it is for the wealthy to be saved?

Our Lord wants us to understand that if we forgive others, the Father will forgive us; if we do his will, he will do ours; if we try to do good, he will do good things for us. But above all, he wants us to ask for the better gifts. Jesus ends up saying, "If you, with all your sins, know how to give your children good things, how much more will the heavenly Father give the Holy Spirit to those who ask him." Here's the gift to ask for day after day: the Holy Spirit of love and holiness and goodness. The Opening Prayer puts it well: God our Father, "Guide us to everlasting life by helping us to use wisely the blessings you have given to the world."

Persistence in prayer is necessary too. We can understand this better if we ask a question: How does a wise father treat his children? Does he give them whatever they want whenever they want it? Or does he give and withhold in ways that will make them grow up and become more like him? Isn't it the greater gift when God helps us to be something rather than merely have something?

Our Blessed Mother at Cana only had to say to Jesus, "They have no wine," and wine flowed. When she sees us praying, may she always back up our prayer with her own. And may she who gave us her Son help us to see that he who is so eager to give his very self to us in the Eucharist will withhold nothing that is for our good if only we have the faith to ask.

"C" — The Transfiguration

Dn 7:9-10, 13-14
2 P 1:16-19
Lk 9:28-36

THE MYSTERY OF THE GOD-MAN

One priest counseling a person with many troubles listened carefully to her account. His best judgment was that she had to bear with her burdens to be faithful to her Christian calling. He suggested that she consider all the sufferings Jesus endured, and pray to him for the strength to carry her cross in his likeness. She retorted, ''O, but he was God!'' In that one sentence she expressed her erroneous belief that because Jesus was God he didn't have to struggle as human beings do.

Today's feast tells us how wrong she was. It reveals Jesus as the true Son of God who is also the true Son of Mary. As her Son he escapes nothing of what it means to be human. Today we enter deeply into the mystery of Jesus to know him better, love him more, and pattern ourselves more faithfully in his likeness.

His Mother Mary can help us begin our reflection. In Bethlehem there is a shrine called the Milk Grotto. There, according to one account, Mary stopped to nurse her Son on their flight into Egypt. If they had not rushed to safety, Jesus would have been killed by Herod's soldiers; if Mary had not nursed him, he would have died of starvation. He was subject to all the trials and tribulations that afflict the rest of us.

The fact that Jesus was human is confirmed by history and the thousands who knew him. We know the identity of his human mother. That is what distinguishes our Lord from the mythical incarnations of gods recorded in various cultures. It is a distortion of our faith, therefore, to let our belief in his divinity undermine our awareness of his humanity.

Jesus worked many miracles to relieve others of their human burdens, but try to find in the Gospels one miracle he worked to escape his own burdens. At his arrest in the garden, when Peter drew his sword, Jesus told him to sheathe it, and added, ''Do you think I cannot call upon my Father and he will not provide me at this moment with twelve legions of angels?'' But Jesus did not ask for the angels. He willed to live human life with all its burdens just as we must. If we don't understand that, we don't understand our religion, the religion in which God became a man to live life as it ought to be lived, and be our way.

Do you recall the legend of the centaur, a being that was man from the head down to the waist, with the body of a horse below? Such a creature would be neither man nor horse. Some people seem to imagine Christ along those lines, as if he were half man and half God, but really neither. That was the heresy of Arius, and it was condemned. The teaching of the Scriptures and the Church is that Christ is complete Man and complete God. He is everything God is and everything we are. He lives his divine life fully divinely, and his human life fully humanly. Not only is he as human as we, he is more human. Sin has dehumanized us. It hardens us until our hearts are not fully human. Christ's heart was the most human of all; his sufferings were more intense than ours, because he was more innocent and sensitive than little children, who are already marked with original sin.

Mary is called the Mother of God because the Son of God came down in his full divinity and joined to himself the full humanity which she bore in her womb. Christ's human and divine natures were not mixed together like batter in a cake. Just as our two arms are distinct and separate and can act separately, but belong to our one person, his divine and human natures act distinctly and separately, but belong to his one Person. This the Church teaches when it says that Christ has a divine intellect and a human intellect, a divine will and a human will. Christ's human will had to struggle like ours to do what pleased his divine will. His divine will was never tempted, but his human will was tempted like ours. His divine nature never suffered, but his human nature suffered more than we will ever suffer.

That is what today's feast is trying to tell us. Peter, James and John were there with Jesus. They knew he was a Man. But suddenly they saw him flare in glory, and they heard the Father say, "This is my Son, my Chosen One. Listen to him." The Father gives witness to Jesus as divine; he knew Jesus' disciples could and would give witness to him as human. The fact that his human body shone in glory did not make him less human. Moses and Elijah shone in glory when they appeared to him, and so will we at the resurrection.

But there is something else that happened on the mountain

which stresses his humanity. Moses and Elijah spoke to Jesus about his ''passage'' which he is about to fulfill in Jerusalem. In blunt language, that ''passage'' is his passing through death after betrayal, torture, and untold agony on the cross. Those are things only Jesus' humanity could suffer, not his divinity. Jesus' coming was foretold by Moses, and his sufferings by the prophets. Moses and Elijah are confirming that he is the one who is about to fulfill all they and the other prophets foretold.

What then should we take with us from these Scriptures? We should take them home and pray over them. There is a powerful way to pray that someone has compared to running your own movies, only better. Find a quiet place, and in your imagination replay the whole event. Go up the mountain with Jesus and his disciples, listen to the conversation, and watch what happens. The grace of God will be there helping you pray, giving you insights, making meaning known to you. Talk over with the Lord your love for him, and how you want what you have learned to affect your life. Ask him to help you know what Christianity is all about so you can live as a true Christian, another Christ.

This event also strengthens our faith by confirming it through the ancient prophecies, the testimony of the Apostles, and the Voice of the Father from heaven. In that second reading, Peter tells how his faith in Christ was confirmed by the transfiguration, the Voice, and the prophets, and how ours should be as well.

We must realize too that in this event Christ is calling us to the sinless life that is the road to glory with him. Finally, we should bear in mind that when Jesus comes to us in the Eucharist he comes in his glory as risen Lord, a glory which is veiled from our eyes so that we may approach him without fear as his disciples did. In that realization we will reverence, honor and love him as true God and true Man.

"C" — Eighteenth Sunday of the Year

Ec 1:2; 2:21-23
Col 3:1-5, 9-11
Lk 12:13-21

PRAYER: THE ROAD OUT OF MATERIALISM

Some years ago, on this eighteenth Sunday, a priest told this story in his homily: When he was hardly a teenager, his father went fishing one Sunday. He was having dinner with his mother when the phone rang. There had been a storm on the river. His father had drowned. The boy went to the parish church and prayed. It didn't change the fact that his father had drowned, but it did change him. The whole experience taught him what St. Teresa of Avila once said: All things pass; God only endures. "And so," he concluded, "I take to heart this parable which Jesus tells in today's Gospel; and so should we all. Otherwise we will not live by the logic of fact and the logic of God."

What is that logic of which he spoke except this: We're conceived, we're born, we live, we die, we stand before God, and he judges whether we are worthy of that eternal life which Christ has won for us. It is only in that perspective that we can live aright. Without it, troubles upset our whole lives, and wealth and other passing things command our whole attention.

Can anyone who makes wealth his life's aim listen to today's readings and not squirm in his seat? We heard of the folly of spending life to gather riches we can't take with us. We heard of the materialist whose heart was created for God, but who made money his god, and died godless. Almighty God calls him a fool.

Isn't the logic of these teachings so powerful that it must convert all present? The answer is no. Perhaps someone present didn't even hear the readings. If asked, "What did you think of that parable of Jesus?" he'd say, "I wasn't paying attention. My mind drifted off to that business deal I have to close."

Even when God's word convinces our minds, our hearts may remain unconverted, and we fail to change.

What, then, will help us? Prayer. Praying is what the inspired author of that first reading is doing. He is meditating on eternal values. To embrace them, we have to join in his meditation. We need to grind his words in the mills of our minds until our hearts taste and love the truths they contain.

God and the Church call us to two different kinds of prayer: the prayer of the community, and private prayer. We're here praying and worshipping together in community at Mass. But unless we brought with us hearts made prayerful by daily *private* prayer, we're only an assembly of distracted people, of pray-ers who can't pray. Public and private prayer support one another. We need both. Private prayer is like the roots of a tree, and public prayer its trunk and branches and leaves.

Let's look more closely at each. Both are communication with God. Both are a response to God, who first spoke to us by public revelation. Christian prayer goes to God through Christ, who is the fullness of revelation. To pray well we need to know Scriptures, doctrine, and Jesus Christ.

Public prayer is liturgical prayer, the prayer of the whole Church, the family of God in Christ. The sacred liturgy is the public worship which our Redeemer, Head of the Church, offers to the heavenly Father; it is also the worship which we his faithful people offer to him, and through him to the eternal Father. It is, in short, the public worship of the whole Mystical Body, Head and members. It is most pleasing to God because it is the prayer of the Church led by its Founder, Jesus Christ.

But liturgical worship is not enough. It is built of individual persons-of-prayer, just as a church is built of individual stones. If we don't bring prayerful hearts, how can we pray collectively? We know by experience that if we don't pray privately we can't pray well publicly. We find Mass a bore, find ourselves alone in a crowd, and even complain that "we don't get anything out of the

Mass.'' Honesty should make us take the blame, and provide the remedy. The Mass is Christ's gift of his sacrifice and himself. There is nothing wrong with it. The wrong lies in hearts closed to it by lack of private prayer.

Private prayer is necessary for our individual life with God. In today's second reading, St. Paul says we have died to a godless life. We're called to set our hearts on that higher realm where Jesus dwells, and where we'll dwell after the resurrection. We must put materialism and all sin to death by joining our minds and hearts to Christ. How? By doing the spiritual thinking about eternal things called meditation, and entering into the conversation and communion with God called prayer.

Jesus commanded both liturgical and private prayer. Of the Mass he said, ''Do this in memory of me.'' Of private prayer he said, ''Go into your room and shut the door and pray to your Father who is in secret. And your Father who sees in secret will reward you.''

Jesus longs for our companionship through the day, and we need his presence to be faithful, so he told us to pray always. ''Here I stand,'' he said, ''knocking at the door. If anyone hears me calling and opens the door, I will enter his house and have supper with him, and he with me.'' Do you see the intimacy he promises you in prayer? We need him within our hearts for strength in temptation, light in darkness, loving companionship in our loneliness, and guidance on our way home to the Father.

Open the door of your heart to Christ in daily prayer. Find new joy in life, and at Mass find new meaning in the readings, a new closeness to Jesus in the Eucharist, and a deeper fellowship with us all. That will benefit every one of us. We know we need one another in many things, but can overlook the fact that we need one another to pray as we ought. Surely you've seen some deeply prayerful person at Mass, and been helped to pray better yourself. Now become that person for others.

Surely I don't need to insist on how much we all need prayer.

As Paul makes clear in that second reading, we can't live by the logic of faith until we break free of the illogic of sin. By meditation and prayer we make the logic of faith our own North Star and compass as St. Paul made it his. If we walk with Christ in prayer, when sorrows come they're not too heavy because we are carrying the cross with him; when joys and triumphs come, they don't sweep us away from Christ because once we have really found him he is our greatest joy and we'll never let him go. Prayer frees us from the world's too-tight grip, and makes us one with the heart of Christ and each other.

"C" — Nineteenth Sunday of the Year

Ws 18:6-9
Heb 11:1-2, 8-19
Lk 12:32-48

FIXED AND FLEETING PRAYER

You may know the traditional act of contrition which begins, "O my God, I am heartily sorry for having offended thee." But many a priest has heard a child in confession render it, "O my God, I am *hardly* sorry." We smile at a child's error, but our eyes would go up if we heard an adult make the same mistake.

So too with other prayers, and prayer in general: Adult prayer should transcend the level of prayer we were capable of as children. In today's Gospel Jesus calls us to mature prayer, to prayer that stands always ready for his return. So today we'll reflect on how to pray maturely.

The first thing to be said is that mature prayer is not simply a matter of asking for things. Prayer of petition is important, but not in first place. In this matter we can learn from children. Their hearts turn easily to love, and in this they remind us that the heart of prayer is loving communion with God. We love him by spending time in his presence, whether in silence or in words of love, praise and thanksgiving.

Mature prayer has the following qualities: It is inspired by love, based on faith, and fed by the word of God. Without the reading and pondering of Scripture and spiritual books based on Scripture, it starves.

Good prayer convinces us that, as the second reading says of Abraham, we are sojourners in this world, pilgrims traveling home to God. Prayer is our food for the journey, and our preparation for going home. Prayer makes us recall daily that Christ may be waiting for us over the next hill. We want to be found ready, and so we look to our responsibilities in Christ. Are we using for his service all we have and are while time remains? Are we uniting our hearts with the will of God?

Prayer calls us to a daily accounting to the will of God. We call it the Examination of Conscience. Never go to bed without one. We begin by thanking God for the good things of the day. Next we ask that by his light we may see ourselves as he does. Then we reflect on our thoughts, words and deeds of the day. Was there sin? Was there service of God and neighbor? Did we let our hearts lead us in the Holy Spirit? When we've examined ourselves, we make the necessary resolution, and an Act of Contrition for our sins. It's sad when people come to the Sacrament of Reconciliation and don't even know an Act of Contrition, since we should say one every day. How else can we go to bed like people ready for their Master's return? Finally, we look briefly to tomorrow and tell our Lord we'll make it his day.

So prayer keeps us faithful to faith. It feeds us on the teaching of Christ until our minds, hearts, voices and lives accord with Christ and his Church. ''Prayer,'' one writer has said, ''is not so much a dialogue with God; it is a duet with him.'' Like a child singing the words he hears his mother sing, we sing in our hearts the words God gives us in the Scripture. We should memorize the passages that appeal most to us to help the duet.

How do we pray such prayer in the concrete? We do it through two basic forms of prayer: fixed prayer and fleeting prayer. Fixed prayer is the period we set aside each day, if possible at the same time, at an early hour, in a quiet place. Make it an hour, a half-hour, even ten minutes. Give it the priority you give to eating each day. It is feeding time for the soul.

During this time of fixed prayer, you recite prayers you know, or read from a book of prayers like the psalms, or you meditate. Meditation is prayerful thinking about divine truths, the way Our Blessed Mother use to ponder in her heart all that happened in her life with Jesus. It has four stages: reading, thinking, praying, and contemplating. Let me describe it.

You read a few words from a Gospel passage: "Do not live in fear, little flock. It has pleased the Father to give you the kingdom." These words are like bread from heaven. Or, put better, they are grains of the finest wheat for feeding the spirit. Now wheat is ground and baked in a fire before you taste its sweetness. Similarly, you have to grind the words of Scripture in the mill of your mind, and let the flour of your thoughts grow hot and savory in the fire of your heart. And suddenly you *realize* what Jesus is saying to you: "Get rid of those empty fears. The kingdom of love, life, resurrection, eternity with God, is really yours!" Then your heart sings, and the fire of your love for Christ pours out to him in words of endearment. Now you have passed beyond meditation to pure prayer. After your loving burst of words, you remain quiet in the presence of God-with-you. Now you are in the prayer of contemplation. You may not reach it often, but when you do it rewards all your efforts.

Distractions plague us in prayer, but they grow less as our hearts grow in love, so persevere. And examine your distractions. They may not be distractions at all, but matters you ought to take up in prayer. Prayer must be practical. You may see, for instance, that you're attached to too many things. You're living a rushed and hectic life you must simplify if you want God and prayer in your life.

During the day, your fixed prayer will be like a storeroom from which rays of fleeting prayer flash out at every spare moment. For fixed prayer helps you fix your heart on God, and a heart in love with God gravitates to God the moment it's free of necessary business. Fleeting prayer is often expressed in some short phrase like, "My Lord, my God, my all," or "Most Sacred Heart of Jesus I implore the grace to love you more and more."

Jesus urged us to pray always. The combination of fixed and fleeting prayer approaches the ideal closer than we realize. St. Augustine explains this in commenting on the phrase of Psalm 37, "In the anguish of my heart I groaned aloud." A person with his heart fixed on God has a hunger for God that makes him at one time groan aloud for longing, and at another laugh aloud with joy. Even when he's otherwise occupied, God sees that hunger as a perpetual prayer, for as St. Augustine says, "The desire of your heart is itself your prayer." We can learn to pray this way. Our hearts are made for it. And if we do, we'll fulfill Jesus' command, "Be like men awaiting their master's return."

"ABC" — The Assumption

Rv 11:19; 12:1-6, 10
1 Cor 15:20-26
Lk 1:39-56

WOMAN VICTORIOUS

Outside Jerusalem, across the Kidron Valley, at the foot of the Mount of Olives, in an ancient burial site, stands the massive Church of the Assumption. Housed within is the tomb presented as the traditional site of Mary's burial. If you look through the glass cover, you see that the tomb is empty. Mary was taken up body and soul into heaven. This is the festive event we celebrate today.

What is the meaning of Mary's Assumption in God's plan? What is its meaning for us?

First, what is the meaning of the Assumption of Mary in God's plan? It means that Mary has been fulfilled and rewarded. It is the day when she from whom the Messiah was born was herself born into eternal life by the power of his redemption.

But it is also meant as a feast of promise. The resurrection is spreading from the Lord to his people, with Mary first. At the Lord's return, we ourselves will rise. In the Opening Prayer we prayed, "All-powerful and ever-living God, you raised the sinless Virgin Mary . . . body and soul to the glory of heaven. May we see heaven as our final goal and come to share her glory."

That is our petition today, and it is made the firmer by the ancient faith of the Church that Mary's body never knew corruption. She was taken up bodily into heaven. Pope Pius XII confirmed that faith on November 1, 1950, in a solemn use of his infallible role as Christ's vicar. "We proclaim, declare, and define it to be a dogma revealed by God," he wrote, "that the immaculate Mother of God, Mary ever Virgin, when the course of her earthly life was finished, was taken up body and soul into the glory of heaven."

Today's readings give insight into the feast we celebrate. The first reading, from the Book of Revelation, is mysterious and full of symbolism. What is the ark of the covenant which John sees in the temple in heaven? The Old Testament ark was a casket about two by four feet which housed the stone tablets of the Ten Commandments. Symbolically, then, it contained the covenant between God and his people. What does John intend the ark to mean to Christians? To find out, we have to go on.

Next appears a great sign in the sky: a child-bearing woman clothed with the sun, crowned with twelve stars, standing on the moon. The moon has always had special meaning for woman, with her waxing and waning in cycle with the moon, as if woman's travail is written by God in the heavens for all to see. But the vision presents something unheard of. The moon is no longer standing over her; she is standing on the moon. Her time of trial is over.

What is the relation of the woman to the ark? The answer is that the woman *is* what the ark only prefigured. As the old ark contained the Old Law, the child-bearing woman contains the new Law, Christ himself. Like the moon lighted by the sun, the woman is clothed in the radiance of the child she gave birth to, the Son of God, the Messiah. The woman has put on the Christ she mothered! O woman, you have been saved by childbearing, as God foretold in the Book of Genesis! The very role which burdened and weakened you has become your strength and your salvation. Your power to give and nurture life has saved and glorified you and brought forth the world's salvation.

Who is this woman of glory, in the sky under the symbol of the ark, and in heaven with her Son in shining glory? First, she is the Jewish people, from whom the Christ rose up. For as Jesus said, "Salvation is from the Jews." But the woman is also their Jewish daughter, Mary, who brought him forth. And so the woman in the sky is the Blessed Virgin Mary, Mother of God.

But the symbolism goes on from the Jewish people to Mary to the Church. Mary is the Mother of the Church, which was founded by Christ on the Twelve Apostles, the twelve stars of the vision. The body of Christ continues to be born from the womb of the Church's baptismal font, and from the wombs of all the Christian mothers who bring their children to her.

The flaming dragon in the sky is the devil. He rages to devour the woman's offspring, but her divine Son is snatched up to God in the resurrection and Ascension. At the time of his vision, John also sees Mary the Ark in heaven, for by then she had probably been taken up in the Assumption.

As figure of the Church, the woman goes off into the desert of earth, living out her role as the Church suffering. That is you and I. We suffer, but in hope. Mary in heaven foretells the victory and the glory of the Church and the Jewish people.

What then is the significance of the Assumption for our own lives? It tells us that as a dying life came to us from the first Adam, the resurrection life is coming to us from the last Adam, the Christ. On his return we will all rise from the dead. If we have been faithful we will rise up like that woman in the heavens, rise up to be clothed in Christ our life, and ascend with him and Mary to God.

In the Gospel we sing with Mary the canticle she sang in Elizabeth's house. John, still in his mother's womb, leaped with joy when Mary came bearing Christ. By her son's leaping Elizabeth recognized Mary as the Mother of the Savior; and we recognize and praise her today, we and the churches throughout the world. We have the honor of fulfilling her prophecy, ''All ages to come shall call me blessed.''

Today we leap with John for joy, joy for Mary, joy for the Son she gave us as Savior, joy for the resurrection he will communicate to us as he has to her.

Christ promised that whoever wins the victory with him will share his throne. Mary shares his throne. Next week on this day we celebrate the Feast of the Blessed Virgin Mary as Queen of all creation. We know from the teaching Church and from her appearances through the ages that she is actively working for our salvation. We go to this mild and merciful Queen with all our needs.

And so today we celebrate with Mary and sing her praises and recite her canticle and ask her prayers that we may be faithful to her Son. Through communion with his risen body in the Eucharist today may we be clothed in glory and come to the resurrection at the appointed time.

"C" — Twentieth Sunday of the Year   Jr 38:4-6, 8-10
                                                      Heb 12:1-4
                                                      Lk 12:49-53

OVERCOMING ALCOHOLISM

"Do you think I have come to establish peace on earth? I assure you the contrary is true; I have come for division." Those words of Jesus shock us. They're meant to. They demand that we reflect on the fact that the easy-going gospel some preach is no gospel at all, and certainly not the Gospel of Jesus Christ. Speaking and living his truth causes division, because some do not receive it. We must expect it, and expect persecution, and accept it as Jeremiah did, and as Jesus himself did. We heard how Jeremiah's life was threatened when he did no more than God had commanded him to do in dealing with those who had gone astray.

We have the obligation to speak the truth of God and the truth of common sense even when it's very difficult. Parents have to correct their children, brothers and sisters one another; the priest must preach the doctrine of Christ and his Church even when it falls on unwilling ears. Few of us take correction gracefully, but there are matters in which it is a religious duty to give or receive correction. I will speak of only one of those matters, the problem of alcoholism in the family.

How hard it is to deal with a loved one who drinks to excess! Unless we act wisely we do more harm than good. Before making a move we need sound knowledge of alcoholism and the way of overcoming it.

First, we have to learn whether a person is an alcoholic. When can we know for sure? The experts define the alcoholic as a person in the grip of a physical, emotional and spiritual disease indicated by dependence on alcohol. We can know a person is an alcoholic when alcohol causes him serious problems and he continues to drink. Many alcoholics don't admit they have a problem even when they begin to lose their jobs, health, moral ideals, faith and self-respect. The tragedy in this is that the alcoholic can begin to overcome his problem only when he is willing to say, "I am an alcoholic."

When an alcoholic denies he has a problem, realize that "alcoholic denial" is a normal part of the alcoholic syndrome. The alcoholic may deny his problem and still be in the grip of despair.

We have to understand and share the suffering of the alcoholic. He feels despair because he's aware his compulsion robs him of his freedom, but is also aware he has enough freedom left to cry for help. So when he doesn't cry for help he feels both enslaved and guilty.

It's hard to admit we need help. It's harder when we don't want help. The alcoholic wants *drink*. He needs a spiritual awakening. He doesn't know how to go from wanting drink to wanting help. He needs prayer, an understanding family, and a support group. He needs Alcoholics Anonymous. We should have sympathy. We're all Sinners Anonymous. We have our support group in the Church of Christ.

Like many sinners, the alcoholic's terrible obstacle is that he has lost self-esteem. He feels it's not worth making the *effort* to recover. One alcoholic priest described at an A.A. meeting how he used to tell himself bitterly that God could never have called him to the priesthood. He wondered what madness led him there. But then, with the help of God and A.A. he won back his sobriety and his priestly life as well. The members of A.A. cried and laughed with him and got great help from his story.

A woman alcoholic joined A.A. On Christmas eve she went out and got drunk. She phoned an A.A. friend and mentor who had given her learned discourses on alcoholism with little effect. Her mentor rushed over gorgeous in her Christmas finery, and gave her hot and cold baths. The Christmas finery got soaked and rumpled. Seeing the sacrifice made for her, that alcoholic told later how she thought, "I must be worth something." And she proved it. She was soon celebrating her first year of sobriety.

We have to understand that the most workable solution found is A.A. Alcoholism is no respecter of persons. It strikes peons and presidents. The two alcoholics who founded A.A. were a broker and a physician. Members of A.A., who ought to know, say the way out is not opened until the alcoholic admits two things and does a third. First, he must admit, "I am powerless over alcohol." Second he must say, "There is a Power greater than myself who can restore me to sanity." Then he must act by saying, "I make a decision to turn my life and my will over to God as I understand him."

Members of A.A., even after decades of sobriety, call themselves alcoholics. They still have an addiction to alcohol. They must practice total abstinence. They agree with the common-sense Catholic teaching that there is nothing wrong with drinking for those who can and do drink moderately. The Christian attitude is: Drink moderately, or practice total abstinence.

The alcoholic requires our support and understanding. He also needs a support group of others who have conquered alcoholism before him. A.A. fills that need. It is free. It is just a phone call away. And there is the organization Alanon to help families to understand and work with their alcoholic loved one.

Despair is the worst enemy. The right attitude is illustrated by a favorite story of an alcoholic who has won victory through Christ and A.A: A cocky little demon, sent on patrol by Satan, leaped on a Christian's shoulder and said, "You're discouraged." The man denied it. "You're discouraged," the demon repeated. "A little," the man conceded. "You're discouraged," the demon persisted. The man's shoulders slumped. "I'm discouraged."

The demon reported to Satan and was advanced. The next day he jumped on the shoulder of a real Christian. "You're discouraged." "No I'm not." "You're discouraged." "Not a bit." "You're discouraged." "No. A day, an hour at a time. The Lord won't let me be tried beyond my strength."

That night Satan asked, "How did it go?" The demon slumped. "I'm discouraged."

With alcoholism or anything else, God is on our side. If we stay on his, we can't lose. Those who have won out with God's help are often better Christians than many of us.

As we Sinners Anonymous turn to share the banquet of Christ, let's pray for ourselves and all sinners, with special concern today for the alcoholic who has not yet won the victory.

"C" — Twenty-first Sunday of the Year

Is 66:18-21
Heb 12:5-7, 11-13
Lk 13:22-30

CONSCIENCE AND AUTHORITY

The old Jewish rabbis had a saying, "If *one* man calls you a donkey, don't get upset; if *two*, get worried; if *three*, get a saddle." Perhaps humor is the best way of making the point that those who don't listen and learn from friend and neighbor and rightful authority have strayed from the right path. In today's Gospel Jesus is condemning just such people.

Some in the Church cry "Freedom of Conscience!" as if it were a declaration of independence from the teaching authority of Pope and bishops. They think conscience is a purely personal matter. This is a dreadful error. Every human conscience is under the same basic law of reality, of truth, and of God; every Catholic conscience is under the guidance of Christ's Church. Catholics who make fundamental decisions about faith and morals apart from the guidance of the Pope and bishops have fallen away from the faith. The Pope is successor of Peter, and to Peter Christ said, "Whatever you bind on earth is bound in heaven, and whatever you loose on earth is loosed in heaven."

The younger U.S. generation doesn't seem to understand that any genuine religion binds us to do God's will. Christians among them don't realize Christ intends us to find God's will through the teaching of his Church. Children from fourth grade through high school were asked in a survey what they would do if they were unsure what was right or wrong. Only sixteen percent said they would do what God or Scripture says is right; only three percent said they would seek advice from religious leaders. Yet when Jesus sent the 72 disciples to spread the Gospel he said, "He who hears you hears me, and he who rejects you rejects me."

Jesus touches on this very issue in today's parable about the last judgment and the locked entrance into heaven. To those clamoring at the door he says, "I don't know where you come from." They try to correct him: "You taught in our streets!" He responds more sternly, "I tell you, I don't know where you come from. Away from me, you evildoers."

Is he denying he taught them? Rather, he's denying that they heard! Or if they heard, they disagreed; or if they agreed, they didn't live by what they learned. They did evil.

Here, then, we confront the issue of conscience and authority. Let's review what conscience is, and how a Catholic conscience is formed.

Conscience is the faculty that calls us to do good and avoid evil. Conscience is guided by God's law written into our hearts. It is the place where each of us stands alone with God as Father, Lawgiver and Guide. Conscience is the watchdog and guardian of our true worth. In eternity we will be rewarded for obeying our conscience, or condemned for disobeying it. Notice the language of obedience. Conscience is not *free*, any more than our eyes are free. When there is light our eyes see. *We* are free, free to accept or reject what conscience sees, free to do good or evil.

Another important point: Conscience commands us to do the right thing, but at times it is unable to tell us the right thing. It sends us out to search for the truth.

To aid that search Christ founded his Church. It is the light and guardian of religious and moral truth. No one is physically forced to join his Church. But, as Vatican II taught in its *Declaration On Religious Freedom,* "All men are bound to seek the truth, especially in what concerns God and His Church, and to embrace the truth they come to know, and to hold fast to it." It also taught that "In the formation of their consciences, the Christian faithful ought carefully to attend to the sacred and certain doctrine of the Church. The Catholic Church is, by the will of Christ, the teacher of the truth." Here we touch on the responsibility of everyone who belongs to the Catholic Church to attend to its teaching in faith and morals.

How does conscience make its judgments? It is guided by reason, authority, and the light of the Holy Spirit. *All* are necessary. In other words, conscience is neither magic, nor a purely natural way of knowing, nor a purely supernatural way. It is a human power of judging that is dependent on all attainable resources, human and divine. Therefore conscience has to be *formed and informed.*

This means we develop a mature conscience only by working at it. As we grow up, our consciences are formed by the Catholic faith. In the course of our lives, when we have to judge in a particular matter of conscience, we need first to inform ourselves on that matter. For it's not enough to follow my conscience; I must try to form a *right* conscience.

There is such a thing as an erroneous conscience; there is also such a thing as a guilty conscience. An erroneous conscience is one that has made a wrong judgment without realizing the fact; a guilty conscience is one that has made a self-deceiving judgment, or one that has rejected the task of really trying to learn the truth. That's why we pray to be delivered from our *hidden* sins. Good people want a right conscience.

In summary, then: The norm of conscience for everyone is right reason; the added norm for Christians is reason illumined by

Christ; the final norm for Catholics is the truth of Christ as defined by the Church. Consider St. Paul. When he was struck blind, he was told to go to a member of the Church to learn what to do. Christ, who could have told him, did not. He speaks through his Church. In accord with his blind conscience, Paul had been persecuting Christ's Church. He was struck blind to lead his conscience to see by the light of the Church.

None of this means we are not free to reflect on faith and morals. Just the opposite: It is a duty. Theologians do it with a special competence derived from training. But only the Pope and bishops have the authority of Christ and the special guidance of the Holy Spirit to interpret Christ's word in a binding way.

When we reflect on this, we may find the Spirit moving us to joy and gratitude that Christ leads us beyond the bedlam of the world to the Church's clear and reliable guidance. We are of the line of martyrs like Thomas More and John Fisher who so treasured faith and conscience and the nobility it brings that they held firm, even to death, against the pressure and tyranny of their king. May Holy Communion inspire us to share with them Christ's own loving desire to find and do God's will always.

''C'' — Twenty-second Sunday of the Year

Si 3:17-18, 20, 28-29
Heb 12:18-19, 22-24
Lk 14:1, 7-14

ELEVATING HUMILITY

Below ground in the Basilica of the Annunciation in Nazareth is the humble little room revered as the place where the Virgin Mary conceived the Son of God. One day a pilgrim gazed at it and whispered in shock, ''I thought she was a king's daughter!'' On this day when Jesus guides us to humility, it will pay us to look at the real Mary. Whatever her line of descent, she was a poor woman. The angel had to come into a poor little home to visit her. True, she was engaged to a man descended from kings. But little good that did Joseph. His lineage was only a memory. He was a poor carpenter. He earned his living by the sweat of his brow. In his day the kingdom, long since lost to foreign conquerors, was under the Roman occupiers.

If we meditate on the life of Mary and Joseph we'll learn about humility; and we'll learn much if we picture Jesus traveling on dusty feet through the desert lands between the towns, tired, hungry, and badly in need of a change of clothes.

Jesus lived humbly. Three days on the road with him would teach us the meaning of humility and help us welcome it into our lives. Since we lack those three days we turn to his word and example, and the examples of the saints who found them enough. "Everyone who exalts himself," Jesus says, "shall be humbled, and he who humbles himself shall be exalted." Here is the strange fact: humility exalts; pride degrades. The dictionary tells us that to be humble is to be neither proud nor haughty, neither arrogant nor assertive. It is to be submissive and unpretentious. The word humility comes from the Latin word, *humus*, which means *earth*. Earth we are and to earth we will return. By humility we recall our origin from dust; we recognize our duty of submission to our Creator as we journey back to him; we embrace dependence on God who alone can give us resurrection and true life; and we admit our dependence on one another during this time of our mortality. Without parents we wouldn't be; without educators we wouldn't know; without industrious people we'd live impoverished lives. All these truths are the source of real humility.

The great source of humility is love. Love opens our eyes. We pour ourselves out in friendship and devotion. We are ready for the lowly tasks of serving our loved ones, as mothers do, and fathers, and loving brothers and sisters. Basically, humility is simply the truth lived out in our lives.

Pride is the contrary. Pride, the first of the capital sins, is a lie. It pretends to more than we are. Its prime example is Satan. Pride is a liar and self-deceiver like him. He presumed to lift himself up to God's place, and fell from his own. He deceived Eve into aspiring to be a goddess; instead she found deterioration and death.

The smell of pride comes from the self-corrupting refusal to subject oneself to God the Lifegiver. Pride draws in its train many other evils. It cuts others down so as to appear taller. It lusts after money and power to evoke the illusion of greatness.

By doing these things it impoverishes the world. In business it knows only the motive of profit, so it mistreats the worker. In politics it knows only the lust for power, so it manipulates and controls the peoples, and provokes wars in the process. In personal relations, it demeans relatives and friends alike, so it destroys families, friendships, and international alliances. In religion it presumes to know more than the Pope, so it spreads error, creates dissension, and destroys unity and peace.

We resist God's call to humility because we neither believe what he tells us nor find the truth for ourselves. When we do believe, we gain, in one act, the door to the whole sweep of truth about life and its values. We see that humility is the basic Christian virtue and fertile soil of every virtue; and pride is the poison that kills them all.

Even if we get this far, we may resist. You might say, ''When I'm pushy and self assertive it gets me places. How can I accomplish what I want if I'm humble?'' Perhaps you can't. But you can accomplish what God wants. Let's not mistake humility for pretense or the depressed state of one who thinks he is worthless. That's not the truth, so it's not humility. Jesus told the parable of the servants who were given various sums of money and expected to produce accordingly. The money is our gifts and talents. Humility doesn't excuse us from using them, only from abusing them.

Many great and accomplished people have been humble people. Pride opens the way to some things we want, but humility opens the way to the best, the things our deepest heart wants.

We're so enslaved to prestige that we won't live humbly without a conversion experience. St. Augustine describes the beginning of his conversion: "Suddenly," he wrote, "all the vanity I'd hoped in I saw as worthless, and with an incredible intenseness of desire I longed after immortal wisdom. I had begun that journey upward by which I was to return to (God)."

How can we dispose ourselves for such a grace? By meditating on Jesus. His whole life is an incarnation of humility. St. Paul says, "Though he was in the form of God, he did not deem equality with God something to be grasped at. Rather, he emptied himself and took the form of a slave."

He clothed himself in the humble garment of human flesh with its pleasures and pains, birth and dying; took human consciousness with its limits and griefs and sense of mortality.

He obeyed human parents and teachers, underwent religious rites at the hands of priests far inferior to himself, and became known as a companion of sinners and wine-bibbers, though he had the noble qualities to hobnob with wise men and kings. He forgot himself in the service of others. He traded his royalty for a crown of thorns, divested himself of dignity and hung disgraced between criminals in a shameful and tortured death. And if that's not enough, he is humble enough today to want union with each of us in Holy Communion, as though each were his only loved one.

With the clarity of crystal he showed that humility is what you see when you look into the face of love. He endured suffering and shame as no more than buzzing gnats to be ignored in his engrossment with the tasks and joys of love. And so "God highly exalted him and bestowed on him the name above every other name." And if we follow him, we, like Mary, will learn the truth of his words, "He who humbles himself shall be exalted."

THE COST OF DISCIPLESHIP

"If anyone comes to me without hating his father and mother, wife and children, brothers and sisters, and even his own life, he cannot be my disciple." These words of our Lord can sound harsh in our ears. So before considering them think of this: A marriage counselor gave a talk in which he described how he deals with a troubled couple. He gives them a homework assignment. They are to spend 24 hours together without radio, T.V., newspapers or children. The hope is that, having nothing to do but communicate, they may find one another again.

After his talk an attractive couple stepped up and told him how happily in love they were, and how much they enjoyed his talk. Then the husband, a lawyer, said, "But there's one thing that troubles me. How do you find time for that intimacy?" The counselor responded, "There's one thing that troubles me. Given how much you're in love, how do you find time to attend to your law practice?" Then the counselor went on to say that we find time for important things like work, and when we decide love is important we find time for it too. Keep that interchange in mind as we meditate on these words of Christ.

We'll look at the fact that God knows our problems and knows how to guide us; that Christ is giving us that guidance in his stern words; and that we have to put Jesus first.

First, God knows our problems and knows only his wisdom can guide us. In the first reading, God is telling us he knows we have all kinds of troubles. We can't walk out on them. We have problems to solve. He can help us solve them. We have many cares, but he cares for us. He is our Father, and he will guide us with his wisdom. He sent his wisdom to us in the person of his Son.

Second, Christ the Wisdom of God is giving us guidance and admonition in those stern words we just heard. What does he intend by them? If you think about it, his words are really not stern; they're just blunt. If he doesn't put it bluntly, we won't even notice what he's saying. How many times does it happen that we're listening to the word of God when suddenly we realize our minds have drifted off? Christ wants to make sure these serious words get through. They hit like sledgehammers.

We might look for an escape hatch by saying, "Those words are just for some chosen people." Notice the Gospel wards that one off by saying it was a great crowd and Jesus turned to them — to all of them — and said these blunt words. Now let me ask you a question. Is he really saying anything more demanding than that marriage counselor said about married love? Our Lord is telling us that love for him is like the deepest love anywhere, only more so, because it comes first. God cannot be second. Surely we all know that Christ is not telling us to love our loved ones less; he's only telling us we must love him more. You know how he said at the Last Supper, "Love one another as I have loved you." The Scriptures connect love of God and one another so closely as to make it clear we can't love God as we ought without loving one another very deeply. We shouldn't go away today with the idea of loving anyone less; the idea is to love more purely, more deeply, more rightly, without any mixture of sin.

What Christ is demanding is loyalty to the highest love, love of God-made-man. Christ is our Way, our Truth, our Life. We have to be loyal to our Way, our Truth and our Life. If God makes certain demands and our family make contrary demands we have to say "Yes" to God and "No" to family. That's not a lack of love. When you say no to your children, is it because you don't love them or because you love them rightly, and wish the best for them? Isn't it only too easy to say yes to them when you should say no? We must put God before family, nation, anything. The martyrs did; we must do it, sometimes in a living martyrdom.

The marriage counselor advised unsettled couples to spend 24 hours alone together. Where did he get the idea? Perhaps from God. God calls us every week to spend 24 hours with him. "Keep holy the Sabbath day." There have to be those times with God or we will drift away from him. We thank our Lord for his blunt words. Perhaps we need them to wake us up before we drift away.

The marriage counselor I mentioned said that after the 24 hours together some couples don't solve their problems. They decide to separate. Jesus said, "None of you can be my disciple if he does not renounce all his possessions." Blunt language. Is separation an alternative? It's too awful to think about. St. Peter couldn't think about it. When Jesus promised the Eucharist, the giving of his body and blood for food, it sounded like madness to many, and they left in droves. Jesus turned to his disciples and asked, "Do you also want to leave?" Peter answered, "Master, to whom shall we go? You have the words of eternal life." If we have faith, we say the same. So we have to find ways to love the Lord and make it easy to put him first .

So let us think about how to put Jesus first. We don't want to say "I have to," or "I wish to;" we want to say "I love to." Isn't that the way Mary and Joseph felt? It's also the way St. Paul felt. "The Son of God," Paul said, "has loved me and delivered himself up for me." Make those words your own. Say to the Lord, "You have loved me, and delivered yourself up for me." Say those words through the day for a week and watch what happens. Feel your heart awakening to that freedom which we prayed for in the Opening Prayer. Love of Christ gives us that freedom. It makes us truly free to put first things first.

There was once a seminarian who would announce at recreation about once a week, "I'm going to clear the air!" Then he would raise troublesome issues among the seminarians that no one had had the courage to bring up. It often helped to clear the air and bring about a more peaceful community. Christ is "clearing the air" today. Those words of his that sound so harsh at first hearing are not harsh at all. They are an earnest statement about reality by God the passionate lover. They insist that to be wholly one with him we have to give ourselves wholly to him as he gives himself wholly to us. There is no other way.

Today at Holy Communion realize that the Lord is giving us everything he has and is to the extent we have the capacity and open-heartedness to receive it. If we enter deeply into that mystery, can we fail to respond? "You have made us for yourself alone, and we cannot rest until we rest in you."

"ABC" — The Triumph of the Cross   Nb 21:4-9
                                                          Ph 2:6-11
                                                          Jn 3:13-17

THE HEALING CROSS

Signs and symbols have great power over our hearts. The Stars and Stripes spanking in the breeze stir a patriot to the depths; the sign of the swastika conjures up dread in the breast of a survivor of Auschwitz. The image of a horn of plenty calls to mind the joys of harvest and the Feast of Thanksgiving.

Most symbols, like the horn of plenty, have a quality that make them naturally suitable for what they represent. The cross, on the contrary, is the most unlikely symbol of salvation in the history of the world. In the Roman age it was a sign of torture, disgrace, degradation and death. How could a mechanism of torture ever be transformed into a symbol of anything good? Each symbol has a story attached to it, so on this Feast of the Triumph of the Cross we reflect on how the cross came to mean salvation.

God and the cross step into the picture when human resources fail. Medical science keeps looking for the perfect curative. It has found wonders, but only within limits. One old woman of 88 was told by her doctor that medicine could do no more. She had to endure what she suffered and faced.

Only the Divine Physician provides the perfect curative. He gives it under the unlikely sign of the cross. The cross is a curative with so many uses we will never discover them all. The spiritual healing it gives leads to the resurrection of the body.

We'll look at the figures under which God reveals the cross's curative powers, then at the way to apply the curative, and finally at how the cross heals religion itself.

First, in figurative language God reveals the cross's curative powers. Adam used the tree against God's will; Christ, the last Adam, used the wood of a tree in obedience to God. The first Adam pursued his own pleasure, the last Adam God's pleasure. This is the symbolism of the saraph serpent in the first reading; what it did by itself was destructive; what God did with it was healing. That is, as Adam used his human nature to wound us, Christ used his to heal us. As Adam used a tree to rob us of our inheritance, Christ used a tree to regain it and more. Adam lifted himself up to strike against God's will; Christ was lifted up on the cross to heal such sinfulness, and lifted in resurrection and Ascension to bring us everlasting life.

All the value of the cross comes from him who hung on it. Christ is our curative. As the Opening Prayer says, God's Son died for our salvation. God's curative is Jesus Christ crucified. Well might he be our cure. He is the God-man, God become Man.

Secondly, we look at the way to apply the curative given us by God. We gain its benefits by looking in faith at Jesus Christ crucified. We who are bitten by our own sins through the induce-ment of that old serpent the devil look at Jesus on the pole of the cross and find healing as the snake-bitten people in the desert were healed by looking at the bronze serpent on the pole. We look at Jesus and say over and over in love, "You have loved me and delivered yourself up to take away my sins." In that trust and repentance our sins are no more.

A second healing comes with that first one. For often when we sin and experience other disasters, we think we are abandoned by God. But when we look at Jesus the Innocent One, the Only Son, in torment, we realize that suffering, pain, and failure are not abandonment by God. We discover we are no more abandoned than he was. Suffering he had to endure, but he endured it freely for our salvation. He was raised up in glory and victory over sin and death. So shall we be. We discover in this the healing freedom to resist sin that comes from pure love.

This heals us by giving suffering value. Suffering endured for love is transferred from the debit column to the gains column of life. Everything we endure in fidelity to God makes us grow in Christ and stores up treasures in heaven. Even suffering for sin is not a punishment but a corrective by a loving Father. This realization pours joy into our sorrows, the way it did for the saints. Jesus told us to jump for joy when we suffer for the sake of goodness. And acceptance of any suffering in obedience to God's will is goodness. How well Our Lady knew that when she endured all things with Jesus. We see all these things if we take God's medicine by meditating on Christ crucified.

Pope John Paul II gives us great insight into the Triumph of the Cross. He says, "In the messianic program of Christ, which is at the same time the program of the kingdom of God, suffering is present in the world in order to release love, in order to give birth to works of love for neighbor, in order to transform the whole of human civilization into a 'civilization of love.' " Here there is no sickly attachment to suffering. The cross and the Christian vision teach us to remove all the suffering we can. They teach us to endure what we must to set all things right in accord with God's will and God's law, as Jesus Christ did.

How well this brings out the fact that the cross teaches us what a privilege it is to walk with Jesus, to endure with him, to have the honor of carrying on our shoulders too the cross of his labor for truth and love and holiness and life for the world.

Finally, we look at how the curative power of the cross heals the sickness which at times afflicts religion itself. Sometimes religions have advocated immoral and unclean practices; sometimes they have afflicted people with neurotic guilt over things that are not sin; and often they have stirred consciences against real sin without giving the power to overcome sin. The medicine of the cross cures them all. The blood of Christ pouring down from the cross cures the wounds of sin, calms consciences, takes away real guilt, and eases false and neurotic guilt.

We sinners can't understand these things simply by listening; only the heart understands them. Hardened sinners are like alcoholics. As one expert said, "You'll never cure them by arguments." Sin, like alcoholism, is madness. The medicine of the cross cures both. We gaze at the crucifix until the love of God gets through and the triumph of mankind over death registers in us and we say to Jesus, "The Father has so loved us all that he has given us you and your love and example as our remedy."

We are here at Mass to renew the Cross of Calvary in our lives by offering the Lord who hung there, and receiving in Holy Communion the remedy of his heart's love. Every time we see a cross, may we remember his saving love and rejoice in it.

"C" — Twenty-fourth Sunday of the Year

Ex 32:7-11, 13-14
1 Tm 1:12-17
Lk 15:1-32

FORGIVENESS IN THE FAMILY

Little children don't always understand this parable of the Prodigal Son. A catechist asked the children, "Who was unhappy when the wayward son returned?" One child said, "The fat calf."

Do we ourselves see clearly that the parable deals with three cases of needed forgiveness? Before looking at them, let's revise the parable: When the prodigal son left, he had a father who said, "If you go off and live a degraded life, never come back. I'll never forgive you." When the son's life went sour he remembered his father's words and gave up hope. He needed money so he sold himself on the street; he felt so degraded he began using drugs; and having no hope, he committed suicide. This is not a fanciful case. It happens repeatedly in our culture. A study some years ago reported that suicide was the third highest cause of death among 18 to 24 year-old young men. Runaways often end up, not back home, but in the grave at an early age.

Now we take up the parable as our Lord told it.

First we consider the forgiving father. His younger son asked him for his share of the estate; perhaps he said brutally, "Dad, why make me wait for you to die before I get my share of that property of yours. Give it to me now." And the father did.

The father probably heard reports of what people thought of his boy: That worthless, no good son. His poor father! I'd have booted that kid out penniless. He deserves anything he gets.

That's not the way his father felt. When his son at last came home, his father saw him a long way off. Why was that except that he changed his habits after his son left? He began to take a long walk every day. Whether he felt like it or not, he climbed the high hill nearby and looked everywhere. "Maybe my son will come home today," he thought. And one day he was rewarded.

When his son said, "Father, I have sinned against God and against you," his father gave no lectures. He was too busy preparing for the celebration. His forgiveness had always been ready, but to be of use, there had to be one who wanted it. Now that his son wanted it, the matter was settled.

So it is with our heavenly Father. The Scriptures tell us his mercy is above all his works. Whose homecoming is the Father awaiting now in his sacrament of reconciliation? If only they would want his forgiveness! Why is his sacrament of forgiveness so neglected? Whatever the reasons, it's tragic. I'll mention one reason when we come to the prodigal son.

But first we look at the stay-at-home son. He seemed a model son until it came to forgiveness of his own brother. Then he was jealous and unforgiving. Jealousy is a horrible sin. It led Cain to murder Abel; it led Joseph's brothers to sell him into slavery; and it led the Jewish leaders to demand that Pilate crucify Jesus. The younger brother sinned from weakness; the older brother from hardness of heart. Whose sin was worse?

Why did Jesus add this part of the story? He could have ended, "And they lived happily ever after." But here the Father who has just forgiven one son has to plead with the other to be forgiving; indeed, the older son needs forgiveness himself now. Isn't Jesus saying, "You all need forgiveness from the Father? Are you then going to refuse forgiveness to your brother?" If we're unforgiving we're in a bad way because Jesus put on our lips the words, "Forgive us our trespasses *as* we forgive those who trespass against us." He added, "If you do not forgive others, neither will your Father forgive your transgressions."

We should remember here how Jesus our Brother forgives us. When we come home to the Father it's because he came out looking for us. When our sins are washed away, it's in the shower of his own blood. When the Father sets out his feast, it's the Eucharistic body of his own Son.

Now we look at the forgiveness of the wayward son. Whom did he have to forgive? Himself! Sometimes that's the hardest. Until he forgave himself he couldn't accept his father's forgiveness. One who can't forgive himself ends up only too often a suicide like Judas. Contrast Judas with Peter. Peter denied Jesus. He wept. He forgave himself. Then he sought Jesus' forgiveness.

So too with Paul. He tells us today how hard-hearted he was. He persecuted Christians. He considered it a religious act. He says, "I did not know what I was doing in my unbelief." That's how the wayward son began. In his own eyes, he wasn't sinning. Those old rules were out of date, and his father hadn't waked up to the fact. Today, that's what happens to many young people, and some not so young. They are brainwashed by a world that denies sin. They listen to neither God nor his Church. They think they haven't sinned and don't need confession. But denying sin is like denying cancer. It doesn't stop eating away at you. Unless you go for treatment, sin kills the soul and cancer kills the body.

Contrast sin with innocence. The word innocent means "not sinful, not harmful." An innocent person is one who doesn't harm himself or anyone else. A sinner harms first of all himself and then others. Only when the wayward son came to admit he had done wrong to himself did he realized that he had done wrong to his Father in heaven and his father on earth.

The beautiful thing about this son is that he really was sorry. He didn't just want to go home. He wanted forgiveness. The proof is in the parable. When his Father ran up and kissed him, he could have said, "Well, I see I don't have to give that fancy little speech I prepared." But instead he said from the heart, "Father, I have sinned against God and against you."

In New Orleans a man came down the aisle of a Catholic Church waving a revolver. Worshippers scattered. The man laid the gun on the altar and left. Perhaps at our next Penance Service we should have a "Bring Them In" ceremony: guns, knives, rolling pins, drawings of sharp tongues, and stones for unforgiving hearts.

Today we're called, especially as families, and the family of the Church, to realize we need to forgive and be forgiven. We're not all members of runaways anonymous or drugaholics anonymous or sexaholics anonymous but we're all members of sinners anonymous. That was our passport to baptism; it's our passport to the sacrament of reconciliation. When we receive Holy Communion today let's admit to our divine Brother, "I have sinned against the Father and against you. Wash away my sins in your holy blood. Lead me home to the Father."

RCIA — THE BUSINESS OF ALL CATHOLICS

The American Nihilism Society had an ad in which they said we used to believe in God, heaven and hell, and John Wayne, but now all we're sure of is that "life is essentially meaningless."

We Catholics respond with the joy of faith in life's meaning as Christ revealed it to us. Today, Christ's parable is about getting home. Make use of money and all else, he tells us, in a way to assure ourselves of a "lasting reception" in our eternal home. And, as St. Paul adds, we should earnestly pray that all others will travel home with us, even the Nihilists.

That's why we have in our parish the Rite of Christian Initiation of Adults, or RCIA for short. What is the RCIA, what is our role in it, and how does it benefit us all? Those are the questions I will probe.

What is the Rite of Christian Initiation of Adults, or RCIA? It's the parish program we conduct for prospective converts. It make them fully-formed members of our Church. It's the most updated program available for people who want to share the faith; yet much of it is almost as old as the Church. The Fathers of the Church must look down from heaven with joy as we restore the long and careful training of converts which they originated.

Some who come to the program have never known Christ; others were baptized in another denomination, but are now called by God to join us in the Roman Catholic Church. In the program we speak to their intellects. They come to a knowledge of the revelation in all its depth; they gain an understanding of that to which God calls them. They are summoned to a conversion of their moral life. They learn the rule of conduct: Don't do things just because they please you, or solely out of obedience to God's law. Do all from utmost love for God and his people and the eternal life with God which awaits us.

We speak to their hearts and their religious sense so they no longer see life in the old way. They discover the mystery of life. It is a gift that involves us in carrying the cross with Christ so we may share his glory. They discover God. He is not an impersonal "Force," as he is described in some modern fiction. No, he is the most personal of all beings whom they are called to know in the most intimate of all relationships. They plunge into the depths of Christianity. They meet Jesus, the living, vibrant, risen Lord who said, "I am with you all days." They commune with him in prayer; they learn he washes away our sins in baptism and penance, and gives himself to us body and blood in the Eucharist; and in an extension of himself, he comes to us and serves us in the persons of his members.

They become acquainted with the Church. They learn it's not an institution out there serving us; we are the Church, the body of Christ, the mystical body, the people of God, the family of the Father, the brothers and sisters of Jesus, his fellow workers as children and servants of the Father. Over the weeks and months they sense and experience this. At last Holy Saturday comes and they are baptized and confirmed and receive the risen body of Christ and become fully one with him and with us the Church.

What is the role of all of us in the RCIA? Surely we can see right off that the candidates will never get a warm sense of belonging to Christ's Church without our help. Our part comes out of our very identity as followers of Christ. He charged us to call all people to share the faith. If we appreciate the gift of God, we thank God by helping others to have what we have. It is our duty and our privilege. The RCIA itself says that "the people of God, represented by the local Church, should always understand and show that the initiation of adults is . . . the business of all the baptized."

Here are some ways to support the RCIA: Pray for the program every day in your Daily Offering. Talk about it at coffee breaks and lunches and in other conversations with family and friends and neighbors. It's *interesting*. And if the Holy Spirit touches them, some will ask about joining it. So the first thing is to do our part in attracting candidates to the program.

Then get to know the candidates. Chat with them, invite them to other parish affairs, especially the ones you're involved in. Offer to be a teacher in the program, or a sponsor at baptism. Invite candidates to your home to get to know you, the Church, the body of Christ. By winning their hearts, you may keep someone from falling away. On Holy Saturday, attend the Vigil Mass to celebrate their reception into the Church as our fellow members. In everything show interest, helpfulness, friendliness, love and good example.

How does the RCIA benefit us all? Let me start with an example. People who've never had an alcoholic problem take sobriety for granted. Alcoholics who have won sobriety back after terrible ordeals thank God for it daily. We who've had the faith from birth can lack gratitude. We may learn it from RCIA candidates who are overwhelmed with gratitude because they have known the hell of life without faith, like the Nihilists.

We see them thrill to learn one mystery after another which we take for granted. Years ago one convert was brought before the Blessed Sacrament by the priest and told our belief. She exclaimed, "Then why don't we fall down on our hands and knees!"

As the light of faith falls on the candidates in one flash after another, they will help us appreciate the gifts of God. They can't help helping us as they discover Christ's light and love. They learn of the Church as the beacon of the light of Christ; they find his truth shining into their lives. They find guidance and hope and revelation given them by the patriarchs and the prophets. They thrill to the Savior and the New Covenant, the law of love, the conversion experience, the road to Rome, the call to holiness, the sacraments, the body of Christ, the rebirth and the Eucharist, the support of the community of faith and the promise of life everlasting. As they progress through these gifts and promises one by one their joy and gratitude and enthusiasm mount. They even rub off on us who have forgotten to thank God endlessly for all we have been given. At last we may begin to thank him in the best way, by beginning to make a better, a deeper, a greater use of the faith to which he has called us.

When the body of Christ grows we all grow. It's what RCIA is all about. Let's do our part as Jesus and the Church invite us.

"C" — Twenty-sixth Sunday of the Year   Am 6:1, 4-7
                                                        1 Tm 6:11-16
                                                        Lk 16:19-31

THE NON-NEGOTIABLE MANDATE TO SHARE

What is today's parable really about? It's clearly about God's command to love our neighbor; but it's also about how obeying that command provides for our social security in eternal life. The rich man didn't provide for his and ended up eternally without it. A reverent fear of God and his commands will free us from the fear of everything else, especially death.

Jesus is calling us to charity, but he's also teaching us that thoughts of death and judgment will confirm us in charity. As a matter of fact, a scientific research project showed that "confronting people with the fact that they will die makes them cling tenaciously to their deepest moral values." That research project's conclusion can already be found in the Book of Sirach: "In all you do remember the end of your life and you will never sin."

What if God had willed Jesus to live as a wealthy man to show the wealthy how to use their wealth? Picture Jesus living in a palace, and Lazarus coming to his door. What would Jesus do for Lazarus? I think we all know. But if Jesus was a wealthy man, we'd all want to be wealthy. He was poor, and still we don't want to be poor. What happened when the poor or the sick knocked at the door of the Holy Family? We're not told, but surely we know without being told.

Shockingly, few take to heart the Lord's words, "It's easier for a camel to pass through the eye of a needle than for one who is rich to enter the kingdom of God." Greed burns bright. It's the mark of the rich man of the parable.

But in some the call of the beatitudes burns brighter. "Blessed are the poor in spirit, for theirs is the kingdom of God." St. Francis of Assisi was poor in spirit. He owned nothing and loved everything. Tens of thousands go to his town of Assisi every year to drink of his spirit. In 1986 the World Wildlife Fund made its pilgrimage there to honor the man who wrote a hymn to brother sun and sister moon, to brother wind and sister water. He loved God, he loved Christ, he loved humanity, he loved nature, and he loved poverty. Unlike the rich man of the parable, he clung to nothing, for in Christ he possessed everything.

In his parable Jesus teaches us how to use what wealth we have. Cain asked, "Am I my brother's keeper?" Christ's answer is a resounding *Yes.* Our eternal destiny hinges on the way we love, and the way we use money. If we love money it becomes our master and we its slave. Christ didn't love money. It was a possession to be used to serve, not a value to be clung to from selfishness. Please observe that the rich man was condemned not for what he did with money but for what he failed to do with it.

Our Lord wants us to take great joy in being members of his body the Church, and of his creation. Like St. Francis we are to love one another and love nature and the animals and the natural order of the earth, and take responsible care of them or they can't take care of us.

The Church teaches this universal extension of charity. We find Lazarus at our door almost every time we watch TV. We have to reach out to him in many ways. We make donations to charities, but we also use our vote and our social influence to bring about the "civilization of love, the kingdom of the Heart of Christ." We can never be like the woman who said, "When I go into the voting booth I leave religion outside." Does she leave both God and Lazarus outside? Does she leave the endangered child in the womb outside to die with Lazarus?

Statistics in the Eighties showed that one percent of Americans owned half the country's wealth; the richest ten percent owned over four-fifths of the nations wealth. That is not acceptable. It must be changed.

In that same decade the U.S. bishops wrote a letter on social teaching. They declared that "From the Patristic period to the present, the Church has affirmed that misuse of the world's resources or appropriation of them by a minority of the world's population betrays the gift of creation, since whatever belongs to God belongs to all."

The environment too belongs to us all, and we are all responsible for it. Greed is ruining it — not just the greed of industrialists, but the greed of all who want too much. The Pope said in his 1990 World Day of Peace message that at root, "the ecological crisis is a moral issue." It reflects a worldwide desire for "instant gratification and consumerism" without concern for the consequences. The Holy Father is calling us to a simpler, less affluent way of life which recognizes that we must share more fairly with our brothers and sisters in this global village of ours.

We must hear these things though they burden us, because it is God's own message. There is no real faith without justice, as we see in all of today's readings. God and his Christ and his prophets and his Church will give us no rest until we take these things to heart and live them.

If the third of the world that is Christian had lived these truths, would atheistic communism ever have risen to try to do by force what should have been done by love? The failure of Christians to live this doctrine in 1,800 years was the opening for Marx and Engels to come with their doctrine of hatred for the wealthy and to promote class struggle. Hatred didn't work. It never does. But maybe it can shame us into trying love.

Why is greed for great personal wealth so ugly in the Christian? It's because Christianity teaches us we are all brothers and sisters in Christ. We're one family. To desire to have it all when we see our little brothers and sisters starving or homeless on the streets is to be not only less than Christian but less than human.

Even worse if possible, it is to reject God the Father's own example. He has shared his greatest wealth in sharing with us the love and very life of his Only-begotten Son. Can we be so mean of spirit as to persist in greed when we possess the Treasure of treasures? We pray today that God's grace may awaken in us true love of Christ and of one another and of eternal life. That is what freed St. Francis of Assisi to live so full of love that he still draws to his way people from around the world. May God grant us the grace to do the same.

"C" — Twenty-Seventh Sunday of the Year

Hab 1:2-3; 2:2-4
2 Tm 1:6-8, 13-14
Lk 17:5-10

THE CHRISTIAN RESPONSE TO ABORTION

How do we react when troubles beset us on every side, and social earthquakes shake the ground under our feet? We witness the prophet Habakkuk's reaction in the first reading. The Babylonians are besieging Jerusalem. He cries to the Lord about ruin and violence and misery, and complains that his prayers are not being heard. The Lord has heard, and gives answer, but not the answer he wanted. The Lord's promises will be fulfilled in their time. Until then, pray, labor, and persevere in faith.

We have our own earthquakes at the horror of abortion. We feel grief, sorrow, anger; we don't know whether to shout in outrage or weep helplessly. We even hear of Catholics in favor of legal abortion. Can they imagine they have the mind of Christ? "Stop the world. We want to get off." But that's no answer. The answer is to persevere in prayer, faith and faithful action. Let us look at the world situation, the need to stir up the grace of confirmation in us, and the call Christ gives us.

The world is disordered by abortion, and we are part of the struggle against it. The first need is to understand what happened and why. In 1970 the pro-choice journal, *California Medicine*, told us three things that were happening. People were worrying about the population expansion; and they were worried about the earth's limited resources; and, finally, they were worried that the higher "quality of life" science was promising would be undermined by the growing population.

So what did people do? The journal says that people and churches began to abandon the long-held teaching that every human life had equal value, "regardless of its stage, condition or status." Then this *pro-choice* journal states with brutal frankness that because killing was still "socially abhorrent," people began pretending that abortion was not killing. "The result," the journal goes on, "has been a curious avoidance of the scientific fact, which everyone really knows, that human life begins at conception and is continuous whether intra- or extra-uterine until death." The journal mocks this pretense as ludicrous. Then it goes on to predict confidently that the "new ethic" would prevail. And in fact, less than three years later, the Roe vs. Wade decision of the Supreme Court legalized abortion.

Please note carefully that this journal which favors the right to abortion admits that abortion is not just a religious issue but a human issue. Abortion raises the question of whether people will respect other human lives equally with their own, or whether self-interest will demote the value of certain lives.

And now a question to think about: Were women given abortion rights for their own good, or to get them to do society's dirty work? Even the feminist Gloria Steinem said that nobody's in favor of abortion. Everyone knows abortion is a tragedy. But some claim it's less of a tragedy than bearing an unwanted child. Our work is to show that abortion is far worse, as sin and tragedy; our work is to help women in distress give birth with dignity.

Now let us look at today's readings and see how they guide us in the issue of abortion and all other difficulties. The prophet Habakkuk learns that prayer does not make his troubles go away. God tells him to bear up by the power of faith, and endure until relief comes. Paul strikes the same note. "Bear your share," he says, "of the hardships the Gospel entails."

Paul also strikes a new note. "Guard the rich deposit of faith," he writes, "with the help of the Holy Spirit who dwells within us." The Holy Spirit shared his power with us in the sacrament of Confirmation. Confirmation is the sacrament that continues the day of Pentecost in the Church. It is normally given us at Mass to show that its grace was won for us by Christ's passion. The anointing gave us a special share in Jesus' role as God's Suffering Servant. He served and he suffered and he triumphed. That is our calling too. The Second Vatican Council said that Confirmation obliges us more strictly "to spread and defend the faith both by word and by deed as true witnesses to Christ." The Holy Spirit gives us many gifts, including the gift of fortitude to bear what we must, and grace to do it with joy.

These activities are all part of faith. Faith means not just to have faith but to be faithful. The Scriptures make it plain that we are not only to hold to the truths called the "deposit of faith," but we are to live to the full what we believe. In the words of St. James, "Faith without works is dead."

Finally, we take a look at the call to outstanding service which

Christ gives us in today's Gospel. I put it that way, but you have to dig out that meaning. Actually, when the Apostles ask the Lord how to increase their faith, he says faith the size of a mustard seed could transplant a tree into the sea; then he seems to change the subject. He talks about service. He says that if we do only what he commands us to do, we should think of ourselves as mere servants who do the least amount possible.

What is the point? The point is that if we're his friends and lovers faith will compel us to do not just what we have to do but all we can do. And that's how to grow in faith! With the help of the other readings we can almost hear Jesus saying, "You, my friends, are servants of the Lord as Habakkuk was and as Moses was and as I am. I have made you a sharer in what I am as Son and servant of the Father. So if the burdens and the sufferings and the persecutions of faith land on your shoulders don't be surprised. Just say, 'Well, what do you know! I'm having the experience of a child and servant of the Lord!' " So, then, let us do all we have the power to do. Only then can we call ourselves children of the Father worthy of the name. That's what true faith is and it's how to grow in faith.

As children and servants of the Father, we are not overwhelmed by abortion. We work to overwhelm it. We don't just denounce abortion; we work to save babies; we work to win parents away from the horror of abortion; we work to bring the civilization of love, the kingdom of the Heart of Christ. With hearts like our Mother Mary's we work to serve love and life. Now we turn to the Holy Sacrifice to offer ourselves with Christ, and we await the Eucharist to be filled anew with his love and life.

"C" — Twenty-eighth Sunday of the Year

2 K 5:14-17
2 Tm 2:8-13
Lk 17:11-19

THE PRAYER OF GLORIOUS THANKSGIVING

The Heismann-trophy winning football star Alan Ameche died at 55 after surgery for a heart ailment. Several years before, a young son was killed in an auto accident. His widow, Yvonne, described the process of loss and bereavement to others who had lost loved ones, and expressed her confidence in God's love for her. A woman who heard her said in amazement that in her shoes she would doubt God's love. When Yvonne recounted the story to a priest, he said simply, "You're a satisfied customer."

We see in today's readings how pleased God is with his "satisfied customers." They are the people who believe he is in charge of their lives. They trust him not only in good times but in bad. Their hearts are full of gratitude, and they know how to spice their prayer with cries of thanksgiving.

If a poll-taker asked the question, "What is the missing virtue of our day?", *thankfulness* might well be one of the answers. Day after day advertisements try to inflame us with so many desires we can forget the blessings we have.

Today's readings are meant to stir in our hearts the prayer of thanksgiving. Jesus is clearly distressed that only one in ten of the lepers he healed returned to give thanks. In the Our Father Jesus included the four element of prayer: Praise, thanksgiving, repentance and petition. He wants us to repent, he wants us to ask, but he also wants us to praise and give thanks.

Naaman the Syrian of the first reading was not a Jew or a believer; but being a leper he went in desperation to ask the Jewish prophet, Elisha, to heal him. The condensed reading we heard omits much of the drama. The prophet told Naaman to bathe in the

Jordan seven times. Naaman went away angry, proclaiming that back in Syria he had better rivers to bathe in than that mud-hole of a Jordan! But his servants reasoned with him, arguing that he should do the easy thing the prophet asked. He did, and "his flesh became as the flesh of a little child," and his leprosy was gone. So Naaman went through a process: He petitioned, disbelieved, criticized, obeyed, was healed, and became a believer so full of thanksgiving he went back with his whole retinue to thank the prophet and offer him a gift. We too have to work at being grateful.

In the Gospel reading Jesus is particularly distressed that of the ten lepers whom he healed the only one who returned was a non-Jew. There is a serious lesson in this. Converts are often far more grateful for the gift of faith than people of the household of God who have been given the gift all their lives. Don't we all tend to take for granted what we've always had, as though it was ours by right? It's a foolish thing to do. St. Paul says pointedly, "What do you have that you have not received?" The longer we've had our gifts, the more grateful we should be.

A group of modern Jews have given us a beautiful example of gratitude. During the holocaust, most Christians seem to have done little or nothing to rescue the Jews. But some did risk their very lives to save them. The Jewish Rabbi Harold Schulweis began to search out and honor the righteous gentiles who came to the rescue. Another Jew, Pierre Sauvage, has founded an organization that searches out these rescuers and helps them financially if they themselves are now in need.

When rescuers were asked why they helped, and non-rescuers were asked why they didn't help, a thought-provoking fact came to light. Some non-helpers said they didn't help because they know who crucified Jesus. Some who risked their lives to help said, "I did it because Jesus was a Jew, and these are his people." So let me ask a question: Which of these Christians was grateful, grateful not only to Jesus but to Mary and Peter and Paul and all the early Jews who built up the Church of Christ?

Now let's consider some of the causes we have for thanksgiving. The first cause is suggested by the story of Naaman. Leprosy is a natural symbol of sin, and the washing in the Jordan is a natural symbol of everything that removes sin. For us, that means Christ's sacraments of baptism and penance.

Do we act like Naaman who, angered by the simplicity of the prophet's remedy, first refused to wash in the Jordan? To reject a gift is the worst ingratitude. Do we confess our sins as often as we need to, and give thanks to God from the heart? Any one who doesn't may have stopped believing what a dreadful thing sin is — worse than leprosy. Leprosy can't block our way to eternal life; sin can and does. Do we all, like the Good Leper, go show ourselves to the priest, and come back praising God?

Have we ever drifted away from giving thanks for the Mass and the Eucharist, gifts so great we can never be grateful enough? Pope John Paul II called it "the mystery of mysteries." He said that to accept it is to accept the whole mystery of Christ and the Church with its doctrine of redemption, Holy Sacrifice, consecrated priesthood, and all the rest. The Mass contains the death and resurrection of Christ our Life. The body of Christ is the "Trojan Horse" beyond all others. Death greedily admitted his body into its walls, but on the third day the walls fell forever, and Christ came forth in risen glory with death lying slain behind him. Do we give thanks by visiting him risen and present in the Blessed Sacrament? Do we participate daily if possible in the Holy Sacrifice of the Mass, our most glorious prayer of thanksgiving?

Our Lord is showing us how much he desires prayer of thanksgiving. We should never stop praying for forgiveness and the healing of the leprosy of sin; but never omit praise and thanksgiving to God for his goodness and mercy.

Reflect for a moment on ingratitude's destructive effect, and the upbuilding effect of gratitude. Negative persons think to upbuild themselves by tearing others down. But the person who feels God has given him nothing will soon come to believe he is nothing.

The person who is always praising God sooner or later realizes he is something special: He has all the gifts for which he's praising God! That leads to self-appreciation. If we want to be praisers, we can keep in practice by praising not only God but all in whom we see good, especially those close to us.

When we receive our Lord in the Eucharist today, let's vie with one another in seeing who can offer him from the heart the most glorious prayer of thanksgiving.

"C" — Twenty-ninth Sunday of the Year

Ex 17:8-13
2 Tm 3:14 - 4:2
Lk 18:1-8

PRAYER, THE ROAD TO FOOL-PROOF JOY

The author Sigrid Undsett, in her great novel, *Kristin Lavransdotter*, recounts a fable that is a perfect lesson in how to be unhappy. It is Christmas day. A mother is weeping because all she has to feed her brood of seven is the little scrap of pork on the table. St. Olav drops in, sees her need and prays, and Lo! There on the table is a whole roast pig. The mother stares at the pig — and weeps because she has no plates.

In the Opening Prayer we begged God for the joy of happy followers of Christ. Now we do our part to find that joy. The readings tell us how. We come to joy by learning through prayer to carry the cross with Christ, by finding in Scripture wisdom and food for prayer, and by persevering in prayer.

First, we learn through prayer how to carry the cross with Christ. In the first reading, Moses teaches us how. He is at war with Amalek. Amalek is a symbol of all anti-God forces. Moses raises his arms in prayer. Now we have a symbol of the cross.

As long as Moses holds up his arms, that is, shares the cross with Christ, he and his people defeat the anti-God forces. When he lets his arms fall, refuses to carry the cross, he begins to lose the war. We too have the victory when we carry the cross with Christ. We learn in prayer to carry the cross.

Did you notice Moses couldn't do it himself alone? Aaron the priest held up one of Moses' arms, and Hur the warrior the other. The priest in us must make the offering of prayer to God; the warrior in us must fight against all the anti-God forces in our hearts: selfishness, disbelief, desire to abandon our obligations to prayer and to the Church, and to give up the fight against sin. To carry the cross means never to give up.

Second, we must find in Scripture wisdom and food for prayer. Only Scripture can guide us to the promised land. As Paul says so clearly in that second reading, Scripture is inspired of God, and useful for every good work. It teaches us how to pray. Christian prayer is not a human invention. Divine revelation is the very substance of our prayer. We pray over God's truths.

Jesus taught us new depths of prayer. Prayer over Scripture teaches us fidelity to the word of God and his Church. Scripture confirms our faith in what the Church teaches because we find its teaching there. While the Church inherited the Old Testament, the Church itself wrote the New Testament under God's inspiration. To pray well, go to the Scriptures daily, and chew them like food. When you find a passage you love, memorize it and say it over and over during the day. It works wonders.

Beware the preacher or teacher who doesn't clearly reflect the word of God and his Church! Jesus says in today's Gospel, ''When the Son of Man comes, will he find any faith on the earth?'' Prayer over the Scriptures undoes the unbelief we contract by contagion. We discover our turnings from God's word, our pretense that we have the true faith when in fact we don't. Don't be like some who, when they make these painful discoveries, turn cowards and run from true prayer.

All of that symbolism in the first reading is telling us of the struggle of prayer. When Moses wearied, he rested on the rock. The rock is Christ. Scriptural prayer rests on that same Rock. Through the use of Scripture, God is our teacher in prayer.

Prayer is a great privilege. We draw ever closer to God; we learn that God walks with us as he did with Abraham and Moses and Mary. Though we can all say with the lips that God is love, prayer teaches our hearts to feel it. The Divine Lover draws us to the Eucharist where he comes to each of us in that personal relationship which is the highest gift of God. But not the only gift: Scriptural prayer teaches us the ways of salvation; it reproves us, corrects us; it trains us in holiness, and in how to do every good work. We discover in prayer that despite appearance the world is losing the war; God is in charge. And that is joy.

Finally, we must learn persevering prayer. Isn't the conduct of the widow in Jesus' parable an example of just the way we act in daily life? When we really want something, we go after it until we get it. Do the same, Jesus is saying, in prayer.

There's an interesting sidelight in the parable. The judge is hard-hearted and uncaring. When prayer goes unanswered, do we have a sneaking suspicion God is that way? Is that why Jesus uses the figure? We have to persist in prayer not because God is hard-hearted, but because we may be. We ask God to do our will while we're not even doing his! We don't know it because we blackjack our consciences about the truth. When we persist in prayer we discover the truth and convert to the Heart of Christ.

We persevere in prayer not just for ourselves but for all. We're supposed to love all people. Prayer is really the only way we can do it practically. By prayer we can reach out to every creature. Don't think it's presumptuous. Tell our Lord that since he commanded you to love all, he has to hear your prayer for all. You can be a missionary to the world, a missionary of prayer, without leaving home. The Little Flower, St. Therese of the Child Jesus, prayed so hard for the missions she was made world patron of missions though she never left her Carmelite monastery.

A perfect mission prayer is the Daily Offering recommended by the Apostleship of Prayer, the League of the Sacred Heart. Each morning we offer Jesus our day. We offer it through the Heart of his Mother, Mary. We offer every prayer, work, joy and suffering for all the intentions of his Sacred Heart, in union with his Holy Sacrifice, and for the intention of our Holy Father. That is prayer for the world. It helps bring the civilization of love, the kingdom of the Heart of Christ.

That brings up daily forms of prayer. You surely know we should pray on rising; and examine our conscience and make an Act of Contrition before going to bed. In between, we pray at meals; and if we obey Jesus' injunction, we pray always. What does that mean? It means to breathe little prayers when we can during the day. And then try to act in a way that pleases God in everything. If we have that intention in our hearts, we are praying always.

The great teacher of prayer St. Teresa of Avila says we should keep before our eyes the loving Jesus; and if he impresses his love on our hearts we'll easily and effortlessly do what he wants and even do great things. And that is joy, the kind of joy we should find now as we turn to Jesus in Mass and Eucharist.

"C" — Thirtieth Sunday of the Year

Si 35:12-14, 16-18
2 Tm 4:6-8, 16-18
Lk 18:9-14

HOW TO PRAY AND NOT TO PRAY

The eminent Protestant theologian, Karl Barth, wrote many treatises that helped bring Christians closer to unity. But he didn't take his work over-seriously. He pictured the angels looking down and smiling indulgently on him as he went about with the wheelbarrow-full of books he had written. Let us picture Barth going round the world with his collection of books crying, "Who will trade me eternal life for my wonderful books?"

That kind of nonsense is just what Barth pictured the angels smiling about, but he was not guilty of it. The Pharisee in Jesus' parable was. At first glance, it looks as though the parable is meant to teach humility. But in fact it goes much deeper; Jesus is teaching the proper attitude toward God, especially in prayer. So we will reflect on humility and prayer. We took up prayer last week, but this week we will go deeper.

Why is humility so important when face to face with God? Because humility is nothing but the truth! The word *humble* comes from the word *humus*, earth. To be humble is to know that dust we are and to dust we shall return. Resurrection can only come from God. That's why God says in Jeremiah that one who puts his trust in human beings is cursed. And that's why, when the Jews asked Jesus what work they needed to do to be saved, Jesus said, "This is the work of God, that you believe in the one he sent."

Pride is folly. If you have money you'll spend it, lose it, or leave it behind. Beauty fades like the grass. As to virtue or intelligence, can they ward off death? Pride destroys brotherly love and childlike prayer for salvation. We're no more than children of the cosmos. Only God the Father can rescue us. Pride blocks faith and submission to God and the Church.

Paul speaks of the "obedience of faith." Faith is the *present* of the mind to God. We believe in order to know as God knows. The proud can't do it. They prefer their own opinions. They cut themselves off from God's word and the Church's faith. They become heretics. Contrast them with St. Thomas Aquinas, a theologian of the greatest learning, wisdom, and prayerfulness. As he grew in prayer he wanted to burn his wheelbarrow-full of books like so much chaff. Three days before he died, he received the sacrament of the body and blood of Christ and said, "I have taught and written much on the Most Holy Body and on the other sacraments, according to my faith in Christ and the Holy Roman Church, to whose judgment I submit all my teaching." Such humble faith can be gained only through deep prayer.

The Pharisee and the tax collector stand for meditation and contemplation, the two stages of mental prayer. Mental prayer is prayer in which we pray with thoughts and affections, not with memorized words. In meditation we think about, and talk to God about, the truths of faith. In contemplation we simply give our attention to God whom we know by faith is with us.

The Pharisee was meditating, but his thoughts went wrong. He thought himself a deeply religious man. In a way, he was. His fault lay in picking and choosing what he would believe and practice of God's law. He didn't keep God's whole law, especially the law of love of neighbor. What if he had prayed like this: "Lord, thanks for helping me struggle to be honest, to fast, and to support the synagogue as I ought. But now help me to find the virtues I lack — the sorrow for my sins which this tax collector clearly has; and compassion for people like him who work in trades that make them so susceptible to dishonesty." If he had prayed that way, he would have been praying truthfully. Humility is not supposed to destroy our self-esteem, but to purify it.

To pray well we need truth and humility. When our Lady sang her Canticle of Praise, she said of God, "He has looked upon his handmaid's lowliness." In other words, he liked her humility. But Mary also says, "The Mighty One has done great things for me." She faced her nothingness without God, and rejoiced in the wonder God was making her. Humility is the truth about both.

Now let's make a meditation of our own on the parable: Lord, you teach us to come to you in the truth of what we are, and of what we need. I need you, Lord Jesus. I need your company, as you lived with your disciples on earth. You came to them in the resurrection, and promised to be with us. Come to me, I pray.

Help me, Lord! My sins are saying to me, "Fool! Do you think you're worthy of such things?" Father in heaven, I offer you the blood of Jesus on the cross to wash away all my sins.

Now my faithless self says, "So you think your poor prayer will be heard?" Father, I offer you Jesus' prayer as my prayer.

Now my cold heart objects, "Why should he come to you, lover of the world? What love do you have to offer him?" Jesus, you gave me to Mary, and Mary to me. I offer you her heart afire. Touch it to mine. Kindle mine with love for you. You won't refuse my prayer, Lord Jesus. It is the best I have to offer. Amen.

Now let us turn to the tax collector as a symbol of contemplative prayer. In this prayer we simply believe in God's presence, and dwell there, like the tax collector. He says the same words over and over. Often we use no words at all as contemplative prayer grows in us. We begin with Scripture, with the promise of Jesus: "Whoever loves me will keep my word and the Father will love him and we will come to him and make our dwelling with him." We say, "Lord, that's what I want, your presence, friend to friend. I know you keep your promise. I'll just stay here without a word, living in your presence as you live in mine. If it pleases you to make me feel your presence, I will be glad. If not, I'll be happy to know of it just by faith, for I have given you the present of my mind. I believe."

Many people spend hours in this kind of prayer, either in their rooms, or before the Blessed Sacrament. And if God pleases, he makes his presence felt to them as truly as you can feel a child you hold in your arms. This is the gift of mystical prayer. It is not given to all, and generally it is given only after years of mental prayer.

We all have a still greater gift of prayer, the prayerful offering of the Mass, and the reception of Jesus in the Eucharist. I'll close with a prayer to the Lord about that: Lord, as we turn to the Mass now, we renew our petition of the Opening Prayer for an increase of faith hope and love to do your will and come to share the life you promise. Amen.

Rv 7:2-4, 9-14
1 Jn 3:1-3
Mt 5:1-12

THE DAY TO LOOK HOMEWARD

If I told you that you were going to be a saint, you might smile and think, ''He doesn't know me.'' So, too, did Abraham chuckle in his beard when at the age of 100 he was told he would father a son; so, too, did Sarah his wife laugh when she heard she was to conceive and give birth at 90. But parents they did become, and they called their son Isaac, which means ''laughed.''

Today the saints we celebrate are spelled with a small ''s.'' They include all who have made it to heaven; and we ourselves are on the way. I hope you pray often to the Saint whose name you bear: St. John, St. Mary, or whoever. Today, address yourself and say, ''Hello, St. Mary, or ''Hello, St. John.'' How does it feel? Laugh if you will, but be a saint you will. It's the only way to enter ''the city which is to come.'' What we leave undone on earth we'll do the hard way in the ''finishing school'' called purgatory, the place we consider tomorrow on the Commemoration of All Souls.

We are the families of the Family of Saints. Today we lift our eyes to see our whole family, the family of God. Families on earth are the Church militant, doing the works of love and fighting the spiritual battles for God; those in purgatory are the Church undergoing the final purification; those in glory are the Church triumphant. From their box seats they're cheering and praying us on. We're one for all and all for one. This is the vision of the meaning of our lives and our tasks. Our lives have the same meaning as theirs had, and lead us to the same home.

If you're still afraid to believe, pay attention to that vision of St. John in the first reading. Before God's throne stand a huge crowd beyond counting. Do you think they were all great heros or heroines on earth? Far from it! Most were ordinary people. One dentist has a sign in his window, "We cater to cowards." So does the Church. Look closely at John's crowd. You will see yourself there, for John's vision was of the future.

Let's remember today that each human family and the whole human family and the family of the saints and angels are a created likeness of the family of the Holy Trinity. The Holy Trinity are our true heaven and home.

The Church is made up of ordinary families, and those families are the seedbed of saints. So special are some saints that they only discourage us; but look closer and get a different picture. Forget their triumphs which we hear so much about. Look at their struggles, sins and failures. Look closely at St. Peter, head of the whole Church. Find a man who denied Christ when Christ needed him most, and only later proved faithful.

The saints had ordinary human parents like us. They shared our trials, darkness, doubts, concerns about how to put food on the table and pay the bills. They had our difficulties, sins, weaknesses. Many turned only gradually to the Lord, and some only on their death bed. They know all about life's ups and downs. It's easy to object that we're different, we're weak, but it's all wrong! St. Paul learned that God is so marvelous he delights especially in glorifying weak and ordinary folk. Ask Mary.

From the beginning of the Church most Christians came from ordinary families. Even the Holy Family looked just like other families to the people of Nazareth. And in many ways they were. They worked for a living, had a poor home, were friendly with neighbors, and did the other ordinary things. The difference is that they did it all for God, and did none of the wrong things. To save the world Jesus lived with Mary for 30 of his 33 years. Then family life must be important beyond measure. Jesus offered all his prayers, works, joys and sufferings of those years to the Father for the world's redemption. We can do the same.

Each Christian family is a miniature of the whole family of the saints. In each family we can often find a comparison with the three stages of the whole family of God. One member is doing good works like the Church militant on earth; one is suffering some ordeal like the Church suffering in purgatory; one is presently finding things easy, like the Church triumphant.

The saints in heaven, including family and friends who were once with us on earth, are praying up a storm for us. If parents and friends were concerned for us on earth, how much more are they praying for us now, when they have no other concerns? Ask their prayers; pray to your loved ones who have gone before you.

Thoughts of our great family in God should inspire us to a deeper love of our families on earth. Are we neglecting anyone? Is any member sad and in need of love? Or in trouble and in need of help and prayers? Do we help them by practicing the beatitudes in our family life? Do we remain poor in spirit, not demanding a lot? Do we sorrow with the suffering, and keep a lowly profile so as not to rouse jealousy? Are we merciful? Do we inspire them by our single-hearted concern for the things of God?

Today we should trust that we belong to the number of the saints we celebrate. In today's psalm we say, "Lord, this is the people that longs to see your face." Each of us should ask the question, "Lord, do I long to see your face?" What lover doesn't?

None of us is far from seeing God's face. What is a lifetime but a fleeting thing? Senior citizens already have one foot in heaven and the other on a banana peel. And if we're living the beatitudes, we're already close to God in holiness as well.

Sometimes world conditions make us doubt Christ's power. St. John's vision ought to dispel that doubt. See through his eyes the billions Christ has won for God by his victory. At the Last Supper he said, "Don't be afraid; I have overcome the world." Here we are building the civilization of love, the kingdom of the Heart of Christ. In heaven the building is complete.

Let us give the Lord love and honor and glory by telling him from the heart that we long to see his face. Live each Sunday faithfully, close to God. It is a dress rehearsal for our eternal Sabbath. It gives us insight into and longing for heaven that increases our faith. Old age is a long Sabbath that is a special gift of preparation for heaven. Use it well.

We close with the thought that we're closest to the saints and loved ones in heaven when we're celebrating together the Eucharistic Sacrifice of praise to God. How close are we, then, when we receive in the Eucharist the same Lord with whom they are united in heaven! Today, when we receive him, let us look homeward and say, "Lord, I long to see your face."

"ABC" — All Souls: First Mass

Dn 12:1-3 (Lect. 789-6)
Ps 23:1-3, 3-4, 5,6 (791-1)
Rm 8:31-35, 37-39 (790-6)
Jn 17:24-26 (793-17)

THE ALMIGHTY TO THE RESCUE

Some years ago (1986) Buffalonians were bombarded with news of an epic marine disaster in the mighty Niagara River. An immense barge had broken loose, swept down the swift river, and crashed into an abutment of the Peace Bridge. Entangled with the abutment, the barge battered it like a mighty mallet in the hands of the waves. The bridge between the U.S. and Canada was threatened. Crews set to work trying to remove the barge.

If you ever took a speed boat up river, you'd understand their problem. It takes a powerful motor just to cancel out the rush of the downstream current. As you pass under the bridge you see the water swirling by, leaping up the abutments. The waters are moving, you are moving, and the very abutments seem to be in giddy motion. How work in such conditions?

For ages Christians have compared with a marine disaster the human condition brought about by the sin of our first parents.

The bridge between heaven and earth was severed.

Busy as bees, we the survivors dike ourselves in and try to forget the cosmic disaster. Then an unwelcome caller sweeps away all our dikes and plunges us back into the maelstrom. The caller is death. You see the shipwreck written on faces at a funeral: grief, shock, confusion, incomprehension, and questions: Why us? Why our loved one? The questions are only more dikes, warding off the more fundamental question: Why death? For once there is death, the question, "Why us" is no more meaningful than, "Why not us?" Before the cosmic dimensions of this shipwreck all our efforts are futile, all our science impotent.

Let's return to the Niagara. Men like ants on the high bridge lower machines. The scene resembles children at work with a huge erector set, getting nowhere. But what if a voice from the sky proclaims, "Children, it's time for supper," and a great hand reaches down, lifts out the barge, and ends the crisis?

This is essentially what God has done for us in our cosmic shipwreck. In prophecy after prophecy he promised to send us a Savior. In the fullness of time he sent him, born of the Virgin Mary. He died for our sins as Scripture foretold, and rose as Scripture had prophesied. He ascended to the Father and with him awaits us. In the course of his salvage operation, he re-routed death into eternity and resurrection. Death is now the road home to the Father. This is the true plot of the story of human life.

Today we remember our loved ones who took the road home before us. We know of the final stop-off called purgatory, and so we offer this Holy Sacrifice in expiation for their sins. We offer it to speed their way to the Heart of the Savior.

As Daniel foretold in that first reading, and as the Gospels confirm, resurrection will reclaim all to life. For some there will be eternal glory, and for others eternal disgrace. Trusting in the great mercy of God, we pray with hope for those who have gone before us. Take confidence! The Church refuses to say that even Judas has been lost.

One year, after a Mass on All Souls Day, a parishioner asked the priest, ''What does this 'they will rest in peace' mean?'' It's an interesting question because too many people think of heaven's peace as such boring inactivity that the other place sounds more interesting. So lets give a little thought to what it does mean.

If, to a little child who had never seen a farm you gave a grain of corn and said, ''Plant this and see what happens,'' he'd be in for an interesting experience. He might think a big grain of corn is going to come up. Instead, he sees a shoot rising in due time, and then ears on the shoot and finally the beautiful corn stalk with its ears of corn full of grains. St. Paul uses a similar comparison to describe our risen bodies. They will be full of surprises, and more glorious than anything we can imagine. And the activities we will be able to engage in will be even more surprising. The word *peace* in the Scriptures does not mean a lack of activity, but only a lack of disorder, sin and suffering. It means the fullness of all the joys God intends.

St. Paul makes another statement that allows me to assure you that if you think of what you like most, heaven's activities will be incomparably more pleasing to you. Paul says, ''Eye has not seen, nor ear heard, nor has it entered into the heart of man, what God has prepared for those who love him.'' Surely, we know less of the joys of God than a child knows of the joys of grownups; yet it is in the very life of God that we will share. These are the mysteries that are in the background of the feast we celebrate.

And if we but will, we shall share them. If we cling to our Good Shepherd as we long to do, and repent if we fall, nothing can stop us from getting home. Nothing can stand in the way of the power of God who loves us. As St. Paul says with such powerful logic, ''If God is for us, who can be against us?'' If a child can assemble things with an erector set, what cannot God, the Author of Life, set in order by his almighty power?

Paul says we are ''more than victors.'' It's a challenging phrase. What does it mean? Doesn't it means that now God has stepped into the picture, there's no contest? That worn out old lion the devil still frightens us with his roar, but he's impotent. His teeth have been worn away biting futilely against the wood of the cross. He has no power to defeat us. Everything is in God's hands and ours. We need only struggle. If we fall, God is our safety net. He will catch us. Disaster is impossible.

Jesus waits for us with love. At the Last Supper he expressed his longing to have us with him, as we heard in the Gospel reading: ''Father, all those you gave me I would have in my company . . . to see this glory of mine.'' We have believed in his glory. He wants us to see it and adore him.

God wills it; we need only will it, and nothing in life or death, present or future, can block our route home or prevent us from arriving. Jesus is our Resurrection and our Justification. Who would want to be in the shoes of Satan arguing with him? It is with this same confidence that we pray for our dear ones who have gone before us, and ask our Lady to intercede for them. In that confidence we turn to the Mass and look to the Eucharist, that foretaste of the joys that await us.

''ABC'' — All Souls: Second Mass

2 M 12:43-45 (Lect. 789-7)
Ps 42:2, 3, 5; 43:3, 4, 5 (791-4)
2 Cor 5:1, 6-10 (790-10)
Mt 25:31-46 (793-4)

A SOUL'S JOURNEY: PURGATORY TO PARADISE

Yesterday we celebrated the whole sweep of the saints from earth to heaven; today we use our ''Zoom Lens'' of faith to focus on the Church suffering, the souls in Purgatory.

Purgatory is likely the next road-stop on our journey to

eternity; it is also where some of our dear ones may now be. We're interested; and doubly so, because one of the few certainties about Purgatory is that we can do much to aid souls there and to bypass it ourselves or at least shorten our stay. In the Mass today we pray that their sins may be washed away so they can enter into the joys of eternal life. As we heard in the first reading, the pre-Christian Jews too sacrificed for their dead.

Purgatory comes from the Latin, "cleansing fire." Even the name involves mystery, as we'll see. It is the condition after death where those who die in the state of grace make any expiation still due for their sins.

When we sin, we offend God and mar his creation. We need to be forgiven and to heal the wounds on self and others by penance and good works. When we die, each is judged by his deeds and treated accordingly, as Jesus says in our Gospel reading, and Paul in that second reading. Those blessed with the lot of heaven can't yet enter if they have unrepented venial sins, or owe a debt of penance they neglected to do on earth. Scripture says of the City where God dwells, "Nothing profane shall enter it, nor anyone who is a liar or has done a detestable act."

God is both merciful and just. Not to seek his overflowing mercy in this life is to face his justice in the next; to refuse our full share of Jesus' redemptive suffering now is to postpone it and do it the hard way in Purgatory. St. Augustine begged God to cleanse him in this life, so he wouldn't have to have it done the hard way by the cleansing fire St. Paul speaks of when he talks of those "who are to be saved, yet so as by fire."

Now let us look at the privileged, strange and terrible state of Purgatory. It is a privileged state. These souls have been judged worthy of eternal life. They can no longer be lost as we can. It is a strange state. It is outside of time and place, which have to do with bodies. These are disembodied souls, stripped by death. It is a terrible state. We, the Church militant, do spiritual battle for Christ, but we have many pleasures and consolations. The suffering souls in Purgatory undergo the final purgation stripped of every material comfort.

What is their suffering like? Is it by actual fire? The Church leaves the question open. We're free to believe either way. But many theologians are convinced the soul's pain is purely spiritual. The Council of Trent forbade exaggerated, uncertain, frightening teaching on Purgatory. In that spirit we proceed.

God has judged them worthy to be his beloved children forever. They will enter his home as soon as they're ready. What is required to make them ready? Let's imagine an actual case. John hears from his divine Judge he is worthy of eternal life! His heart, bursting with joy, longs to behold God. Then, in the flame of God's love, he sees them — his sordid, ugly wounds from venial sins never repented, and his debt of unpaid good deeds he owed for his forgiven sins. He can't go to God like that!

How did he fail to see the twistedness of clinging to money, the ugliness of not going where love called him to serve?

He pours out his contrition, shamed by the trifles that drew him from God. Now he burns with love for God but his will is like a tree bent too long by the winds of selfishness. With wrenching effort he tries to straighten it. It resists, as if he were arm-wrestling with himself. Now flashes the remembrance of the thousands along the river banks of his life crying for the help he too often refused. Behind them hangs Christ crucified whom he refused in them. Here, there is no dinner bell, no cool drink, no night of rest to distract him from this terrible awareness.

Nor does he want to turn from his sins. He faces them. Love wells up, making his sorrow bottomless. From now on he'll do what is right! Then comes the stunning realization: He will indeed, but can no longer receive merit for doing it from faith, because now he *knows* there is a God. He has seen the Judge. Nor does he have any choice but to suffer. There is no material thing to tempt him, and the grace and love of the Holy Spirit are so full now that temptation is impossible. Here he is only paying his debt as he must. Hardly can he bear this sorrow, that he left so much good undone, and failed to help so many. And yet, he'd willingly bear still more to cry out to God and his creation his desire to heal all he has wounded. And how he thirsts for God!

He's so absorbed he fails to sense the dawning change. Then radiance flows from him. Divine hands reach down and draw him up. Suffering is over forever. He is with and within the Glory.

Is this a fictional concept of Purgatory? Not likely. St. Catherine of Genoa thought that Purgatory's "Fire" is God's love finally taking flame in souls too waterlogged with creature comforts to burn with it in this life. Her experiences as a mystic made her see that mystical experiences are the closest parallel to Purgatory. The mystic's soul, illumined by the light of God's loving presence, is drawn almost irresistibly, yet hangs back, tortured by its own sinfulness exposed by the divine light. St. Catherine's interpretation is theologically sound.

We should make intercession for the souls in Purgatory, especially our loved ones. We can do much by prayer, by attending Mass, by having Masses offered for them; we can also give to the poor and do other good works they omitted. These are most pleasing to the Blessed Trinity, for they help to bring the civilization of love that is the Kingdom of the Heart of Christ. And on this feast we can gain a plenary indulgence for a poor soul by a devout visit to a Church, where we recite the Our Father and the Creed, make sacramental confession, receive Holy Communion, and pray for the Holy Father.

It's a holy and pious thought to pray for our dead. We speed them to the Heart of Jesus and the arms of our Lady and the Church Triumphant, to the glory of the Father. When we're close to Jesus in Holy Communion today, let's not forget the sufferers in Purgatory. Be sure they won't forget us. They are saints.

THE FAITH THAT UNDERLIES CONVERSION

Toward the end of the last decade the New York Times carried an unusual op-ed article on spiritual conversion by a man of the baby-boom generation. He cited statistics showing that many of his age group had grown more spiritual in the last five years. It was his experience that "the deliverances of life lead us to the idea that God loves the world and acts within space and time." He saw that grace was active "whenever much is done with little." And family life came into the picture. He observed that "babies focus love and so offer healing." He was reminded of the saying of the author Willa Cather that "Wherever there is great love, there are always miracles."

Today's Gospel is about conversion to a deeper life with God. Has it occurred to you that the reason we don't live a life more afire with God is that our faith is weak? Even if we don't doubt God's existence, we may not really believe that he loves us personally and passionately. Zacchaeus' conversion prompts us to reflect on the reasons for our faith in God and his love for us.

The first reason is the evidence from creation. The Book of Wisdom condemns as foolish those people who from the good things seen do not come to know the good God who created them; and from the works of creation do not come to appreciate the Creator. St. Paul adds that God's power and divinity are evident through the things he made, and God is angry with those who pretend otherwise. In our own time science claims to have traced the origin of the universe all the way back to the "Big Bang." This discovery all the more makes the mind look for the First Cause of that marvelous event, and find it in God alone.

The next reason for our faith in God is God's revealed word to us in Scripture. Faith is belief in God and his truths on the basis of God's own testimony. From the happenings foretold by God in Scripture, and from their fulfillment, we have evidence of his infinite wisdom and power and love and goodness.

Our Catholic faith is founded on the life of Christ and the divinity revealed in him. He embodies everything good that the Scriptures said of God in the Old Testament. His solitary life has changed and is changing the world more and more each age. His disciples said to him, "Now we realize that you know everything . . . Because of this we believe that you came from God." And after his resurrection, Thomas said, "My Lord and my God!"

The moral miracle of the Church is a further reason for strong faith. Despite her sinners and crises of faith and attacks on her doctrine even from within, she speaks her truth and produces her saints age after age. God himself testifies to his Church and his saints by miracles only he can work.

Finally, we grow in faith from the experience of divine providence overseeing our lives, as that *New York Times* writer said. The inspired author of today's first reading is reflecting on that same experience, and precisely along the lines of conversion as Zacchaeus experienced it. The Lord and lover of souls who fashioned everything, he says, loves everything he has made, or why make it, or preserve it? He spares us and blames us for our sins only with discretion and care, even overlooking them until we're able to take his correction. Someone we live with and love may always be throwing up our faults in our face, and that only makes for bitterness and despair. God does not do that. He is patient; he gives us time. His corrections come from pure love, not from his own hang-ups, as ours often do. He wants us not only to have faith, but to witness to it as practicing Catholics.

Patience is not easy. One dentist said to his priest-patient, "I tell people how to save their teeth, but it goes in one ear and out the other." God might have said to that dentist what the priest said:

''You have an experience much like me. I tell people how to save their souls, and it goes in one ear and out the other. Keep up the good work, as I do.''

We're invited today to take a lesson from Zacchaeus. He was a business man, a tax collector accused of crookedness. He had faith, but wasn't living it well. Probably he didn't believe God was really interested in him. But when he heard of Jesus, and heard he was in town, something stirred deep in him. The stories they told about this man! The love that radiated from him! The healing power of that love! He had to learn more. But when he got out there, he was lost in the crowd because he was such a little man. So he climbed a tree as he did when he was a boy. It couldn't have been easy, but it was worth it anyway.

Jesus saw him and invited him down. We can imagine his excitement and be sure he dropped down fast — perhaps right into Jesus' arms! Jesus invited himself to his home. That started the critics carping. With all the deserving people in town, why honor this bum? Is this Jesus really all he's said to be? But Zacchaeus came through. He's going to give half his wealth to the poor. Anyone he may have cheated will get it back four times over. Picture the line of claimants at his door that offer generated. How his wonderful conversion justified Jesus' love for him!

Paul prays in that second reading that we too may be converted and become worthy of our call. Then we'll glorify God and draw others to him as Zacchaeus still does. How do we glorify God except through living by his loving commandments?

Be aware that just when we try most, the devil most attacks our faith. One young woman said, ''I read the Bible daily. It's amazing how the more I read the more Satan works on me trying to tell me God isn't real. He never used to do that when I was living so sinfully.'' No, he was too satisfied with her.

If we believe enough in the Son of God's love, we'll act like Zacchaeus. The miracle of love will take hold of us too. We'll look daily into his divine face, gaze at the wound in his side, and awake to the love and joy that holds nothing back. We'll understand Jesus where he says that the ones who observe his commandments are the ones who love him. That was surely what Zacchaeus did. It's what every true lover does.

Today when Jesus visits our town and parish by descending on our altar, he will say to each of us, "I mean to stay at your house today." Make no mistake about it: His offer of coming to us in Holy Communion is a greater gift than his visit to Zacchaeus. Will we justify his goodness to us as nobly as did Zacchaeus? Zacchaeus, what a challenge you've set us!

"ABC" — Dedication of St. John Lateran

Ezk 43:1-2, 4-7 (Lect. 701-6)
Ps 95:1-2, 3-5, 6-7 (703-3)
1 Cor 3:9-13, 16-17 (704-1)
Jn 2:13-22 (706-3)

GOD'S HOME AND OURS

Why, with all the problems we have to solve and the truths of faith to meditate, do we set aside this Sunday to commemorate the dedication of a church? Why do it even if the church we commemorate is the basilica of St. John Lateran, even if it is the cathedral of the Holy Father in Rome, even if it was originally built over 1,600 years ago, and has come to be called the mother church of Christianity? It's a good question. Be sure the Church has a good answer. I can best head us toward the answer by asking another question: What is religion all about? Is it not about coming home? About God coming to our home, and we to his? The cathedral of St. John Lateran, and every church, including our own, is an expression of that coming home to God.

Each church, and The Church, *is the home of God.* Of course, as the Old Testament already makes clear, God Almighty doesn't really dwell in buildings. But he is present in a special way in our churches, consecrated places where we his people come to pray and offer sacrifice. Our church is the home of our parish family. Great artists, architects and craftsmen have built our finest churches to help us express the awe we should feel toward God.

Awe is a feeling of wonder tinged with reverential fear in the presence of the sublime and the mysterious. A woman under instruction in the faith expressed this awe when taken into the parish church by a priest. Told that she was before the presence of the Son of God in the Blessed Sacrament, she exclaimed, "Then why don't we fall down on our hands and knees!"

Devout Catholics show awe and reverence in Church by outer and inner silence, devout attitude, and genuflection before the Blessed Sacrament. Where awe and reverence are lacking, faith lacks deep roots and edifies no one. Can strangers to our faith think the irreverent believe what they profess? Won't they at best consider them religious savages who have no sense of the honor and reverence due to Almighty God? Go to the Last Supper Room in Jerusalem. See the reverence of pilgrims there. Realize that our church is a Last Supper Room with Christ present.

In a larger sense each of our churches stands for the whole Catholic Church throughout the world. It is the Church where God speaks, for Jesus said, "He who hears you hears me." It is the Church of unity under the Pope and bishops as successors of Peter and the Apostles. It is the people of God to whom Jesus promised, "I am with you all days." All of this is what we celebrate today.

If a church is a home of God, then each child of God is a living church. You heard Christ speaking of his own body as the Temple of God. In the hymn which begins, "Mary the dawn," we find the phrase, "Mary the temple, Christ the temple's Lord." Our bodies, like Mary's, are temples of God. You heard Paul say we are God's building, God's temple, the home of the Holy Spirit. In fact, we are the temple of Father, Son and Holy Spirit.

Over the ages, the Basilica of St. John Lateran was damaged

by earthquakes, fire and sword. It even collapsed from neglect; yet it was always restored. We see in this a likeness to the whole Church and to each of us. In his day, St. Francis of Assisi was called by God to restore the collapsing Church. Pope John Paul II has been restoring the collapsing faith of our day. Each of us too has been damaged by the spiritual earthquakes and fire and sword of sin. To be restored we need to use the spiritual construction equipment of prayer, sacrifice and confession.

Be sure to get the picture. If you walked into this church consecrated to God and found it full of filth, wouldn't you be shocked? What if God came into any of us consecrated to him by creation and baptism and the Eucharist and found the filth of moral corruption? Wouldn't he be shocked and outraged? In today's Gospel Jesus is angry because the Temple is used as a place of business. We are God's temples day and night. Does God find nothing but secular business going on during the week? Do our thoughts and conversations deal only with worldly things, or do we often turn to God like loving children phoning home?

Pagan temples of old were often centers of prostitution blasphemously operated in the name of God. Does God find in our bodies the purity without which he cannot approach us?

Years ago, when Pope John Paul II beatified a priest, a sister and a layman, he said no one is excluded from sanctity. In fact, no one is *excused* from sanctity. "You," our Lord said, "must be perfect as your heavenly Father is perfect."

Mary entered the Temple of Jerusalem to pray, but far more often she entered the temple of her own heart. Do we imitate her? Do we keep daily company with the Lord who said the Blessed Trinity would come and live with us?

The Church as the house of God is a symbol of heaven. After all, what church is suited to God, or large enough to accommodate God? God must be his own house! And what kind of house is it? It is the house of love! "God is love." In that sense, our homes are churches too, as was the home of the Holy Family. In a good home we learn that religion is joyous, happy, friendly, kind and thoughtful. We discover that love is the only cement which can bind together the building blocks of the temple of God.

Some churches were so great and strong they served as fortresses in times of war. Each of us is a spiritual fortress. We worry about the army of evil in the world, as though it could seize our fortress. It never can. Never! For, "where sin increased, grace overflowed all the more." God is in our fortress. He hands us the mighty weapons of prayer and sacrament and the invincible power of the Holy Spirit. We're as strong as God while we remain faithful to God. Our Commander in Chief said, "Fear not, for I have overcome the world." Our fortress can't be taken unless we betray it from within, as Judas did.

In our churches we have a foretaste of the heavenly Jerusalem where we will live in the House of Love with the angels and the other saints. When we enter the temple of Christ's body worthily in Holy Communion we go there to worship God. In doing so, we are already paying a visit home. Our Church, then, reminds us that we have a Father and an eternal home, where he awaits us. Need I remind you to tell the Father of your longing to get home at last?

"C" — Thirty-second Sunday of the Year

2 M 7:1-2, 9-14
2 Th 2:16 - 3:5
Lk 20:27-38

REMOVING ROADBLOCKS TO RESURRECTION FAITH

In the Gospel reading Jesus rivets our eyes on those words of the Nicene Creed which we will say today as always: "We look for the resurrection of the dead."

The Pharisees believed in the resurrection; the Sadducees did not, on the claim that Moses did not teach it. Jesus points out that Moses did teach it where he says, "the Lord is the God of Abraham, and the God of Isaac, and the God of Jacob." For, Jesus explains, "God is not the God of the dead but of the living." The souls of Abraham, Isaac and Jacob were alive and well and waiting for Jesus to bring the resurrection of their bodies.

The meaning of our faith lies in the truth that Jesus died for our sins and rose for our justification and our resurrection. Life and love always come through a person. Resurrection life and love come only through the person of Jesus. When his side was pierced, the water of our rebirth in baptism flowed out, and the blood of our Eucharistic food, and the Holy Spirit of Pentecost. That's why Jesus said, "Let anyone who thirsts come to me and drink," for "rivers of living water will flow from him." Later he said to Martha, "I am the resurrection and the life."

Jesus appeared repeatedly to his disciples after his resurrection to embed the fact of it into their faith. They learned well, for when it came time to choose a disciple to take the traitor Judas' place, Peter thought of it at once. He said that the one chosen must be a disciple who had been with them during Jesus' whole public life, death and resurrection, so he could "become with us a witness to his resurrection."

And St. Paul, when confronted with doubters of the resurrection, said that if there is no resurrection, Jesus didn't rise, we give false witness when we say God did raise him, we are still in our sins, and so "we are the most pitiable of people." Clearly, then, one who does not believe in the resurrection is neither Catholic nor even Christian.

Jesus also brings into the picture the need to be worthy of the resurrection. He says that "those who are deemed worthy" will be children of God and children of the resurrection. The seven brothers in the first reading were worthy. They died as martyrs to God and God's law and their faith in the resurrection.

We most likely won't have to die as martyrs to the faith, but we have to live as "martyrs" to it. The word martyr means "witness." We have to witness to faith by a faithful life.

This brings up the need to remove the roadblocks to faith in the resurrection. The saint-theologian Thomas Aquinas said that sexual impurity undermines faith in the resurrection. The reason? Impure people develop a dislike of the flesh and don't want to believe in resurrection. The widespread impurity in our culture may explain why many have lost their faith in the resurrection. There is a tragic fittingness to that loss. A sin against sex is a sin against life and love, for the gift of sex is a special power of loving and life-giving. People who abuse their own life-giving power tend to lose faith in God's life-giving power of resurrection. The heartfelt advice I would give them is simple: Go to confession. When the soul is purified, the flesh is purified, and faith and longing for the resurrection return.

We need all the help we can get to live pure lives. The Church warns us over and over against premarital sex, adultery, illicit marriages, homosexual acts, masturbation, contraception. They are all against God's law. Chaste marriages are the witness to purity we all need. They are part of the fidelity between Christ and his bride the Church that we all must live.

Pope after pope, aware of the need married couples have for a moral method of family planning, urged medical scientists to find one. They were confident our provident God had provided one, if only we could discover it. And discover it we did. This discovery of a moral way to control fertility in marriage is a greater landmark in human history than the discovery of control over the atom. The greatest of human triumphs is control of self.

Modern natural family planning, or NFP for short, is a moral way to control fertility by observing the signs God has implanted in a woman's body. When God told our first parents to be fertile and multiply and fill the earth, he implanted those signs to prepare in advance for the day when his command would be nearly accomplished. That is the greatness of his providence. It is our God-given greatness that we discovered those signs and have the self-control to use them. Using NFP within marriage for a serious reason is a virtuous act that merits divine grace.

Modern NFP is as effective as contraceptives, with none of their moral or biological defects. NFP, said Pope John Paul II, accepts the woman's nature, respects it, and calls couples to shared responsibility and self-control. NFP accords with both the bodily and spiritual nature of marriage, with its tender love and affection that express sex in its "truly and fully human dimension." It respects the marriage power of life-giving, and controls it without corrupting it.

If the infertile woman in today's Gospel had known NFP, she might have conceived. The knowledge of the high point of fertility it makes known has enabled many low-fertility couples to conceive. In one backward country couples refused to believe in NFP until it helped one couple conceive. Then they realized profound truth was at work in the method. Because NFP helps both to plan a conception and to postpone one, it is the only true family planning method (NFP can be learned through the sessions conducted by our diocesan Family Life Bureau. Refer to this week's bulletin for further information).

The hope for resurrection of the body cannot be separated from the respect for the body that makes us desire resurrection. Lives of chastity, like lives of love, promote faith in the resurrection. It may be that the average family can best forward the faith by living purely and helping others to do so, in the likeness of the Holy Family. A great service is to teach NFP.

When we receive Holy Communion today we can please Christ by praying for vocations to virginity, for purity for the young, and for faithful chastity for all. Lets make the Church, the bride of Christ, a shining example to the world that gives Christ pride before his Father and hastens the day he will call us to the resurrection of the body as sons and daughters of the Father.

STOCK-TAKING FOR THE FINAL REPORT

A man who had visited Israel was describing to a friend one of their problems. They have, he said, three Sabbaths each week: Friday for Muslims, Saturday for Jews, Sunday for Christians. His friend said, "Did you hear of the atheist who was converted? He was tired of being the only one who didn't have a day off."

The readings today are a call to prepare for the age when every day will be a Sabbath. God gives us the Sabbath rest to practice for that eternal Sabbath. Our work will be behind us, our trials over, and our joy never-ending. It is time to think of these things. The liturgical year is ending. That symbolizes the end of our time on earth and the beginning of our eternity.

The readings tell us it's time to take stock of our lives. What's the state of affairs? We must take stock with the same good sense secularists do. Businesses do it at year-end, if not because good sense requires it, then because the income tax report does. On January first, the newspapers sum up world conditions: wars and rumors of wars, social and ecological and economic problems and prognoses, and where we're at in general. The President gives his required State of the Union address.

Christ demands that we be no less practical. We need to make more than the usual slip-shod examination of conscience. It's time to examine the whole trajectory of our lives. Never mind whether we said our morning prayers, or used a curse word. Something more thorough is afoot. Is our life really on the right path? Are we buried in concerns for this life like the materialists? Or truly pilgrims on the way to eternal life?

Once a priest was standing on Forty-third street in New York waiting for a bus when a troubled Jewish man who needed to talk came up to him and said, ''After 3,000 years of Judaism and 2,000 of Christianity why are people so bad? God said, 'Thou shalt not kill,' and still war.'' The priest said it was because people had the freedom to choose, and were choosing wrongly. The man said, ''If the Pope told people to do this and that, wouldn't they do it?'' The priest responded, ''If they won't obey God, why would they obey the Pope?'' The man went on: ''All these single women having babies! Why should I support them?'' The priest said, ''For the reason you just gave: 'Thou shalt not kill.' ''

''I'm a materialist,'' the man said. ''You're not. My father is dead. I'll never see him again.'' ''Who told you you'll never see him again?'' the priest asked. ''You will see him again.''

Let's stop there. Who did tell the man he'd never see his father again? How we misinterpret nature! We see dead bodies decay, and say, ''Nature says when they're dead, they're dead.'' Does nature say that? If an alien came to earth in the fall and saw all the beautiful vegetation dying and the leaves falling, wouldn't he think the trees had died? Yet when spring came he would see they had not died at all. He would see them re-clothed more beautifully than before. If he saw a pond dry up in the heat of summer he might say, ''I'll never see that water again.'' Yet on the first chill morning he would see the drops of dew on the rose petal and the thorns. The water has come back. Let the rose petals be a symbol of heaven, and the thorns a symbol of hell. If we read nature aright, it confirms rather than denies our faith. Things change more than they are taken away. So it is with life itself. In death life is changed, not taken away.

Our Lord warns of disasters, persecutions and martyrdom. But did you notice that after he spoke of martyrdom he added, ''Yet not a hair of your heads will be harmed''? Isn't that interesting? What can he mean except that what people do to our bodies is only for a moment because God will raise our bodies forever? By patient endurance we will save our lives for eternity.

Our Lord is calling us to meditate on the last things, and to order our lives accordingly. Death, judgment, heaven and hell are the final realities. Beloved Pope John Paul XXIII, when a boy, memorized the words, "Nothing is more certain than death . . . more strict than judgment . . . more delightful than heaven." That is exactly what God revealed, what Christ taught, and what his Church insists on. It is the faith. St. Augustine said of hell that we can't escape it by disbelieving but by believing. St. Ignatius urged us to meditate on hell so that if love of God doesn't keep us from going there, at least fear will.

The famous artist Salvador Dali was commissioned to do a painting of hell as shown to Lucy by our Lady of Fatima. He went to Fatima and did the painting, and while there he made a good confession and returned to the sacraments. His dreadful painting of hell hangs in Washington, N.J., at the Ave Maria Institute.

St. Ignatius wants us to picture the souls in hell being burned by their own wickedness, the screams and blasphemies against Christ and his saints, the corrupt smell of sin, the bitter remorse of conscience, the hatred of all that is innocent, holy and good, the malicious cursing of God, and the refusal to repent of sin. He wants us to recall that this good earth is the land of beginning again. We turn to God and ask for mercy.

Consider the real mood and attitude our Lord is invoking. We have it in the several readings: The Psalm invites the rivers of people to clap their hands, for the Lord is coming to bring justice to the world. Paul calls us to imitate him, who worked so hard in human labors to support himself, and in preaching the Gospel to bring salvation. In the Opening Prayer we ask for the same grace when we say, "Father of all that is good, keep us faithful in serving you, for to serve you is our lasting joy."

Our Lord tells us there will be sufferings, but by bearing them patiently we will possess our lives forever. Fear sin, not death. Sin separates us from God. Death is the trip home to him.

Today we remember that "the world as we see it, disfigured

by sin, is passing away.'' Christ is our way. We are the children of the resurrection. Heaven is our eternal home.

Today, do this: Offer Mass for your sins. Stand by Mary on Calvary offering the crucified Christ to the Father in atonement for sin. He has loved you and delivered himself for you. What do you have to fear except that you won't say yes to his love? Ask Mary to help you be so repentant you won't repeat your sins. And after you have offered the Lamb of Sacrifice, partake of him at the Father's table, as you will in eternal life. In him you will grow in love, and that is the surest road home.

"C" — Solemnity of Christ the King

2 S 5:1-3
Col 1:12-20
Lk 23:35-43

KNOWING THE HEART OF OUR KING

Kings by the thousands have held scepters in the course of the ages. And if "a man's home is his castle," millions have pictured themselves as kings over their own tiny domain, and devoted their lives to promoting their own little kingdom.

And so a question: What drives you? Are you trying to be a king or to serve Christ your King? When Bishop St. Ignatius of Antioch was on his way to martyrdom he begged Christians not to interfere. "The delights of this world will not profit me," he said. "I would prefer to die in Jesus Christ than to rule over all the earth . . . If anyone has God in him, let him understand what I want and have sympathy for me, knowing what drives me."

Today the Church puts Christ before us, not on a throne, but on the cross. Why, except to help us know the Heart of our King? Today's *Liturgy of the Hours* says, "Crown him the King, to whom is giv'n / The wondrous name of Love."

King St. Louis of France knew his King's Heart. To his son he wrote, "My dearest son, you should permit yourself to be tormented by every kind of martyrdom before you would allow yourself to commit a mortal sin." Louis realized that a worthy soldier of Christ must stand and die rather than betray the innocence and godliness which make up the kingdom of Christ. Though he was a king, he lived as the servant of Christ his King.

In the first reading, King David's people set us an example. They acknowledge that David is of their flesh, that is, born of their tribe and people, and that God has chosen him to be their king. We in our turn confess that God sent his Son to be our King, and that he took our flesh as Son of the Virgin Mary.

In the second reading St. Paul further illumines our faith in Christ our King. He is the beloved Son of God and Son of man, the firstborn of creation and the firstborn of the resurrection. He is the head of his body the Church who poured out his blood to unite heaven and earth and everything in them.

In the Gospel reading, the Heart of our King lies revealed. Though all-powerful, he's not greedy for power. He strips himself of power; he takes the worst job in the kingdom. He accepts being treated as a powerless fool. He took the job of love. He knew he would win in the end, for he said, "When I am lifted up from the earth I will draw everyone to myself." Though all-powerful, he knew his greatest power is love.

His game plan didn't square with the popular definition of Savior. Many Jews and non-Jews present rejected him. They mocked the placard which read, "King of the Jews." We understand, don't we? If we're not wise about what we demand of God, we repeat their folly and their lack of faith, and slide down into their darkness. Let us learn from their error not to tell God what it means to be King and Messiah; let us listen to him tell us.

The crucified criminal we call the Good Thief did an astounding thing. He escaped their unbelief. He discovered Christ in this impossible situation. He leaped out of the darkness into wonderful light. Where most of the others saw only a dying pretender, he discovered the triumphant King of Love.

Let us study him to help ourselves. Crucified and dying, how did he discover in the crucified and dying condemned criminal beside him the King of kings? How did he ever do that? He began with his own sins. He admits he deserves what he's getting. But this Man beside him wasn't like him! This noble man wasn't cursing and screaming. Even as he was nailed he kept saying, "Father, forgive them. They don't know what they do." He even makes excuses for his torturers! Truly, he has the nobility of a Lord and King. Amazed, the thief listens and looks through his pain, observing everything. And his faith begins to build.

But there was another factor involved. As a Jew, he knew his Scriptures, and as a man who had knocked about he knew that just men suffer. Perhaps he recalled Isaiah's prophecy of the faithful servant of God who would die for the sins of others. And so in his dying hour he made that great leap of faith and called out, "Jesus, remember me when you enter upon your reign." The noble King did not fail him. Forth from his lips came the matchless promise, "I assure you, this day you will be with me in paradise." Who of us can match the faith of the Good Thief, or merit such a promise? But at least let us try.

Unlike his unbelieving fellow criminal the Good Thief never said, "Save yourself and us!" No, the Good Thief accepted the Messiah's game plan of salvation, and didn't demand his own be accepted. He joined the game plan of suffering.

Let us recall, then, the game plan of Christ's kingdom. In teaching after teaching he makes it clear that we are to share his yoke of love. We are to labor with him to bring what Pope John Paul II called the "civilization of love," the "kingdom of the Heart of Christ." Our King's Heart was pierced not so much by a lance as by the suffering he saw and foresaw. He wants us to do away with all needless suffering. He wants us to suffer and sacrifice to do away with all sin and suffering. He is the Good Shepherd, the ideal

King, who suffers to see his people suffer. Sacrifice and suffer that there will be no more suffering! That is his strategy. The more we cooperate, the more earth will become the image of heaven, and the more we will look forward to heaven as the perfection toward which we were striving.

We turn now to think of his deepest love of all. Our King gave himself to us for our food. Our minds cannot grasp the meaning of this gift. It goes beyond anything of earth's. But our hearts can understand it when we surrender our minds in faith. And then we understand the Heart of our King.

We close with the prayer of consecration to the King of the Universe. It gains us a plenary indulgence if we add prayers for the Holy Father, and confess and receive Communion. Here is our prayer: Most sweet Jesus, Redeemer of the human race, look down upon us humbly prostrate before you. We are yours, and yours we wish to be; but to be more surely united with you, behold each one of us freely consecrates himself today to your Most Sacred Heart. Many indeed have never known you; many, too, have rejected you. Have mercy on them all, most merciful Jesus, and draw them to your Sacred Heart.

Be King, O Lord, not only of the faithful who have never forsaken you, but also of the prodigal children who have abandoned you; grant that they may quickly return to their Father's house, lest they die of wretchedness and hunger.

Be King of those who are deceived by erroneous opinions, or whom discord keeps aloof, and call them back to the harbor of truth and unity of faith, so that soon there may be but one flock and one Shepherd.

Grant, O Lord, to your Church assurance of freedom and immunity from harm; give tranquility of order to all nations; make the earth resound from pole to pole with one cry: Praise to the divine heart that wrought our salvation; to it be glory and honor for ever. Amen.